The
Princeton
Review®

Cracking the

SAT

Subject Test™

in Literature

16th Edition

The Staff of The Princeton Review

PrincetonReview.com

Penguin
Random
House

The Princeton Review
555 West 18th Street
New York, NY 10011

E-mail: editorialsupport@review.com

Published in the United States by Random House LLC, New York, and simultaneously in Canada by Random House of Canada Limited, Toronto.

A Penguin Random House Company.

ISBN: 978-1-5247-1078-1
ISSN: 1944-379X
eBook ISBN: 978-1-5247-1094-1

Editor: Sarah Litt
Production Editor: Emily Epstein White and Ali Landreau
Production Artist: Gabriel Berlin

Printed in the United States of America on partially recycled paper.

10 9 8 7 6 5 4 3 2 1

16th Edition

Editorial
Rob Franek, Editor-in-Chief
Casey Cornelius, VP Content Development
Mary Beth Garrick, Director of Production
Selena Coppock, Managing Editor
Meave Shelton, Senior Editor
Colleen Day, Editor
Sarah Litt, Editor
Aaron Riccio, Editor
Orion McBean, Associate Editor

Penguin Random House Publishing Team
Tom Russell, VP, Publisher
Alison Stoltzfus, Publishing Director
Jake Eldred, Associate Managing Editor
Ellen Reed, Production Manager
Suzanne Lee, Designer

Acknowledgments

The Princeton Review would like to give special thanks to Susan Swinford for her tremendous contributions to this title.

A special thanks to Adam Robinson, who conceived of and perfected the Joe Bloggs approach to standardized tests and many of the other successful techniques used by The Princeton Review.

Contents

Get More (Free) Content

1 Go to **PrincetonReview.com/cracking.**

2 Enter the following ISBN for your book: 9781524710781.

3 Answer a few simple questions to set up an exclusive Princeton Review account. (If you already have one, you can just log in.)

4 Click the "Student Tools" button, also found under "My Account" from the top toolbar. You're all set to access your bonus content!

Need to report a potential **content** issue?

Contact **EditorialSupport@review.com**.
Include:

- full title of the book
- ISBN number
- page number

Need to report a **technical** issue?

Contact **TPRStudentTech@review.com** and provide:

- your full name
- email address used to register the book
- full book title and ISBN
- computer OS (Mac/PC) and browser (Firefox, Safari, etc.)

The Princeton Review®

Once you've registered, you can...

- Take a full-length practice SAT and/or ACT

- Get valuable advice about the college application process, including tips for writing a great essay and where to apply for financial aid

- If you're still choosing between colleges, use our searchable rankings of *The Best 382 Colleges* to find out more information about your dream school.

- Access comprehensive study guides and a variety of printable resources, including additional bubble sheets, score conversion tables, and lists of key terms

- Check to see if there have been any corrections or updates to this edition

- Get our take on any recent or pending updates to the SAT Subject Test in Biology E/M

Look For These Icons Throughout The Book

 ONLINE ARTICLES

 PROVEN TECHNIQUES

 MORE GREAT BOOKS

 COLLEGE ADVISOR APP

Part I
Orientation

Chapter 1
The Route
to College

This chapter provides a brief explanation of the SAT and SAT Subject Tests and their role in the college admissions process. Have you been wondering what Score Choice™ is? We'll explain that too!

WHO WRITES STANDARDIZED TESTS?

If you've purchased this book, you are probably preparing to apply to college. Part of the long and arduous college admissions process will almost certainly include some standardized tests. For most of you, these tests will come from a company called the College Board. This company has hired the Educational Testing Service, or ETS, to administer and grade its exams.

WHAT IS THE PRINCETON REVIEW?

Tick Tock
We don't waste your time. We tell you what you need to know and, more importantly, what you don't need to know.

The Princeton Review is a test-preparation company. We have branches all over the United States and abroad. We've developed the techniques you'll find in our books, courses, and online resources by analyzing several years' worth of actual exams. We've seen the effectiveness of our techniques in action with thousands of our students.

Our approach is what makes our techniques unique. We base our principles on those used by the people who write the test. We don't want to waste your time with information that you don't need to know. We know you're busy. We're not going to teach you "How to Appreciate Fine English Literature" (although that's a wonderful thing to know), but rather the information you'll need to get great score improvements on this test. You'll learn to recognize and comprehend the relatively small amount of information that's actually tested. You'll also learn to avoid common traps, to think like the test writers, and to find answers to challenging questions.

You need to do only three things: trust the techniques, practice them, and then practice some more.

THE SAT AND SAT SUBJECT TESTS

For General Prep
Preparing to take the general SAT? Pick up a copy of *Cracking the SAT 2018 Premium Edition*, which has 8 (!) practice tests.

What Is the SAT?

The SAT is a multiple-choice exam used by colleges to provide a standard measure of high school students around the country. The composite scores on the SAT range from 400 to 1600 and combine an Evidence-Based Reading and Writing score (on a scale from 200–800) with a Math score (also on a scale from 200–800). The SAT also has an optional essay, which is scored separately.

What Are the SAT Subject Tests?

These are a series of one-hour exams administered by ETS. Unlike the SAT, the SAT Subject Tests are designed to measure specific knowledge in specific areas. There are tests in many subject areas, such as biology, history, French, and math. They are each scored separately on the familiar 200–800 scale.

Should I Take the SAT Subject Tests?

According to the College Board (which, since it sells you the tests, really has an interest in inflating these numbers), only 160 institutions require or recommend that you take (usually two) SAT Subject Tests. Of course, these are widely considered to be the most selective institutions in the nation. Many schools will waive the requirement if a student takes the ACT with writing in lieu of the SAT Reasoning test. If you are applying to an engineering program, you will usually be asked to take two tests: Math (generally Level 2) and a science (you usually have the option of Chemistry or Physics). Your first order of business is to visit the websites of the colleges you're interested in, which have the most up-to-date information about their individual policies.

How Are the SAT Subject Tests Used by College Admissions?

Since the University of California stopped requiring two SAT Subject Tests for admission, there's almost no data publicly available. Engineering programs tend to find subject test scores a more reliable indicator of a future student's performance than the SAT Reasoning Test, so they take the scores very seriously. At the other end of the spectrum are schools that ignore the scores altogether in the admissions process, and simply use them for placement purposes (usually in foreign language and math) when a student arrives on campus. To find out exactly how the colleges you are considering will use the scores, visit their websites or contact their admissions offices via phone or e-mail.

SAT Subject Tests are not just used for college admission and placement. For example, if you live in New York State, you may be able to use SAT Subject Test scores to substitute for a Regents examination score. Speak with your counselor or teacher to see whether this might be appropriate for you. In addition, some colleges allow you to use SAT Subject Test scores to meet minimum subject-based requirements to be eligible to apply for admission (for example, University of California's "a-g" requirements and Arizona State University's subject competency requirements).

SCORE CHOICE™ IS BACK!

For the past several years, you have been able to choose which SAT Subject Test scores you want colleges to see. This is great news! For one thing, if you take more than one SAT Subject Test on a given test date, you'll be able to choose which tests from that date you'd like to submit to colleges. So if, for example, you take the French Subject Test followed by the Chemistry Subject Test, but don't think the chemistry test went very well, you can simply opt to have that chemistry score withheld from the schools to which you are applying. However, before you start testing haphazardly, remember that many colleges request that you submit your entire testing record. (Again, contact the specific colleges that interest you—policies are constantly changing.) You are on the honor system to submit your full record, but we advise that you provide colleges the information they request.

Score Choice will be optional for students. This means that you aren't required to opt in and actively choose which specific scores you would like sent to colleges. If you decide not to use Score Choice, then all of the scores on file will automatically be sent when you request score reports.

For more information about Score Choice, go to **sat.collegeboard.org.**

Summary

Did you get all that?

- Like the SAT, SAT Subject Tests measure how well you take standardized tests, NOT how smart you are!

- Find out whether you need SAT Subject Test scores for the colleges to which you plan to apply.

- If you do need to take at least one SAT Subject Test, you should find out how your schools will use your scores.

Chapter 2
Approaching the SAT Subject Tests

This chapter includes general information about the SAT Subject Tests that are offered and how to decide which one(s) to take. We'll also tell you which test administrations offer SAT Subject Tests and where you can register.

WHICH TEST(S) SHOULD I TAKE? WHEN?

Which test(s) should you take? The answer is simple.

- Take the tests that are required by the colleges to which you are applying.
- Take the SAT Subject Tests that you will do well on.

Some colleges have specific requirements; others do not. Again, start asking questions before you start taking tests. That means you should check with the school's admissions office or website. College guidebooks, catalogs, and guidance counselors should also have this information. Once you find out which, if any, tests are required, part of your decision making is done.

The next step is to find out which of the tests will show your particular strengths. Generally (although, again, check with the colleges you want to apply to) colleges will require (or "strongly suggest") two SAT Subject Tests: usually Math Level 1 or 2 and something else.

An Offer You Can't Refuse
Some schools will "strongly suggest" that you take certain tests. It's wise to follow their suggestions, as they are the ones who will ultimately be judging your application for admission.

Subject tests are given in the following areas: literature, U.S. history, world history, biology, chemistry, physics, math, and a variety of foreign languages.

Your number one concern is to determine which tests you will score well on. Then you will want to think about the purposes for which the test will be used. If you plan to major in biology, you should probably take the biology test. If you're a whiz at anything, take that test (no, there is no test in video games, or pancake eating, or marathon sleeping).

After you've checked your requirements and examined your needs, take a diagnostic test like the ones at the end of this book. See how you do, and with that in mind, determine whether the test is for you.

Try to take the tests as close as possible to the completion of the corresponding coursework you are taking. If you plan to take the SAT Subject Test in Chemistry, for example, and you are currently taking high school chemistry, don't postpone the test until next year. Take it while the information is still fresh. (Are you really going to study over the summer? Come on. *Really?*)

WHEN ARE THE SAT SUBJECT TESTS OFFERED?

Remember!
You cannot take the SAT Subject Tests and the SAT on the same test date.

In general, you can take from one to three SAT Subject Tests per test date in October, November, December, January, May, and June at test sites across the country. Check the dates carefully, as not all subjects are offered at each administration. For example, the only language tests administered in November are the language-with-listening tests. (Note: You can take only one listening test per test date, and the November administration is the only test date when listening tests are offered.) French and Spanish are the only languages that are tested on every test date. You'll want to sit down with a calendar and plan, as there are limited dates and a lot of tests to take. For instance, you may want to retake the SAT on one of those days, or you may want to apply early to a school and have all your scores before your application is due in early fall. Register for the test early so you get the location you want.

> SAT Subject Tests are offered in May, June, August, October, November, and December.

Love Lit?
If you're planning to take or already registered for one of the AP English exams, you're in luck! Check out the 2018 editions of our AP English titles, *Cracking the AP English Literature & Composition Exam* and *Cracking the AP English Language & Composition Exam*.

SHOULD I TAKE THE SAT SUBJECT TEST IN LITERATURE?

The SAT Subject Test in Literature will test your knowledge of basic literary terms and your ability to understand selected literary passages (prose, poetry, and drama) written in English. You don't have to know specifics about literature originally written in English to do well on the test.

If you're unsure about whether you should take this test, start perusing college catalogs or contact the college(s) you will probably be applying to. Admissions offices should be able to tell you whether this test is necessary.

If you feel confident about your ability to analyze and interpret literature, are a good reader, do well in English class, or plan to major in English in college, consider taking the SAT Subject Test in Literature.

Registration

The easiest way to register is via **www.collegeboard.org** (you'll need a credit card). This site contains other useful information such as the test dates and fees. You can also register by mail (remember regular mail?) by picking up a registration form and Student Bulletin at your guidance counselor's office. If you have any questions, call 866-756-7346. If you need to register for extended time or make special arrangements due to learning differences or disabilities, you can speak with a representative at the College Board by calling 609-771-7137. Start this process early, as the paperwork is fairly extensive.

On test day, you can take a single one-hour test and leave or take two or three different one-hour tests. When you register, you must select the SAT Subject Test(s) you intend to take; however, on the actual test date, you can take additional tests (up to three total), fewer tests, or even different tests from the ones you originally selected. The only exception is any language-with-listening test—you can't decide to take one of these on the day of the test. Also note that the College Board will charge you for any additional tests you take. You may have the scores sent to you, your school, and up to four colleges of your choice. Additional reports can be sent to additional colleges for, yup, additional money. Your scores are usually posted online and sent to colleges three weeks after the test date. Official scores are mailed to you and your high school about five weeks after the test date. Unfortunately, the Student Answer Service and Question-and-Answer Service are not available for the SAT Subject Tests. For information about these services for the SAT, visit the College Board's website, **www.collegeboard.org**.

What's a Good Score?

Very few colleges release any data regarding how they use subject tests in admissions. Additionally, since such a wide range of subject tests is available, your score can only be compared with students who took the same subject test.

What's important to schools is your percentile ranking (which will be sent along with your scores). This number tells colleges how you scored relative to other test takers who took the same test over a longer period of time (not just the day you took the test). In other words, a percentile rank of 60 means that 40 percent of test takers scored above you and 60 percent of test takers scored below you. The mean on the SAT Subject Test in Literature—and on most SAT Subject Tests—is 600.

Is Any Other Material Available for Practice?

The College Board publishes a book called *Official Study Guide for All SAT Subject Tests,* which contains full-length tests for almost all of the SAT Subject Tests offered. You can also go to the College Board's website, **www.collegeboard.org**, for more information and practice questions.

For book updates and more information, visit PrincetonReview.com.

Summary

Did you get all that?

- Find out which tests are required and/or recommended by the colleges to which you are applying.
- Take the tests on which you'll do the best.
- Plan ahead!
- A "good" score is relative—it depends on which test(s) you take and your percentile ranking.

Part II
Practice Test 1

Chapter 3
Practice Test 1

PRACTICE SAT SUBJECT TEST IN LITERATURE 1

TEST 1

Your responses to the SAT Subject Test in Literature questions should
be filled in on Test 1 of your answer sheet.

LITERATURE TEST 1

Directions: This test consists of selections from literary works and questions on their content, form, and style. After reading each passage or poem, choose the best answer to each question and fill in the corresponding oval on the answer sheet.

Note: Pay particular attention to questions that contain the words NOT, LEAST, or EXCEPT.

Questions 1-9. Read the following passage carefully before you choose your answers.

Maman-Nainaine said that when the figs were ripe Babette might go to visit her cousins down on the Bayou-Lafourche where the sugar cane grows.
Line
(5) Not that the ripening of figs had the least thing to do with it, but that is the way Maman-Nainaine was.

It seemed to Babette a very long time to wait; for the leaves upon the trees were tender yet, and the figs were like little hard green marbles.
(10) But warm rains came along and plenty of strong sunshine, and though Maman-Nainaine was as patient as the statue of la Madone, and Babette as restless as a hummingbird, the first thing they both knew it was hot summertime. Every day
(15) Babette danced out to where the fig-trees were in a long line against the fence. She walked slowly beneath them, carefully peering between the gnarled, spreading branches. But each time she came disconsolate away again. What she saw
(20) there finally was something that made her sing and dance the whole long day.

When Maman-Nainaine sat down in her stately way to breakfast the following morning, her muslin cap standing like an aureole about her
(25) white, placid face, Babette approached. She bore a dainty porcelain platter, which she set down before her godmother. It contained a dozen purple figs, fringed around with their rich green leaves.

"Ah," said Maman-Nainaine arching her
(30) eyebrows, "how early the figs have ripened this year!"

"Oh," said Babette. "I think they have ripened very late."

"Babette," continued Maman-Nainaine, as she
(35) peeled the very plumpest figs with her pointed silver fruit-knife, "you will carry my love to them all down on Bayou-Lafourche. And tell your Tante Frosine I shall look for her at Toussaint—when the chrysanthemums are in bloom."

(1893)

1. In the passage, the ripening figs are symbolic of
   (A) the fruits of labor
   (B) the maturation of Babette
   (C) the difficulty of life
   (D) the enigma of nature
   (E) the battle between Maman-Nainaine and Babette

2. The phrase "but that is the way Maman-Nainaine was" (lines 5-6) suggests which of the following about Maman-Nainaine?
   (A) She was not aware of the seriousness of the situation.
   (B) She was an overly strict woman.
   (C) Her actions had their own logic.
   (D) She doled out punishment for no reason.
   (E) Figs were her favorite fruit.

3. The phrases "patient as the statue of la Madone" (line 12), "her stately way" (lines 22-23), and "like an aureole about her white, placid face" (lines 24-25) serve to
   (A) illustrate that Maman-Nainaine is completely out of touch with the present
   (B) suggest that Maman-Nainaine's patience is a positive characteristic
   (C) indicate that Maman-Nainaine is as virtuous as a saint
   (D) suggest that time has little significance in the world of the story
   (E) make Babette seem unattractive by comparison

GO ON TO THE NEXT PAGE

4. In the passage, Maman-Nainaine's attitude toward Babette can best be characterized as

   (A) contemptuous
   (B) flippant
   (C) reluctantly accepting
   (D) joyously optimistic
   (E) wisely patient

5. All of the following pairs of words illustrate the difference between Maman-Nainaine and Babette EXCEPT

   (A) "patient" (line 12) and "restless" (line 13)
   (B) "early" (line 30) and "late" (line 33)
   (C) "purple" (line 27) and "green" (line 28)
   (D) "danced" (line 15) and "sat" (line 22)
   (E) "ripe" (line 2) and "bloom" (line 39)

6. Which is an effect of the last sentence of the passage?

   (A) It shows that Maman-Nainaine is clearly illogical.
   (B) It serves as ironic counterpoint to the rest of the story.
   (C) It reinforces the suggestion that Maman-Nainaine is attuned to the rhythms of nature.
   (D) It introduces a literary allusion.
   (E) It advances the story beyond its scope.

7. Maman-Nainaine's peeling of "the very plumpest figs" (line 35) illustrates that Maman-Nainaine

   (A) appreciates the value of appropriate timing
   (B) is gluttonous
   (C) has used her knife so often it's become misshapen
   (D) is testing their ripeness
   (E) has a sly and unpleasant sense of humor

8. The word "though" (line 11) implies which of the following in the context of the sentence?

   (A) The two women were in disagreement.
   (B) Patience is a virtue when waiting for something.
   (C) Figs were not really important.
   (D) Their patience and impatience had no effect on nature.
   (E) Maman-Nainaine's patience was annoying to Babette.

9. The narrative point of view of the passage as a whole is that of

   (A) a disapproving observer
   (B) a first-person impartial observer
   (C) the protagonist
   (D) an unreliable narrator
   (E) a third-person objective observer

GO ON TO THE NEXT PAGE

Questions 10-18. Read the following poem carefully before you choose your answers.

"On His Deceased Wife"

Methought I saw my late espoused Saint
　Brought to me like Alcestis from the grave,
　Whom Jove's great son to her glad husband gave,
Line　Rescu'd from death by force though pale and faint.
(5)　Mine as whom wash't from spot of childbed taint,
　Purification in the old law did save,
　And such, as yet once more I trust to have
　Full sight of her in Heaven without restraint,
Came vested all in white, pure as her mind:
(10)　Her face was vail'd, yet to my fancied sight,
　Love, sweetness, goodness, in her person shin'd
So clear, as in no face with more delight.
　But O, as to embrace me she inclined
　I wak'd, she fled, and day brought back my night.

(1658)

10. "Whom Jove's great son" (line 3) acts as which of the following?

　(A) A play on words
　(B) A contradiction
　(C) Hyperbole
　(D) Mythological allusion
　(E) Allegory

11. The primary effect of "as to embrace me she inclined" (line 13) is to

　(A) suggest that the speaker's wife was unsure of whether to embrace him
　(B) emphasize the difference in status between the speaker and his wife
　(C) make clear why the speaker was so unhappy to awaken when he did
　(D) show that the speaker's wife let her own inclinations guide her
　(E) undermine the speaker's assertions about his wife's goodness

12. In context, the word "save" (line 6) means which of the following?

　(A) Preserve
　(B) Keep in health
　(C) Deliver from sin and punishment
　(D) Rescue from harm
　(E) Maintain

13. The last line of the poem has which of the following effects?

　I.　Emphasizes the contrast between dreaming and waking states
　II.　Introduces a paradox
　III.　Affirms that the speaker still misses his wife

　(A) I only
　(B) III only
　(C) I and III only
　(D) II and III only
　(E) I, II, and III

14. In context, "my fancied sight" (line 10) suggests that the author is

　(A) imbuing his deceased wife with qualities she did not have
　(B) unable to separate reality from dreams
　(C) capriciously conjuring up his wife's image
　(D) dreaming
　(E) suffering from delusions

GO ON TO THE NEXT PAGE

15. The author's attitude toward his wife can best be described as

    (A) inconsolable
    (B) reverential
    (C) hopeful
    (D) incongruous
    (E) obsequious

16. The poem is primarily concerned with

    (A) the mourning process
    (B) the struggle against dying
    (C) the injustice of death
    (D) the nature of mortality
    (E) a belief in heaven

17. What is the primary effect of "Mine as whom wash't from spot of childbed taint" (line 5)?

    (A) It explains why the speaker's wife is wearing white.
    (B) It contrasts the condition of the speaker's wife with that of Alcestis.
    (C) It suggests how the speaker's wife had sinned.
    (D) It explains why the speaker's wife was "pale and faint" (line 4).
    (E) It makes clear why the speaker's wife needs to be purified.

18. Which of the following are terms of opposition in the poem?

    (A) "embrace" and "inclined" (line 13)
    (B) "day" and "night" (line 14)
    (C) "Full sight" and "without restraint" (line 8)
    (D) "wash't" (line 5) and "Purification" (line 6)
    (E) "sight" (line 10) and "shin'd" (line 11)

GO ON TO THE NEXT PAGE

Questions 19-27. Read the following passage carefully before you choose your answers.

Keenly alive to this prejudice of hers, Mr. Keeble stopped after making his announcement, and had to rattle the keys in his pocket in order to acquire the necessary courage to continue.
Line
(5) He was not looking at his wife, but knew just how forbidding her expression must be. This task of his was no easy, congenial task for a pleasant summer morning.

"She says in her letter," proceeded Mr.
(10) Keeble, his eyes on the carpet and his cheeks a deeper pink, "that young Jackson has got the chance of buying a big farm…in Lincolnshire, I think she said…if he can raise three thousand pounds."

(15) He paused, and stole a glance at his wife. It was as he had feared. She had congealed. Like some spell, the name had apparently turned her to marble. It was like the Pygmalion and Galatea business working the wrong way round. She
(20) was presumably breathing, but there was no sign of it.

"So I was just thinking," said Mr. Keeble, producing another *obbligato* on the keys, "it just crossed my mind…it isn't as if the thing
(25) were speculation…the place is apparently coining money…present owner only selling because he wants to go abroad…it occurred to me…and they would pay good interest on the loan…"

(30) "What loan?" enquired the statue icily, coming to life.

(1924)

19. Which of the following is the intended effect of the pauses in Mr. Keeble's conversation?

(A) It demonstrates that he is a feeble man.
(B) It makes his speech disjointed.
(C) It shows his hesitancy in approaching his wife.
(D) It slows the rhythm of the conversation.
(E) It elucidates his main point.

20. Which of the following expresses a mythological allusion made in the passage?

(A) "interest on the loan" (lines 28-29)
(B) "no sign of it" (lines 20-21)
(C) "turned her to marble" (lines 17-18)
(D) "in Lincolnshire" (line 12)
(E) "the Pygmalion and Galatea business" (lines 18-19)

21. All of the following represent metaphors or similes used by the author EXCEPT

(A) "She had congealed" (line 16)
(B) "enquired the statue icily" (line 30)
(C) "coming to life" (line 31)
(D) "presumably breathing" (line 20)
(E) "Like some spell" (lines 16-17)

22. The phrase "the place is apparently coining money" (lines 25-26) is meant to imply

(A) the farm is presently engaged in illegal activities
(B) the farm is profitable
(C) the investment is unnecessary
(D) the farm serves as a bank for the local people
(E) Lincolnshire is a profitable place to live

23. Which of the following expresses Mr. Keeble's wife's feeling toward the loan?

(A) Amused detachment
(B) Utter disgust
(C) Preformed opposition
(D) Blatant apathy
(E) Neutrality

GO ON TO THE NEXT PAGE

24. All of the following are physical manifestations of Mr. Keeble's anticipation of his wife's response EXCEPT

    (A) "Keenly alive" (line 1)
    (B) "had to rattle the keys" (line 3)
    (C) "was not looking at his wife" (line 5)
    (D) "his eyes on the carpet" (line 10)
    (E) "producing another *obbligato*" (line 23)

25. The phrase "in Lincolnshire, I think she said" (lines 12-13) implies that which of the following is true of Keeble?

    (A) Keeble is unaware of the location of the farm.
    (B) Keeble thinks the location is unimportant.
    (C) Keeble's memory is failing.
    (D) Keeble is attempting to appear casual.
    (E) Keeble wants to conceal the location from his wife.

26. Keeble's relationship with his wife is such that

    I. He seeks her affection
    II. He is disgusted by her
    III. He is intimidated by her

    (A) II only
    (B) III only
    (C) I and III only
    (D) II and III only
    (E) I, II, and III

27. The last line implies which of the following?

    (A) Mr. Keeble's wife is not interested in lending money.
    (B) Mr. Keeble's wife is tempted by the proposition.
    (C) Mr. Keeble has succeeded in his mission.
    (D) Mr. Keeble's wife is keeping an open mind about the loan.
    (E) Mr. Keeble's wife wants to hear more about the loan.

GO ON TO THE NEXT PAGE

Questions 28-37. Read the following passage carefully before you choose your answers.

[*A street in London*]

Enter LORD MAYOR *(Sir Roger Otley) and* EARL OF LINCOLN

LINC: My Lord Mayor, you have sundry times
　　　Feasted myself, and many courtiers more;
　　　Seldom or never can we be so kind
Line　To make requital of your courtesy.
(5)　But, leaving this, I hear my cousin Lacy
　　　Is much affected to your daughter Rose.

L. MAYOR: True, my good Lord, and she loves him so well
　　　That I mislike her boldness in the chase.

(10) LINC: Why, my Lord Mayor, think you it then a shame
　　　To join a Lacy with an Otley's name?

L. MAYOR: Too mean is my poor girl for his high birth;
(15)　Poor citizens must not with courtiers wed,
　　　Who will in silks and gay apparel spend
　　　More in one year than I am worth by far;
　　　Therefore your honour need not doubt my girl.

LINC: Take heed, my Lord, advise you what you do;
(20)　A verier unthrift lives not in the world
　　　Than is my cousin; for I'll tell you what,
　　　'Tis now almost a year since he requested
　　　To travel countries for experience;
　　　I furnish'd him with coin, bills of exchange,
(25)　Letters of credit, men to wait on him,
　　　Solicited my friends in Italy
　　　Well to respect him; but to see the end:
　　　Scant had he journey'd through half Germany,
　　　But all his coin was spent, his men cast off,
(30)　His bills embezzl'd, and my jolly coz,
　　　Asham'd to show his bankrupt presence here,
　　　Became a shoemaker in Wittenberg.
　　　A goodly science for a gentleman
　　　Of such descent! Now judge the rest by this:
(35)　Suppose your daughter have a thousand pound,
　　　He did consume me more in one half-year;
　　　And make him heir to all the wealth you have,
　　　One twelvemonth's rioting will waste it all.
　　　Then seek, my Lord, some honest citizen
(40)　To wed your daughter to.

L. MAYOR: I thank your lordship.
　　　(*Aside.*) Well, fox, I understand your subtlety.—
　　　As for your nephew, let your lordship's eye
　　　But watch his actions, and you need not fear,
(45)　For I have sent my daughter far enough.
　　　And yet your cousin Rowland might do well
　　　Now he hath learn'd an occupation;
　　　(*Aside.*) And yet I scorn to call him son-in-law.

LINC: Ay, but I have a better trade for him;
(50)　I thank His Grace he hath appointed him
　　　Chief colonel of all those companies
　　　Muster'd in London and the shires about
　　　To serve His Highness in those wars of France.
　　　See where he comes.

　　　　　　　　　　　　　　　　(1599)

28. The word "sundry" (line 1) most nearly means

　　(A) groceries
　　(B) numerous
　　(C) provisions
　　(D) infrequent
　　(E) few

29. It can be inferred from the passage that the primary reason the Lord Mayor sent his daughter "far enough" is that he

　　(A) believes she is chasing after a man who is not interested in marrying her
　　(B) regrets the state of poverty in which his family lives
　　(C) does not wish to have his daughter marry Lacy
　　(D) fears what the Earl of Lincoln might do
　　(E) looks down on the trade of shoemaking

30. What reason does the Earl of Lincoln give for his opposition to Lacy and Rose's marriage?

　　(A) Rose is not a pleasant person.
　　(B) Courtiers cannot marry.
　　(C) The wedding will be too expensive.
　　(D) Lacy does not love Rose.
　　(E) Lacy will not be able to provide for Rose.

31. The Earl of Lincoln's attitude toward his cousin can best be described as

    (A) censoriousness
    (B) apathy
    (C) romantic love
    (D) dislike
    (E) affection

32. It can be inferred from the sentence "A goodly science for a gentleman/Of such descent!" (lines 33-34) that

    (A) the profession of shoemaker is not appropriate for someone of high birth
    (B) shoemakers often declare bankruptcy
    (C) the Earl of Lincoln admires the profession of shoemaker
    (D) as a shoemaker, the Earl of Lincoln's cousin will make a thousand pounds a year
    (E) shoemaking is a scientific occupation

33. The Lord Mayor's attitude toward Lacy can best be described as

    (A) reluctant affection
    (B) avuncular indulgence
    (C) cautious approval
    (D) undeserved respect
    (E) disguised disapproval

34. The line "Well, fox, I understand your subtlety" (line 42)

    (A) allows the Lord Mayor to speak to the Earl of Lincoln without others hearing them
    (B) provides privileged insight into the Lord Mayor's attitude
    (C) alienates the audience by prevarication
    (D) creates an atmosphere of unease in the play
    (E) insults the Earl of Lincoln

35. All of the following words are used to describe Lacy EXCEPT

    (A) "affected" (line 6)
    (B) "high" (line 13)
    (C) "poor" (line 13)
    (D) "unthrift" (line 20)
    (E) "jolly" (line 30)

36. This scene reveals a conflict between

    (A) generosity and frugality
    (B) prodigality and profligacy
    (C) youth and age
    (D) joy and melancholy
    (E) expression and emotions

37. The author has the Earl of Lincoln mention the French wars (line 53) in order to

    (A) reveal Lacy's new profession
    (B) foreshadow a military death
    (C) elucidate the causes of the conflict
    (D) explain a system of privilege
    (E) home in on a national debate

GO ON TO THE NEXT PAGE

Questions 38-45. Read the following poem carefully before you choose your answers.

"Fable"

In heaven
Some little blades of grass
Stood before God.
Line "What did you do?"
(5) Then all save one of the little blades
Began eagerly to relate
The merits of their lives.
This one stayed a small way behind,
Ashamed.
(10) Presently, God said,
"And what did you do?"
The little blade answered, "O my Lord,
Memory is bitter to me,
For if I did good deeds
(15) I know not of them."
Then God, in all his splendor,
Arose from his throne.
"O best little blade of grass!" he said.

(1899)

38. It can be inferred that the speaker(s) in line 4 is/are

(A) an angel
(B) St. Peter
(C) the blades of grass
(D) God
(E) the one little blade of grass

39. God's attitude toward the last little blade of grass may best be described as

(A) condescending
(B) neutral
(C) admiring
(D) disdainful
(E) morally superior

40. The main idea of the poem is that

(A) it is better to do nothing than too much
(B) it is better to forget if you have done something wrong
(C) it is better to be modest than to be boastful
(D) it is better to keep your problems to yourself
(E) if you need to tell your bad deeds to someone, you are not worthy of respect

GO ON TO THE NEXT PAGE

41. The word "presently" (line 10) means which of the following in the context of the poem?

    I. As a gift
    II. After a while
    III. Changing the topic

    (A) I only
    (B) II only
    (C) I and III only
    (D) II and III only
    (E) I, II, and III

42. It can be inferred that the small blade was "ashamed" (line 9) because

    (A) it was smaller than the others
    (B) it was disgusted with the other blades of grass
    (C) it didn't feel worthy of God's attention
    (D) it was bitter and lonely
    (E) it thought its acts greater than the others' acts

43. The fact that God called the one blade "'O best'" (line 18) can best be characterized as

    (A) unexpected
    (B) satiric
    (C) tragic
    (D) comic
    (E) unfortunate

44. Which is the effect of lines 16-17 in relation to the rest of the poem?

    (A) They reveal God's egotism.
    (B) They heighten anticipation for the last line.
    (C) They shift the narrative voice.
    (D) They echo the last lines of the first stanza.
    (E) They reveal the poet's true feelings.

45. God's attitude toward the blades of grass as a group is

    (A) shameful
    (B) unstated
    (C) disgusted
    (D) disapproving
    (E) melancholy

GO ON TO THE NEXT PAGE

Questions 46-54. Read the following passage carefully before you choose your answers.

Everybody at all addicted to letter writing, without having much to say, which will include a large proportion of the female world at least, *Line* must feel with Lady Bertram, that she was out of
(5) luck in having such a capital piece of Mansfield news, as the certainty of the Grants going to Bath, occur at a time when she could make no advantage of it, and will admit that it must have been very mortifying to her to see it fall to the share of
(10) their thankless son, and treated as concisely possible at the end of a long letter, instead of having it to spread over the largest part of a page of her own—For though Lady Bertram, rather at home in the epistolary line, having early in her
(15) marriage, from the want of other employment, and the circumstance of Sir Thomas's being in Parliament, got into the way of making and keeping correspondents, and formed for herself a very creditable, commonplace, amplifying style,
(20) so that a very little matter was enough for her; she could not do entirely without any; she must have something to write about, even to her niece, and being so soon to lose all the benefit of Dr. Grant's gouty symptoms and Mrs. Grant's morning calls,
(25) it was very hard upon her to be deprived of one of the last epistolary uses she could put them to.
There was a rich amends, however, preparing for her. Lady Bertram's hour of good luck came. Within a few days from the receipt of
(30) Edmund's letter, Fanny had one from her aunt, beginning thus:
"My dear Fanny,
I take up my pen to communicate some very alarming intelligence, which I make no doubt will
(35) give you much concern."

(1814)

46. The narrative tone in the above piece can best be described as

(A) wry
(B) bitterly ironic
(C) detached
(D) melodramatic
(E) secretive

47. What is implied by the phrase "could make no advantage of it" (lines 7-8)?

(A) Lady Bertram could use the news to suit her best interest.
(B) Lady Bertram was unable to write about the news.
(C) Lady Bertram could not relay the news in a pleasant light.
(D) Lady Bertram could convey only part of the news.
(E) Lady Bertram was bound to secrecy.

48. In context, the word "want" (line 15) means

(A) requirement
(B) desire
(C) poverty
(D) lack
(E) defect

49. What is the "benefit" referred to in line 23?

(A) Friends with whom to visit
(B) The ability to assist others
(C) A house full of visitors
(D) People willing to write letters
(E) News to write about

50. The "amplifying style" (line 19) is one in which

(A) things sound more important than they are
(B) small bits of news are stretched in importance
(C) the speaker's voice is very loud
(D) people are made to sound grand
(E) one writes in a large, bold print

GO ON TO THE NEXT PAGE

51. It can be inferred that Sir Thomas is

    (A) Lady Bertram's son
    (B) Lady Bertram's husband
    (C) a boarder at Mansfield
    (D) a relative of the Grants
    (E) a friend of Lady Bertram

52. The last three lines serve to illustrate which of the following about Lady Bertram?

    (A) She has found something to write about.
    (B) She is spreading malicious rumors.
    (C) She is concerned about the news she is sending.
    (D) She is unaware of Fanny's feelings.
    (E) She is worried about her niece.

53. Lady Bertram is best described as

    (A) a social pariah
    (B) an unwanted family member
    (C) a disenfranchised member of society
    (D) a gossipy member of the gentry
    (E) a disillusioned elderly woman

54. The phrase "even to her niece" (line 22) shows that Lady Bertram

    (A) doesn't much care for her niece
    (B) is unhappy with her niece
    (C) is uncomfortable around her niece
    (D) doesn't need to have much to say to her niece
    (E) dislikes the prospect of writing to her niece

GO ON TO THE NEXT PAGE

Questions 55-61. Read the following poem carefully before you choose your answers.

"Blue Girls"

Twirling your blue skirts, travelling the sward
Under the towers of your seminary,
Go listen to your teachers old and contrary
Without believing a word.

Line
(5)   Tie the white fillets then about your hair
And think no more of what will come to pass
Than bluebirds that go walking on the grass
And chattering on the air.

Practice your beauty, blue girls, before it fail;
(10)   And I will cry with my loud lips and publish
Beauty which all our power shall never establish,
It is so frail.

For I could tell you a story which is true;
I know a woman with a terrible tongue,
(15)   Blear eyes fallen from blue,
All her perfections tarnished—yet it is not long
Since she was lovelier than any of you.

(1927)

55. The tone of the poem can best be described as

(A) cautionary
(B) mythic
(C) sarcastic
(D) optimistic
(E) hopeful

56. The poem is primarily concerned with

(A) the importance of beauty
(B) the lesson to be learned from the past
(C) the fleeting nature of youth
(D) telling a story for the girls' benefit
(E) the permanence of death

57. "Blear eyes fallen from blue" (line 15) is most probably meant to suggest that

(A) the woman's beauty has deteriorated
(B) the woman is tired
(C) the woman is going blind
(D) disease can happen suddenly
(E) the girls are responsible for the woman's loss of beauty

GO ON TO THE NEXT PAGE

58. "And chattering on the air" (line 8) refers to

    I. the girls
    II. the bluebirds
    III. the teachers

    (A) I only
    (B) I and II only
    (C) I and III only
    (D) II and III only
    (E) I, II, and III

59. It can be inferred that the girls to whom the poem is addressed are most likely to see the speaker as being like

    (A) their "teachers old and contrary" (line 3)
    (B) people who chatter like bluebirds
    (C) the woman mentioned in the final stanza
    (D) older women who are jealous of their beauty
    (E) a poet who fails to get his work published

60. The phrases "Without believing a word" (line 4) and "think no more" (line 6) illustrate the girls'

    (A) innate sense of suspicion
    (B) inherent difficulty with understanding subjects
    (C) lack of concern about weighty subjects
    (D) frail nature
    (E) disregard for the feelings of others

61. The poem's theme could best be described as

    (A) she who hesitates is lost
    (B) beauty is a fading flower
    (C) all that glitters is not gold
    (D) beauty is truth, truth beauty
    (E) a penny saved is a penny earned

STOP

**IF YOU FINISH BEFORE TIME IS CALLED, YOU MAY CHECK YOUR WORK ON THIS SECTION ONLY.
DO NOT TURN TO ANY OTHER SECTION IN THE TEST.**

Chapter 4
Practice Test 1:
Answers and
Explanations

- Practice Test 1 Answer Key
- Practice Test 1 Explanations
- How to Score Practice Test 1

PRACTICE TEST 1 ANSWER KEY

Question Number	Correct Answer	Right	Wrong	Question Number	Correct Answer	Right	Wrong
1	B	___	___	32	A	___	___
2	C	___	___	33	E	___	___
3	B	___	___	34	B	___	___
4	E	___	___	35	C	___	___
5	E	___	___	36	E	___	___
6	C	___	___	37	A	___	___
7	A	___	___	38	D	___	___
8	D	___	___	39	C	___	___
9	E	___	___	40	C	___	___
10	D	___	___	41	B	___	___
11	C	___	___	42	C	___	___
12	C	___	___	43	A	___	___
13	E	___	___	44	B	___	___
14	D	___	___	45	B	___	___
15	B	___	___	46	A	___	___
16	A	___	___	47	B	___	___
17	B	___	___	48	D	___	___
18	B	___	___	49	E	___	___
19	C	___	___	50	B	___	___
20	E	___	___	51	B	___	___
21	D	___	___	52	A	___	___
22	B	___	___	53	D	___	___
23	C	___	___	54	D	___	___
24	A	___	___	55	A	___	___
25	D	___	___	56	C	___	___
26	B	___	___	57	A	___	___
27	A	___	___	58	B	___	___
28	B	___	___	59	A	___	___
29	C	___	___	60	C	___	___
30	E	___	___	61	B	___	___
31	A	___	___				

PRACTICE TEST 1 EXPLANATIONS

1. **B** This is a good example of a "least bad" answer. There is no labor involved (A). All we see Babette do is "dance" (line 15), so life is not very "difficult" (C). Nature is not "enigmatic" (a mystery) (D). The differences between Maman-Nainaine and Babette can hardly be called a "battle" (E). So by Process of Elimination, the answer must be (B).

2. **C** Choice (C) is the best answer, because Maman-Nainaine says Babette's visit depends on the figs, which have nothing to do with the visit. So she must have her own reasons for linking the two—"her own logic." Babette wants to visit her cousins, so the situation is hardly "serious" (A). She may be "overly strict," but we don't have enough information to affirm that (B). Choice (D) cannot be the answer because there is no "punishment." And nothing suggests that "figs were her favorite fruit" (E).

3. **B** Choice (B) is the correct answer. Words like "patient," "stately," and "placid" emphasize Maman-Nainaine's patience, not a general saintly virtuousness (C); comparing her patience to a statue of the Virgin Mary makes clear that these are meant as positive references, not as illustrations of Maman-Nainaine's aloofness (A). Time does have significance in the world of the story, which is why it is admirable that Maman-Nainaine can be patient as time passes (D). These phrases focus on Maman-Nainaine's mode of behaving, and while Babette behaves impatiently, there is no evidence that her restlessness is unattractive (E).

4. **E** Maman-Nainaine is patient (line 12) (E). Maman-Nainaine does not look down on Babette, so she is not "contemptuous" (A). Nothing she says to Babette is "flippant" (B). She does not give in to Babette's wishes, so she is not "reluctantly accepting" (C). There is neither joy nor optimism in the passage (D).

5. **E** "Ripe" and "bloom" both refer to later stages of life—they refer to Maman-Nainaine, not Babette, so the answer is (E). It is true that Maman-Nainaine is "patient" and Babette is "restless," so (A) is not the answer. Babette is young; she wants to make the visit "early," while Maman-Nainaine is "late" in life (B). The unripe figs represent Babette—they are "green," while Maman-Nainaine is like a ripe fig—"purple" (C). Maman-Nainaine is older—she "sat" while Babette is young and "danced" (D). (Note: Remember to circle "EXCEPT" and mark each answer with a "Y" for "yes" or an "N" for "no" to find the odd man out.)

6. **C** When the figs are ripe, according to Maman-Nainaine, Babette will be ready to visit her cousins; likewise, when the chrysanthemums are in bloom, Maman-Nainaine will expect to see her sister, so the final line reinforces Maman-Nainaine's awareness of nature's rhythms (C). It is not illogical for Maman-Nainaine to mention chrysanthemums, since throughout the passage she has measured time by the progress of nature (A). There is nothing ironic about her statement (B), and she does not reference a literary work (D). The sentence does not advance the story beyond the boundaries of Maman-Nainaine's relationship with Babette (E).

7. **A** By peeling the ripest figs, Maman-Nainaine chooses the fruit that is most ready to be eaten—thus she is acting on her appreciation of the value of acting at the appropriate time (A). There is no suggestion in the passage that Maman-Nainaine is being gluttonous by eating those figs (B), nor does the passage suggest that there is anything wrong with her knife (C). Before she peels them, Maman-Nainaine remarks on the figs' ripeness, so she isn't peeling them in order to test their ripeness (D). The passage doesn't suggest that Maman-Nainaine's humor is unpleasant (E).

8. **D** The two women are different, yet nature forges on, so (D) is the correct answer. In the context of the sentence the word "though" does not show disagreement (A). No moral is given (B). There is no evidence that the figs were not important (C). Babette is restless, not annoyed (E).

9. **E** The narration is that of an impartial observer (E). It is not disapproving (A), nor is it first person (B). The protagonist (either Maman-Nainaine or Babette) does not narrate the story (C), nor do we have any evidence that this narrator is unreliable (D).

10. **D** Who's Jove? Who cares! This is obviously a reference to someone, so the word "allusion" is our best bet (D). There is no "play on words" (A), nor any "contradiction" (B). Although the poem might be fanciful, there is no "hyperbole" (exaggeration) (C). There are no underlying symbols, so the poem is not an "allegory" (E).

11. **C** The quoted phrase describes what is happening right before the speaker "wak'd" (line 14), so the correct answer is (C). In this context, "inclined" means something like "leaned toward," rather than "personal preference," so eliminate (D). The previous lines describe how the speaker intuits his wife's "delight," so it is unlikely that she seems unsure about whether to embrace him (A), and the phrase does not challenge the speaker's earlier assertions about his wife's good character (E). The phrase does not distinguish between the "status" of the speaker and that of his wife (B).

12. **C** The poem says that the wife was purified and that the speaker plans to see her in heaven, so "save" means "deliver from sin and punishment" (C). Because she is dead, she is not preserved (A), nor is she kept in health (B). She is neither rescued from harm (D) nor maintained (E)—don't fall into the trap answer just because one definition of "save" is "maintain."

13. **E** The final line of the poem explains what happened when the speaker woke up: the vision of his deceased wife "fled," as he returned to the "day" (wakefulness), the speaker's sadness ("night") returned to him. The first part of the line introduces the contrast between dreaming and waking (Statement I), while the second part introduces the paradoxical notion that daytime brings night back to the speaker (Statement II), at the same time affirming the sadness the speaker still feels about the loss of his wife (Statement III). Because the line has all three listed effects, the correct answer is (E).

14. **D** He is asleep and sees a ghost, so it is reasonable to infer that he is "dreaming" (D). There is nothing in the poem to suggest that she did not have these qualities in life (A). The fact that he knows it is "fancied" suggests that he knows he is dreaming (B). He is dreaming, so there is nothing capricious about the image, which comes to him unbidden (C), and he realizes it is a dream, so he is not delusional (E).

15. **B** He clearly loves his wife a great deal, so he is "reverential" (B). He may be "inconsolable," but not in his attitude toward his wife (A). Again, she is dead, so he does not have a "hopeful" attitude toward her (C). Neither "incongruous" (bizarre) (D) nor "obsequious" (fawning) (E) makes sense in this context.

16. **A** The poem is about how the speaker is mourning the loss of his wife, so (A) is the correct answer. He misses his deceased wife, but there is nothing to suggest that the speaker is struggling with the process of dying (B), nor does he lament that death is itself unjust (C). The speaker considers the nature of the immortality he and his wife will experience, but he does not theorize the nature of mortal existence (D); while he mentions seeing his wife in heaven, the poem is not primarily concerned with the fact that the speaker believes in it (E).

17. **B** Line 5 primarily serves to distinguish the speaker's wife ("Mine") from Alcestis (B). While line 2 suggests that the speaker's wife seems to have been "Brought" to him like Alcestis was brought back from the dead, the speaker then distinguishes his wife, who has been saved through "Purification in the old law" (line 6), from Alcestis, who was "Rescu'd from death by force though pale and faint" (line 4). The phrase "pale and faint" does not describe the speaker's wife (D). Line 5 suggests that the speaker's wife has been washed, but not that she is wearing white (A); the phrase "childbed taint" suggests not that the wife had sinned, but that she was tainted by (death in) childbirth (C). It seems to the speaker that "Purification" already "did save" his wife (line 6), so line 5 does not suggest that his wife needs to be purified again (E).

18. **B** The day (and the light of his wife) contrasts with the night that the speaker feels (B). The wife was inclining (leaning) over to embrace the speaker when he awoke, so these are not opposites (A). "Full sight" and "without restraint" mean the same thing (C), as do "wash't" and "purification" (D). "Sight" and "shin'd" don't have a relationship (E).

19. **C** Mr. Keeble is stuttering because he is afraid of his wife (C). There is no evidence that he is a "feeble man" (A), just that he is afraid of his wife. Disjointed speech (B) is an aftereffect; the cause is his fear. It does not serve to slow the conversation (D). It does not elucidate (explain, shed light on) the main point; in fact, it obfuscates it (hides, makes more confusing) (E).

20. **E** A mythological allusion refers to something—usually a work of literature in the myth genre. Pygmalion and Galatea are characters in mythology (E). Lines 28–29 do not refer to anything (A), nor do lines 20–21 (B). In lines 17–18 the narrator is exaggerating but not referring to myth (C), while (D) refers to a place, not a work of literature.

21. **D** Breathing is the only one of these examples that is a normal human characteristic, so (D) is the answer. Choice (A) compares her to a liquid that has turned solid, while (B) compares her to a statue. Choice (C) continues the statue comparison, while (E) suggests that the word "Lincolnshire" is "like some spell" (simile).

22. **B** "The place is apparently coining money" is a figure of speech meaning that the farm is making lots of money (B), which is why Mr. Keeble wants to invest in it. There is nothing to suggest the farm is doing something illegal (A). The investment may or may not be unnecessary, but that has nothing to do with "coining money" (C). Choice (D) takes the turn of phrase too literally. The farm is in Lincolnshire, but there is nothing to suggest that Lincolnshire itself is a good place to make money (E).

23. **C** Mrs. Keeble reacts "icily" before Mr. Keeble can even explain—so she is opposed to the idea (C). She is not amused (A), nor is she disgusted (B). She obviously cares, so she is not apathetic (D), and she is icy, so she is not neutral (E).

24. **A** Mr. Keeble is fiddling nervously while he talks, so all of the examples are physical illustrations of fidgeting except "keenly alive," which simply means he's aware (A). He rattles keys nervously (B) and (E), and doesn't look at his wife (C) and (D) because he thinks he knows how she'll react.

25. **D** Mr. Keeble has put a lot of thought into this, so he must be pretending he isn't sure of the location in an attempt to make it appear as an afterthought or to de-emphasize it (D). He obviously knows where it is (A), and if he didn't think the location was important, he wouldn't have mentioned it (B). There is no evidence that he is forgetting (C), and if he had wanted to conceal the location, he would not have said it (E).

26. **B** Mr. Keeble is clearly intimidated by his wife (Statement III)—he requires "courage" to speak to her about the loan (line 4). The passage does not suggest that he is seeking her affection (Statement I). There is also no evidence that he is disgusted by her (Statement II)—he has "feared" (line 16) her response, not resented or rejected it.

27. **A** Because Mrs. Keeble asks the question "icily," we can infer that she is not excited about the idea of lending money (A). The coldness of her response does not suggest that she is tempted by the suggestion (B), that she is keeping an open mind about it (D), or that she wants to hear more about the possibility of the loan (E). We do not know what Mr. Keeble's mission actually is (C).

28. **B** The Lord Mayor has invited the Earl of Lincoln to dinner several times; therefore, "numerous" is the best answer (B). "Groceries" (A) is too literal of a synonym for "sundries," as is "provisions" (C). There have been many dinners, so "infrequent" (D) is not correct, nor is "few" (E).

29. **C** In his aside in line 48, the Lord Mayor reveals that he "scorns" to have Lacy as a son-in-law; sending his daughter away would help to keep her from interacting with Lacy and thus make their marriage less likely (C). Since the Lord Mayor instructs the Earl of Lincoln to "watch" Lacy's actions so he "need not fear" the two will wed (line 44), it must be that the interest between Lacy and Rose is mutual and not only on Rose's part (A). The Earl of Lincoln notes that the Lord Mayor has many times "feasted" the Earl and "many courtiers," which suggests the Lord Mayor has wealth and there's no evidence elsewhere to suggest his family lives in poverty (B). There is also no evidence that the Lord Mayor looks down on the shoemaking profession (E). The Lord Mayor says he "understand[s]" the "subtlety" of the Earl, not that he fears what the Earl will do (D).

30. **E** The Earl of Lincoln says that Lacy spends too much money, so he won't be able to provide for Rose (E). By saying Rose is "mean," Lord Mayor means that she is of a lower class, not that she isn't nice (A). There is no evidence that courtiers cannot marry (B). No mention is made of the cost of a wedding (C). Lacy *does* love Rose: "He is much affected" (line 6) (D).

31. **A** The Earl of Lincoln does not approve of his cousin's spendthrift ways (A). He is not apathetic, because he obviously cares about his cousin's welfare (B). Romantic love (C) would not describe the relationship between the Earl of Lincoln and his cousin, but rather the relationship between Lacy and Rose. He does not necessarily "dislike" his cousin (D). Affection (E) is not the Earl of Lincoln's primary emotion, as he insults Lacy.

32. **A** The Earl of Lincoln does not approve of Lacy's new profession—the line is sarcastic (A). There is nothing that tells us how much shoemakers earn, (B) and (D). The Earl of Lincoln does not want his cousin to be a shoemaker, so he obviously does not admire the profession (C). Shoemaking is not a scientific occupation (E).

33. **E** The Lord Mayor claims his daughter is too common for Lacy, but his aside shows that he does not think that Lacy is a good match: "I scorn to call him son-in-law" (line 48), although he does not admit this (E). He doesn't feel affection (A), nor does he feel like an uncle (avuncular) (B). He never approves the match (C), nor is there any evidence that he respects Lacy (D).

34. **B** An aside is when a character speaks directly to the audience while the dramatic action "freezes." The aside reveals that the Lord Mayor believes the Earl of Lincoln is a "fox"—and so is behaving deceptively (B). The nature of the aside means that the other characters cannot hear the comment (A). While the aside diverts from the general flow of dialogue, it is not a prevarication (a transgression or departure from the norm) that alienates the audience, since the audience is provided with more information than the other characters receive (C). No additional unease is evoked by the aside (D), and while the comment criticizes the Earl of Lincoln, it is not meant to directly insult him, since he is unable to hear it (E).

35. **C** Lacy is never described as "poor" but Rose is, so the correct answer is (C). As you reread the dialogue, be careful to note exactly which character is being described. Lacy is described as "affected" (line 6) (A), "high" (line 13) (B), "unthrift" (line 20) (D), and "jolly" (line 30) (E).

36. **E** Neither of the characters is saying what he is thinking—as revealed by the asides (E). No one is described as frugal (A). "Prodigious" means extreme wastefulness or generosity, whereas "profligacy" means dissipation or licentiousness (B); Lacy is described as profligate, but no one is extremely generous (A). There is no conflict between the younger and older generations (C). There is no contrast between happiness and sorrow in this passage (D).

37. **A** The Earl of Lincoln most likely mentions the wars because Lacy has just been appointed a soldier (A). We can't know whether there will be a death (B). The Earl does not explain why they are fighting the French (C). The lines do not explain the class system in place (D). There is no mention of a national debate (E).

38. **D** The blades of grass are standing before God, so presumably God is talking to them (D). There is no angel (A), nor is St. Peter in the poem (B). God is asking the blades to justify their entry into heaven, so God—not the blades of grass—is speaking (C) and (E).

39. **C** God is happy at the one little blade's comments, so (C) is the best answer. God is not "condescending" (A), "neutral" (B), or "disdainful" (D). God does not show that He is "morally superior" in this poem (E).

40. **C** God rewards the one little blade of grass for his modesty in contrast with the other blades' boastfulness (C). There is no evidence that it is better to do nothing (A). The blade is not rewarded for his forgetfulness (B). The blades are boasting of their accomplishments, not their problems (D). There is no mention of having to tell your bad deeds to someone (E).

41. **B** The word "presently" means "after a while" (Statement II). It has nothing to do with presents or gifts, nor does it mean that the speaker is changing the topic.

42. **C** The other blades were all boasting, so the one little one is ashamed and hanging back because he does not feel worthy (C). All of the blades of grass were little; their heights are not compared (A). There is no evidence of disgust (B), or bitterness or loneliness (D). Choice (E) is incorrect because the blade thought his acts were less worthy than the others, not more worthy.

43. **A** God's declaration that the one little blade is the best is surprising ("unexpected") because it was the one blade that did not admit to any accomplishments (A). There is nothing "satiric" (making fun of) about the phrase (B). It is neither "tragic" (C) nor "comic" (D), nor, since the blade is probably headed to heaven, is there anything "unfortunate" (E).

44. **B** God rising up is a dramatic pause which heightens the suspense of the poem (B). There is no evidence that God is egotistical (A), nor is there a shift or change in how the narrator sounds (C). These lines do not echo anything in the poem (and it's hard to tell whether there is more than one stanza) (D). We cannot know the poet's true feelings (E).

45. **B** We do not hear about how God reacts to the other little blades of grass, so His attitude can best be described as "unstated" (B). God is not ashamed of the blades of grass (A), nor is He "disgusted" (C) with or "disapproving" (D) of them. He does not feel "melancholy" when considering the blades of grass (E).

46. **A** The narrator is poking fun at Lady Bertram so that the reader will laugh, so the tone can best be described as "wry" (A). There is no bitterness in the passage (B). The narrator clearly has opinions regarding Lady Bertram, so "detached" is not correct (C). Although Lady Bertram herself is "melodramatic," the narrator is not (D). And the narrator is free with her opinions and words, so "secretive" is not correct (E).

47. **B** Lady Bertram likes to write about gossip. She can't write about this news (because the son already has), so it is of no use to her (B). Lady Bertram could not use the news (A). There is nothing that suggests Lady Bertram would relay the news unpleasantly (C). There is no evidence that she could write about only part of the news (D), nor are we told that she was bound to secrecy (E).

48. **D** "The want of other employment" means she lacked anything else to do, so (D) is the best answer. She did not require other employment (A). "Desire" (B) is a trap answer because it is a common synonym for "want." There is no mention of finances (C), and we are not told that her employment is defective (E).

49. **E**   The Grants are going away, so Lady Bertram won't be able to write about Dr. Grant's illness or things that Mrs. Grant says when she comes over; in other words, she'll have no news (E). There is no evidence that she enjoys the Grants, except for the gossip they provide (A), and she does not assist them (B). There is no evidence that her house is full, nor that they stay with her (C). She has many correspondents (D).

50. **B**   The phrase is explained in the text that follows it: "so that a very little matter was enough for her" meaning that she could make a small bit of gossip go a long way in her letters (B). She does not inflate the importance of things (A). Choice (C) is a too-literal synonym of "amplifying." There is no evidence that she tries to make people sound more important than they are (D), nor is there any mention of her penmanship (E).

51. **B**   Sir Thomas must be Lady Bertram's husband (B) because she is left with nothing to do when he is in Parliament (plus, if she is a lady, then he must be a lord). There is no evidence that he is her son (A), nor that he is a boarder (C), nor that he is at all connected to the Grants (D), and his Parliament attendance affects her too much for him to be just a friend (E).

52. **A**   At the end of the passage, Lady Bertram writes to Fanny, so she must have something to say (A). We don't know what the news is, so we cannot say it is "malicious" (mean) (B). She is not concerned about the news, but rather predicts that Fanny will feel concerned (C), so she is aware of Fanny's feelings (D). If she were really worried about her niece (E), why would she be telling her the news?

53. **D**   Lady Bertram likes to gossip, and she is a woman of leisure and title (D). She has friends; she is not a "social pariah" (A). We don't know what others in her family think of her (B). She seems to be very connected to society (C), and we don't know anything about her age, except that she has a niece (which says little about how old she is) (E).

54. **D**   The phrase implies that she needs the least amount of news to write her niece, but doesn't even have that (D). We have no evidence that she doesn't like her niece (A), or that she is mad at (B) or uncomfortable around (C) her niece. Lady Bertram loves writing letters to anyone, so (E) is not correct.

55. **A**   The poem is a warning to young women about the pitfalls of vanity (A). There are no myths in the poem (B). The poet is not "sarcastic" (C). The poet warns of fading beauty, so the poet is neither "optimistic" (D) nor "hopeful" (E). Think: Because "optimistic" and "hopeful" are synonyms, they can't both be the right answer, so they should both be eliminated.

56. **C**   The poem is a warning to young women that beauty fades (C). There is no discussion of the importance of beauty (A). There is no "past lesson" to be learned (B). The primary purpose is not to tell a particular story (D). There is no discussion of death (E).

57. **A**   The last two lines of the poem describe the woman as someone who used to be pretty and is now old and faded, of which her eyes are an example (A). There is no evidence that the woman is tired (B). That she is blind is a too-literal interpretation of the line (C). There is no mention of disease, only old age (D). Girls cannot be responsible for someone's loss of beauty (E).

58. **B**   The vain girls are compared to bluebirds—the two groups chatter among themselves (Statements I and II). The teachers are not the carefree chatterers that the poem mentions (Statement III).

59.　**A**　The speaker assumes that the girls will "Go listen to [their] teachers old and contrary / Without believing a word" (lines 3-4); since the speaker, too, is offering to share a cautionary lesson with the girls, in the form of the "story which is true" (line 13), it is reasonable to assume that the girls might ignore the speaker's lesson just as they seem to ignore their teachers' (A). Chattering like bluebirds is an image the speaker assigns to the girls, not that the girls seem to be assigning to anyone else (B). There is no evidence in the poem that the speaker has actually told the girls about the woman in the final stanza, so it is unlikely that the girls would compare the speaker to her (C), nor do the girls, in the speaker's observation, think about older women who might be jealous of their beauty (D). There is no evidence that the speaker is a poet seeking publication or that the girls would assume as much (E).

60.　**C**　The girls don't listen to their teachers because the teachers are old, and they don't worry about the future ("weighty subjects") (C). There is no sense of suspicion (A) or the notion that subjects are hard to understand (B). They are not described as frail (in fact, they "twirl" their skirts) (D). There is no evidence that they disregard others' feelings (E).

61.　**B**　The theme of the poem is that people should not waste time on beauty because it does not last (B). Acting quickly is not a theme (A). Neither are the trappings of wealth (C). Truth (D) is not a theme, nor is frugality (E).

HOW TO SCORE PRACTICE TEST 1

When you take the real exam, the proctors will collect your test booklet and bubble sheet and send your answer sheet to a processing center, where a computer looks at the pattern of filled-in ovals on your answer sheet and gives you a score. We couldn't include even a small computer with this book, so we are providing this more primitive way of scoring your exam.

Determining Your Score

STEP 1   Using the answer key, determine how many questions you got right and how many you got wrong on the test. Remember: Questions that you do not answer do not count as either right or wrong answers.

STEP 2   List the number of right answers here.   (A) _____

STEP 3   List the number of wrong answers here. Now divide that   (B) _____ ÷ 4 = (C) _____
number by 4. (Use a calculator if you're feeling particularly lazy.)

STEP 4   Subtract the number of wrong answers divided by 4 from the   (A) – (C) = _____
number of correct answers. Round this score to the nearest whole number. This is your raw score.

STEP 5   To determine your real score, take the number from Step 4 and look it up in the left-hand column of the Score Conversion Table on the next page; the corresponding score on the right is your score on the exam.

PRACTICE TEST 1 SCORE CONVERSION TABLE

Raw Score	College Board Scaled Score	Raw Score	College Board Scaled Score
61	800	25	520
60	800	24	510
59	800	23	500
58	800	22	490
57	800	21	490
56	800	20	480
55	790	19	470
54	780	18	460
53	780	17	450
52	770	16	440
51	760	15	430
50	750	14	420
49	740	13	410
48	730	12	410
47	720	11	400
46	710	10	390
45	700	09	380
44	700	08	370
43	690	07	360
42	680	06	350
41	670	05	350
40	660	04	340
39	650	03	330
38	640	02	320
37	630	01	310
36	620	00	300
35	620	−01	300
34	610	−02	290
33	600	−03	280
32	590	−04	270
31	580	−05	260
30	570	−06	250
29	560	−07	240
28	550	−08	240
27	540	−09	230
26	530	−10	220
		−11	210
		−12	200
		−13	200
		−14	200
		−15	200

Part III
Content Review and Strategies

Chapter 5
Overview of the SAT Subject Test in Literature

In this chapter, you'll learn what the SAT Subject Test in Literature comprises and how it's scored. We will also explain how best to use this book and what you can expect from the test.

WHAT DOES THE TEST LOOK LIKE?

You'll have one hour to answer approximately 60 multiple-choice questions. You will read six to eight passages (usually seven), each followed by a series of multiple-choice questions. The content will be varied: prose fiction, autobiography, personal essays, excerpts from speeches, poetry, and drama. You may be asked to compare two passages.

What's on the SAT Subject Test in Literature?

All SAT Subject Tests are only one hour long—it's impossible to test a broad range of topics in so short a time. As a result, the SAT Subject Test in Literature is relatively easy to prepare for.

You will be asked to interpret certain excerpts from literature. You will need to be familiar with some of the basic literary terms your teachers have been tossing around in your English classes all these years: common terms such as *metaphor*, *tone*, and *imagery* will be covered; obscure terms such as *enjambment* and *metonymy* will not.

Do NOT sit down with a reading list and a dictionary of literary terms (at least, not to prepare for this test). Instead, concentrate on pinning down literary terms that sound vaguely familiar and learning some great techniques for analyzing the types of passages that will be on the exam.

What's NOT on the SAT Subject Test in Literature?

The good news: You're not expected to be familiar with any specific works of literature; in fact, the test writers try hard to make sure they provide pieces that few students will have read. There's no official reading list for the SAT Subject Test in Literature. You won't be asked who the author is, when the piece was written (the year of publication is provided to you), or where the piece fits within the history of literature. This is simply a one-hour test of your ability to read and comprehend literature and of your familiarity with basic literary terms.

How to Use This Book

We recommend three simple ways to prepare for the SAT Subject Test in Literature.

- **Start early.** The key to cracking the test is practice. Practicing for six hours the day before the test won't do a whole lot of good (and may fry your brain). Instead, give yourself plenty of time to read this book thoroughly.

It's All in the Technique
To crack the SAT Subject Test in Literature, you need to do two things: First, become familiar with some basic literary terms; second, learn some techniques for analyzing a literary passage.

- **Read this book in order.** Inside, you'll find an overview of the information you need to know to get a great score on the test. Terms and techniques are explained, and there are drills and practice questions that ask you to apply them. Each technique builds on a skill we've previously taught you.

- **Trust us.** We've been in the business for a long time. Some of the techniques may be new to you. They might feel unfamiliar at first, but with practice they will become easier. They may even contradict some things you've learned in English class. Remember that English class is designed to educate you. This book is designed to help you do well on a specific test.

HOW IS THE TEST STRUCTURED?

The SAT Subject Test in Literature consists of about 60 multiple-choice questions (the specific number varies on each test). Each of the six to eight passages of prose, poetry, or drama is followed by 4 to 12 questions. Most of the passages come from English and American literature. On occasion, you'll see a passage from another English-speaking culture. All passages are from texts originally written in English—no translations of Cervantes or Baudelaire. Texts may be taken from any time period, but there will be no Middle or Old English (such as *The Canterbury Tales* or *Beowulf*) on the test.

The general breakdown is as follows:

Source

British literature	3–4 passages
American literature	3–4 passages
Other literature (from Australia, New Zealand, English-speaking Africa, Jamaica, and Canada, for example)	0–1 passages

Time Period

Pre-18th century	2–3 passages
18th and 19th centuries	2–3 passages
20th and 21st centuries	2–3 passages

Genre

Prose	3–4 passages
Poetry	3–4 passages
Other (usually drama)	0–1 passages

HOW IS THE TEST SCORED?

The SAT Subject Test in Literature is scored like the other SAT Subject Tests. You get a raw score based on the following formula:

$$
\begin{aligned}
&1 \quad \text{point for each correct answer} \\
-\,&\frac{1}{4} \quad \text{point for each wrong answer} \\
=\,&\phantom{\frac{1}{4}} \quad \text{raw score}
\end{aligned}
$$

Blank answers neither add nor take away from the raw score. Test administrators then calculate what each score corresponds to on a scale from 200–800, which gives you the familiar "out of 800" score you're used to.

For the most part, every raw point translates to approximately 10 points on the scaled score.

HOW SHOULD YOU PREPARE FOR THE TEST?

This book is designed to be a comprehensive resource and guide to the SAT Subject Test in Literature. It doesn't just give you the information you need; it also gives you the practice, with four practice tests in Parts II and IV. But it's important that you take these tests the right way by trying to recreate the test conditions as closely as possible. This means no water breaks, no texting breaks, and no yelling-at-your-little-brother breaks. Sit down in a place where you won't be interrupted and get a reliable watch or clock to measure one hour. Cross off answers as you eliminate them, and practice bubbling your answers on the sheet provided at the very end of the book. If you do this, you'll get a good idea of how the test works and in which areas you need the most improvement.

As you take the test, mark questions that you guess on with a "G." This will help you gauge how well you're guessing.

After Each Practice Test, Ask Yourself …

Did You Get a Lot of "Painless" Questions Wrong?

Sometimes, when you look back and review, you can't believe you got such a straightforward question wrong. Slow down. Did you read the question correctly the first time around? Did you pick the right answer but bubble an incorrect choice? Rushing is the major cause of avoidable errors.

Did You Mismark Answers on Your Answer Sheet?

It's pretty easy to mismark answers when you're skipping around (as you should be). Don't forget to pick a bubbling method (see Chapter 6) and stick with it. It is really a huge bummer if you get the answers right but don't get credit because you filled in the wrong bubble.

Assessing Your Performance

Don't just sit back and drink a glass of lemonade after you complete your practice test. Study your results so you can improve your score. Fill in the lines below. It'll help—really!

1. How many straightforward questions did you get wrong? (These are questions you can't believe you got wrong.)

   _____

2. Why did you get these wrong? (Maybe you didn't read the question closely enough, didn't read the right place in the passage, or misread the answer choices.)

   _____

3. How many knotty questions did you get wrong? (These questions are the ones you really have to study to understand why the right answer is right.)

   _____

4. How many questions did you guess on?

   _____

Slow Down!
Don't rush. This only results in careless errors.

5. How many of those did you get right?

_____

Wrong?

_____

6. If you got the guessed answers wrong, did you narrow down the answer choices to two or three (or even four)?

_____

Was the right answer among those?

_____

If so, guessing was the right move. How can you improve your guessing?

_____

7. Did you feel more comfortable with the poetry or the prose?

_____

8. What parts of the book should you go over again before you take the next practice test or the real SAT Subject Test in Literature?

_____

Summary

Did you get all that?

- Common terms will be tested; obscure terms will not.
- You don't need any outside knowledge of literature.
- Start studying early.
- You get one raw point for a correct answer and $-\frac{1}{4}$ point for each wrong answer.

Chapter 6
General Test Strategies

In this chapter, you'll learn some general test strategies, from determining how many and which passages to attack—and in what order—to effectively using Process of Elimination, eliminating careless errors, knowing how and when to guess, and getting your answers onto the score sheet with accuracy.

TEST STRATEGIES THAT WORK

The Princeton Review has developed effective and time-saving strategies to optimize your study time and improve your score. Some of the strategies will be unfamiliar at first, or you may not be convinced that they'll work. But give them a try—our methods have improved thousands of scores.

Don't Rush

No Loitering
Don't linger too long on any one question—it's worth only one point!

Some students think they need to finish every question to get a good score on the SAT Subject Test in Literature. Not at all. Don't be afraid to skip a few questions as you go along. You don't get any more points for answering questions you find a bit more difficult than ones you find easy. So there's no reason to bust your, well, you know. If you race through the test, you run the risk of making careless errors, misreading questions, or not choosing the right answers, when spending just a little more time on the questions would have gotten you those crucial extra points instead of those quarter-points off.

On the flip side, you don't want to linger on any one question for too long. Don't get bogged down by one complicated or onerous question. It only takes away from time you can use to answer more straightforward questions. If you come across a stumper, eliminate obviously wrong answers and take an educated guess. If you really can't eliminate anything, skip it completely. Move on to a question that you know you can get right.

Since the questions are not in order of difficulty, it is up to *you* to decide the order in which you'll tackle them. Go ahead and judge a book by its cover. If the question looks very time-consuming to you, reminds you of an unpleasant childhood experience, or nauseates you, skip it. You can always return to it if you have time.

In other words, pace yourself. Don't go too fast or too slow. Consult this handy chart to see how many questions you can leave blank and still get the score you want.

Scoring Chart

Scaled Score	Raw Score	# of Questions to Do	# Wrong	Percentile
800	56–61	all	4	99+
750–790	50–55	58–60	6	95–99
700–740	45–49	53–55	6	82–94
650–690	39–43	49–52	8	66–81
600–640	33–38	43–48	8	49–65
550–590	28–32	38–42	8	33–48
500–540	23–27	36–39	10	21–32
400–490	11–22	24–34	10	1–20
300–390	1–10	18–28	15	< 1

ORDERING THE PASSAGES

Now that you see that you don't need to answer every question to get a good score, let's discuss how to choose your battles wisely.

You are taking the test—the test is not taking you. You have 60 minutes to take this exam. So don't waste time on a passage you hate and then never get to a really great passage you would have loved tackling (love, of course, being a relative term—we understand it's a standardized test). Think about the types of passages you like and those on which you tend to score highest. If poetry is the first passage on the test, and poetry is your weak area, move on to a selection you feel more comfortable with and come back to the poetry passage later. You'll get that all-important boost of confidence right away. Sixty minutes is not a long time. It's a sprint, not a marathon. Try to hit your stride in the first five minutes, not halfway through.

Decide in which order you want to tackle the passages. Is prose, poetry, or drama your strong suit? Are you more comfortable with contemporary passages, or do you like older themes? Do you appreciate the sparseness of poetry? The flow of prose? Poems about nature? Excerpts from stories? Knowing what you're good at will help you choose which questions to do as you come to them and which questions to shelve until later. For example, if you're a slow reader, get shorter passages out of the way first.

Once you've settled on a passage, decide what kind of question you want to do. There's no law that says you have to go in order. Skip Roman numeral questions until later (more on these in Chapter 7). If you come across a word you're not familiar with, save that question for later; do something you're more comfortable with instead. There's bound to be something that looks a little better. Nothing feels better than getting questions right at the start. If you meet more challenging questions later in the test, who cares? You're allowed to leave some blank anyway.

Once you've decided which questions to do, how do you go about getting the answers right? The following is a discussion of general strategies for multiple-choice tests. Feel free to apply these techniques to other standardized tests you may take.

Eliminate and Guess

You may have heard that you get penalized for guessing on the SAT and the SAT Subject Tests. This is only partly true. The test administrators dock you 1/4 of a point for wrong answers, but that doesn't mean you should leave an answer blank if you absolutely aren't 100 percent sure it's correct. If this worries you, let's say you must take "educated guesses." That sounds like an intelligent plan. How does this benefit you?

You may be tempted to leave blanks when you don't know the answers, but a little examination of ETS's scoring system should convince you to blacken those ovals a bit more frequently than you have in the past.

Let's say that when the test begins, you have the overwhelming urge to take a nap. You put your head down on the desk and close your eyes, only to awaken when the proctor announces that there are five minutes remaining in the test. Wiping the drool from the side of your mouth, you decide to take your chances and fill in the same letter all the way down. In a statistically perfect world, you would probably get about one in five questions correct (and the Chicago Cubs would win the World Series every thirty years or so).

Here's what statistics predict would happen if you guessed on every question.

12 correct answers earn 12 points.

48 wrong answers results in $(\frac{1}{4})(48)$ points or 12 points being deducted.

Points earned – points deducted = 12 – 12 = 0.

0 points receives a scaled score of 300 points.

So ETS has achieved its goal—a monkey (or a nap-prone student) trained to fill in choice (C) all the way down the page gets a score of 300. The point is: You're not penalized for making random guesses. In fact, nothing happens when you guess.

Now let's say you wake up from your nap and have enough time to eliminate one obviously wrong answer to each question (never mind logistics, we're doing statistics here). With one bad answer gone, you now have a one-in-four chance of getting the answer right.

So out of 60 questions you get:

15 correct answers earn 15 points.

45 wrong answers result in $(\frac{1}{4})(45)$ points or 11.25 points being deducted.

Points earned – points deducted = 15 – 11.25 = 3.75

3.75 points receives a scaled score of 340.

This score will not get you to the Ivy League, but remember, every extra point earns you approximately 10 points on the scaled score. In other words, if you get one right and then three wrong, you're still up a quarter of a point. Four of those earns you one whole extra point.

Did we lose you on the math stuff? After all, we're supposed to be studying for the SAT Subject Test in Literature, right? It all boils down to this:

> Any time you can eliminate even one wrong answer, you must guess, even if the other answers don't make any sense to you at all. It's mathematically proven.

PROCESS OF ELIMINATION (POE)

Process of Elimination (POE) is your weapon of mass destruction, if you will. If you're good at POE, you never have to know the right answer to a question. You just have to be able to identify the wrong answers. For example:

Line 47 of the poem is a good example of

(A)   French cheese
(B)   tap-dancing shoes
(C)   prize-winning barbecue technology
(D)   clean socks
(E)   synecdochical symbolism

Although slightly silly, the question illustrates the idea: If you know what the answer can't be, you are left with the correct answer by default. (Don't worry; you don't have to know what "synecdochical" is.)

Cross Out Wrong Answers

This may seem too obvious for words, but it's extremely important. A lot of students get lazy and just read down the list until they get to an answer they like. Don't be this student. In your test booklet (not your answer sheet!), put a line through the letter of each answer you eliminate. Get into this habit early, so it will be second nature to you by the time the test date rolls around. Imagine yourself at the end of this test. It is your third test today. You're very tired. Your brain is reeling. It would be easy to make a mistake and pick an answer you've already eliminated or fall for a trick answer in the same way that you might accidently grab grapefruit juice instead of orange juice when you're in a hurry at the grocery store. So put lines through the letters of the answer choices you've eliminated, to keep your focus on the decisions you're making.

If an answer is clearly wrong, cross it out. If you have no clue what is meant by an answer choice, put a question mark (?) next to the letter. If you like an answer, put a check mark (✔) next to it. If you really like it, put two check marks (✔✔).

Thus, a sample answer set might look like this:

✓   (A) I like this answer.
         (B) This answer is wrong.
?   (C) I don't understand this answer.
         (D) This answer is wrong.
✓✓   (E) I really love this answer.

Once you've cleared the proverbial air of bad answers, you can make an educated guess among the choices that are left.

Try POE
The Process of Elimination (POE) approach may vary based on question type, but the general idea is always the same.

AVOIDING TRAP ANSWERS

Trap answers are those that ETS puts into the answer choices to try to trick you. They look like great answers because ETS thinks it knows how you think and teases you with an answer that off the top of your head might look right. On tougher questions, be suspicious of easy answers. Look for a trick. Here's an example:

> As it is used in the passage, the word "rare"
> (line 22) means
>
> (A) uncommon
> (B) rude
> (C) exaggerated
> (D) undercooked
> (E) irrelevant

Someone who isn't familiar with the kinds of traps that appear on the test might see the word "rare" and, knowing it means "undercooked," pick (D). But think: The question begins with the words "As it is used in this passage…" This is not a vocabulary test; it's a test of reading and interpreting literature. Even if you've never seen the word "rare" before, you will probably be able to tell its meaning from the context. Without the passage in front of you now it'll be hard to figure out, but the correct answer is (A), "uncommon," a secondary definition of "rare."

SKIPPING QUESTIONS

Skip It!
Be ready to
skip questions.

Unlike those on some standardized tests, questions on the SAT Subject Test in Literature are not in order of difficulty. Some passages are more challenging than others, and within each passage, some questions are more challenging than others. If you feel uncertain about the answer to a question, circle the question number and return later. Sometimes after you've answered simpler questions on a passage, the difficult ones make more sense. If you're still uncertain after you've finished the passage, move on. Return when you've completed the other passages. Nothing is worse than struggling with a difficult passage early in the test, only to discover that the most accessible passage was hiding at the end.

Shirk Work

Each test has at least ten questions that 60 percent of students get wrong. Don't bother with these questions unless you have extra time—they're not worth it.

On the second pass, do the questions you skipped the first time. If you want, you can do three or four passes, but don't spend too much time deciding on the difficulty level of a question. You should be able to determine the difficulty level within a second or two.

You can also do multiple passes within a passage. Sometimes doing the fifth or sixth question in a passage gives you a better idea of what the second question in the passage is asking. We'll talk more about this in Chapter 7.

Don't neglect to keep track of your time. Look at how many questions there are for each passage. If you're trying to decide between two passages at the end, you might want to opt for the one with more questions so you don't have to read two passages. Or you may opt for the passage that has easier questions (usually specific or line-reference questions, not general or reasoning questions).

THE ART OF BUBBLING

Bubbling is the art of transferring your answers onto the score sheet. When you bubble, be sure to fill in the oval completely so that the computer can give you the credit you deserve. When skipping around, pay special attention to where you bubble. It would be horrible to start recording your answer for question 55 and realize you're bubbling in an answer for question 54 on the score sheet. It's like misbuttoning your shirt, only worse.

There are two methods you can use to ensure you're bubbling in the right place. Pick one, and stick with it, and you'll never get lost bubbling again.

Method 1: The Rat Pack

Answer all the questions for one passage in the test booklet by circling the letter. Save up your answers, and every time you get to the end of a passage, transfer your answers to the bubbles on the score sheet.

Method 2: The Worry Wart

Answer questions directly on the bubble sheet. Every time you do a multiple of ten questions, check back to make sure that your answers correspond to the questions you did. Then you'll never be more than ten questions out of whack. This method takes more of your precious time, but if you're prone to misbuttoning your shirt, or making bubbling mistakes, use this.

It doesn't matter which method you use, as long as you pick one and stay with it. It's important to have a reliable system in place *before* test day.

Practice Your Bubbling
Test forms for the practice tests are located at the back of the book. Use them when you take the tests so that you can also get in some bubbling practice.

Summary

Did you get all that?

- Slow down.
- Order the passages.
- Make educated guesses.
- Use Process of Elimination (POE).
- Avoid trap answers.
- Skip challenging passages and/or questions.
- Bubble wisely.

Chapter 7
Strategies
for the SAT
Subject Test in
Literature

This chapter familiarizes you with each type of question that appears on the test and with the best strategies to answer specific, general, and trap questions correctly.

TAKING THE TEST

You may have noticed that the SAT Subject Test in Literature bears a startling resemblance to the critical reading section of the SAT. This is a good thing—it means you may already be familiar with the test format. The main difference between the SAT critical reading section and the SAT Subject Test in Literature is that the latter does *not* contain sentence completion questions and *does* contain poetry. There's less of an emphasis on vocabulary (except for literary terms—we'll get to those in Chapter 8) and more of an emphasis on inference and interpretation questions on the SAT Subject Test in Literature. This means that the answers you need are in the passages. They may be buried or confusingly worded, but they are in there. So the SAT Subject Test in Literature is like an open-book exam.

It's important to remember that often you won't see an answer you love. That's okay. You're not necessarily looking for the "right" answer; the interpretation of literature is subjective. What you are looking for is the best answer. The "least bad" answer is the one you want. If you remember this, you'll find yourself a lot less frustrated. There's bound to be one answer choice that's better than the others, and that will be the correct response to the question. We'll discuss the approach for how to read the passages when we get to the specific chapters for each type of passage (prose, poetry, drama).

HOW TO APPROACH A LITERATURE PASSAGE

This is a literature test, so, naturally, the answers lie in the literature passages that precede each set of questions. Therefore, the importance of knowing how to approach these passages cannot be emphasized enough. Below are some simple steps for navigating literary passages so that you can arrive at the right answer.

1. **Look at the date.** How long ago was the passage written or published? Art usually reflects the preoccupations and conditions of the time period and culture in which it is produced. If you happen to have a sense of the timeline of literary movements, try to place the piece within that context. If you don't, don't worry! Just make use of all the work you've been doing in your history classes. You can look to your sense of American, European, and World histories to provide possible context. The rise of many reform movements in the nineteenth century, for instance, is paralleled in literature by a blossoming of stories written by and about the working class, immigrants, women, black people, and others.

2. **Read the passage.** You don't have to study it carefully; just read enough to know what is basically going on in the passage. Remember: You can (and must) go back to the passage when you answer the questions, so you're just reading to get a sense of where to find the answer when it comes time to search for it. You should read just closely enough so that you can summarize the main theme and tone.

> ### Theme and Tone
> **Theme** is a unifying idea that is a recurrent element in a literary or artistic work. One of Shakespeare's favorite themes is unrequited love.
>
> **Tone** is the attitude of a writer (or narrator) toward a specific subject, event, or audience, as reflected in the literary work's style or manner of expression.

3. **Select a question.** Questions come in three types: **specific questions** (line-reference, almost-line-reference, and vocabulary-in-context questions), **general questions**, and **trap questions**. Questions are usually worded in ETS-speak. That means they have extra words or a complicated structure to confuse you. Get rid of this verbiage by translating the question into your own words. Simplify things by rephrasing the question so that it begins with *who, what, where, when, why,* or *how.*

4. **Return to the passage.** Always go back to the passage to find the answer to the question. Don't rely on your memory of the passage; make sure you can point to the answer in the text.

5. **Answer in your own words.** If you don't use your own words, you won't know exactly what you're looking for in the answer choices. When you've got the answer in your own words, turn to the answer choices and look for a match.

> **Be Original**
> Use your own words to answer the question.

6. **Use Process of Elimination (POE).** Get rid of bad answers—answers that don't match *your* answer. Once you've eliminated the wrong answers, you're left with the right one!

TYPES OF QUESTIONS

As we mentioned earlier, questions come in three basic types: specific questions, general questions, and trap questions. In this section, we've broken down each category so you can familiarize yourself with the kind of question structure and verbiage you'll likely see on the SAT Subject Test in Literature.

Specific Questions

Line-Reference Questions

Specific questions generally take the least time. They usually give a specific line reference for you to find. Read a few lines above and below the reference in the passage, and answer the question *in your own words*.

DRILL 1

Here are some examples of line-reference questions. Try putting the questions in your own words.

1. Which of the following best restates the meaning of lines 3–4?

   _____

2. The second quoted sentence (lines 7–10) is characterized chiefly by

   _____

3. The speaker's tone in lines 11–15 is

   _____

4. The simile of the "distant shadow" (line 29) suggests

   _____

5. In lines 27–30, the narrator can be best described as

   _____

6. In describing the response of the "careless birds" (line 30) to the "venerable hunter" (line 34), the author suggests that they

   _____

Answers can be found in Part IV.

The reason that these questions often take less time to answer than others is that they tell you exactly where to look for the answer. Generally, specific questions are in chronological order, so that a question about line 4 will come before a question about line 17.

Almost-Line-Reference Questions

Sometimes questions are line-reference questions in disguise. They don't mention a specific line number, but nonetheless they offer clues as to where you can find the answer. Usually there's one word or phrase that will help:

> The author mentions *Vanity Fair* in order to

Here, just scan the text for the words *Vanity Fair* (conveniently italicized). Then reread the passage—five lines above and five lines below—for the context.

> Sue Anne considers the Bali tariffs unfair because

Now you'll have to scan the text for the words "Sue Anne" or "Bali" or "tariffs." Other than the fact that no line number is given, this question is still a line-reference question, and the answer should be relatively easy to locate in the passage.

Vocabulary-in-Context Questions

Vocabulary-in-context questions ask you what a word means. These will almost always test a secondary or tertiary (third) meaning of a word or a word that has changed meaning since the original text was written.

If you come across one of these questions, go back to the text and cross out the word. Then write in your own word for the word on which you're being tested. Go through the answer choices, and pick the one that best matches your word.

Do NOT go directly to the answer choices and simply choose a synonym for the word in question. That approach is likely to give you the wrong answer.

Suppose the question says:

> In context, the meaning of the word "favored"
> (line 20) is closest to

First, to translate the question you might reword it as "What does favored mean?"

Then you'd return to the passage and find that line 20 says, "Clearly Amahl favored his father; it was almost as though his mother was not involved in his birth." Reading a few lines above and below would help you to understand the context in which "favored" is being used. When you cross out "favored" in the sentence, you might replace it with something like "looked like," since the passage notes that Amahl and his father were often mistaken for each other.

"Translate" the Question
Putting a question into your own words will help you clarify and focus your thinking.

Now go through the answer choices:

(A) resembled
(B) presented
(C) was partial to
(D) prioritized
(E) supported

Choice (A) best matches the predicted meaning, so it's the best answer. (Note that only looking at the answer choices might have led to picking (C), as "was partial to" is a familiar meaning of "favored," but that is not the correct answer in this context.)

General Questions

General questions ask about the themes, structure, tone, or style of the piece as a whole. They may or may not ask a question about the attitude of a character, the narrator, or the passage's overarching argument. Pick an answer only if you can point to the specific place in the text that supports your answer. (If your justification is "I don't know where, but I feel like it's in there," you're probably not choosing the right answer, or you need to look harder in the text.)

Point It Out
Make sure you can point to the answer in the text.

If you answer these questions after you answer specific questions, you should have a good idea of what the passage is about—you may not even have to go back to the text. Don't worry if you need to consult the passage, however. That's what it's there for.

One trick to watch out for is the old theme-versus-structure question. Theme questions ask about what the passage is trying to say. Structure questions ask about how it's being said.

Some theme questions:

> The primary theme of the poem is
>
> The passage is primarily concerned with
>
> Mr. Beetlegeuse's attitude in the passage can best be described as

Some structure questions:

> The structure of the narrative can best be described as
>
> The author uses incomplete sentences most likely to
>
> The two stanzas are most different in that they

Don't try to answer a structure question with a theme answer.

The procedure for approaching general questions is the same as for specific ones: Translate the question, find the answer in the passage, put the answer in your own words, and use POE.

Trap Questions

Trap questions come in two flavors: NOT/LEAST/EXCEPT and Roman numeral. They are usually (although not always) more complicated than other types of questions. They are also considered time suckers, and are best skipped. Glance at them to see whether they are straightforward or more time-consuming, and don't be afraid to come back to them at the end or to leave them blank.

NOT/LEAST/EXCEPT Questions

Whenever you see a NOT/LEAST/EXCEPT question, circle the word that is capitalized so you don't forget that this question is inside out. Instead of finding one right answer, you are looking for the one wrong answer. Avoid careless errors by writing a "T" for "True" next to each answer choice that is correct or true, and an "F" for "False" next to the ones that are incorrect or untrue. You should end up with four of one letter and one of the other. That one is the right answer.

For example:

Avoid the Trap
One way to work your way through NOT/LEAST/EXCEPT questions is by marking each answer choice with "T" or "F." Remember, you're looking for the one *wrong* answer (the "F").

> All of the following are true of bunny rabbits
> EXCEPT:
>
> T   (A) They have four legs.
> T   (B) They are soft.
> T   (C) They eat carrots.
> F   (D) They have wings.
> T   (E) They have long ears.

Because (D) is the only "F," it is the correct answer.

Roman Numeral Questions

Roman numeral questions are three questions rolled into one. Here's an example:

> The author suggests that bunny rabbits are
>
>   I. Good pets
> II. Yxzmkls
> III. Smaller than most dogs
>
> (A) I only
> (B) II only
> (C) III only
> (D) I and III only
> (E) II and III only

Go through the listed statements one by one. It's not a bad idea to begin with the Roman numeral that appears most frequently or with the one you know is true. In this case, you know that rabbits are good pets because you've read the passage. So Roman numeral I has to be in the answer. Right away you can get rid of (B), (C), and (E) because they don't contain "I." Now, be smart. The only choices that are left involve I and III. All you have to do is see whether III is true. Don't even worry about II (good news, because you don't know what Yxzmkls means). So go back to the passage and see whether bunnies are smaller than most dogs. They are. Choice (D) is the correct answer.

If you do this carefully, you can avoid doing extra work. You may not need to try every Roman numeral, just a couple of them. This will save you time and effort.

DRILL 2

Make sure you can answer the following questions before you move on.

What are the six steps for tackling questions?

1. _____

2. _____

3. _____

4. _____

5. _____

6. _____

What are the three kinds of questions on the SAT Subject Test in Literature?

1. _____

2. _____

3. _____

What are the two kinds of trap questions on the SAT Subject Test in Literature?

1. _____

2. _____

Answers can be found in Part IV.

Summary

Make sure you can

- differentiate between specific and general questions
- identify the type of question: line-reference, almost-line-reference, vocabulary-in-context, theme, structure, tone, NOT/LEAST/EXCEPT, or Roman numeral question
- quickly decide which questions to do first
- handle trap questions

Chapter 8
Literary Terms and Concepts

This chapter covers everything you need to know for the test. Yup, that's it. Some of the terms will be familiar to you, others may be new, but you can make use of them all in English class. We've also included a list of the main concepts you'll be tested on and some practice drills to wrap it all up!

INTRODUCTION TO ANALYZING POETRY, PROSE, AND DRAMA

The SAT Subject Test in Literature doesn't review your knowledge of literature in general, but there are some terms that are helpful to know. To begin, let's define the following categories:

POETRY: A poem is a rhythmic expression of feelings and ideas, kind of like the lyrics to a song. It may or may not rhyme.

PROSE: This one's easy—if it's not poetry, it's prose. Prose is generally broken down into two categories: fiction and nonfiction.

DRAMA: A play; something that is intended to be acted out. Plays can be written in verse or in a more conversational style.

CONCEPTS YOU'LL BE TESTED ON

Generally speaking, questions on the SAT Subject Test in Literature are rooted in six major literary concepts. In other words, questions on the test usually ask about one of these six categories. Although it's not important for you to memorize these, a short discussion of their meanings should help clarify what will be on the test.

1. Meaning

Of course, the biggest thing that you will be tested on is the meaning of the passage, especially if it's obscure. Many questions will be devoted to seeing whether you understand the plot and motivation of the characters. If the passage is making an argument, the test writers will want to see whether you understand its claims.

The test will also ask you for the meanings of words in context. You can expect that a secondary or tertiary (third) definition of a given word will apply. The word's meaning depends upon the words that surround it. Make sure you look for its meaning in the passage. Never assume a definition without considering its context.

2. Form

Although the test won't ask you to distinguish a sonnet from a sestina, you might have to judge whether a passage is a fable or an allegory. Also, the test will ask you about the overall structure or organization of each passage. Do the events of the passage unfold chronologically? Does the passage follow the development of an argument? How does the author manage transitions from one paragraph or stanza to the next? In some cases, being able to identify a passage as elegy or satire may help with assessing its tone or its use of figurative language (see next page).

Questions about form may also ask about how the author constructs sentences. Is the syntax in the passage simple or convoluted? Do sentences in a poem tend to end in the same places the lines end, or do the sentences tend to continue across line-breaks? Does the author use a lot of parallel sentence constructions?

3. Tone

Tone is a broad term referring to how the passage's language reflects a specific attitude toward a specific subject. Questions about tone will focus on things like diction (word choice) and syntax (sentence structure), asking you to recognize how an author's vocabulary or formal decisions factor into the description of a character or the framework of an argument. Is the passage's diction high-falutin' or fairly colloquial? Does the dialogue sound like how people talk today, or does it sound more like it comes out of a historical movie? What techniques does the author use to place emphasis on certain ideas or relationships rather than others? These techniques may be visual (are certain kinds of words frequently italicized?) or sonic (does the poem feature a lot of alliteration or a particularly sing-songy rhyme scheme?).

4. Figurative Language

Questions about figurative language will test your ability to identify similes, metaphors, personification, and other kinds of descriptive imagery. Some questions will also ask you to assess how those techniques affect the themes, tone, or argument of a passage.

5. Narrative Voice

Narrative voice describes how the teller of a story is positioned relative to that story: does the passage describe characters' experiences as if the narrator had a bird's-eye view of the setting and events, or is the speaker recounting an event that happened to him/herself? (These differences are also called differences in point of view.) Does the narrator seem to be addressing a specific audience? Are there certain experiences or perspectives the narrator focuses on or excludes?

Don't forget that we can't assume any overlap between author, narrator, and characters: assume that the opinions expressed by an "I" are those of a narrator (in prose)/ speaker (in poetry) the author has created, rather than those of the author her/himself.

6. Characterization

This is a less frequently explored topic on the SAT Subject Test in Literature. Characterization refers to how the author represents his or her character(s) in the piece. Sometimes authors describe their characters. Sometimes they let the characters speak for themselves. Sometimes authors let us hear about a character from other characters in the text. Characterization questions ask about the ways in which you learn about how a character thinks and acts.

Again, it's not necessary to have these six areas memorized. But we've outlined them here so that you have an idea of what to expect on exam day.

Learn This
Become familiar with
the basic literary terms
listed on the next
few pages.

LITERARY TERMS YOU SHOULD KNOW

Here's a list of the basics. Each is followed by a discussion of the term, sometimes with examples. If you're familiar with a given term, move on to the next term. Concentrate on any that are unfamiliar to you or on which you feel you could use some work. Make flash cards to help you memorize these terms.

ALLEGORY: A story with underlying symbols that really represent something else. A character can be allegorical.

> Example: The nursery rhyme "Humpty Dumpty" was really a political allegory in which the characters represented people in government who were falling from power.

ALLITERATION: The repetition of a consonant sound at the beginnings of multiple words in close succession.

> Examples: *Silently stalking her sister on the stairs…Falling, falling, fearfully falling…*

ALLUSION: An indirect reference to something or someone (usually from history or literature).

> Example: …but once put out thy light,
> Thou cunning'st pattern of excelling nature,
> I know not where is that Promethean heat
> That can thy light relume…

In this speech from William Shakespeare's *Othello*, Othello alludes to the myth of Prometheus (who stole fire from the gods for human use) as he considers the permanence of murder (putting out Desdemona's light).

ANACHRONISM: The placement of a person, event, or object in a historical or chronological time to which it does not belong. The technique can be deliberate or unintentional.

> Example: George Washington drove his limousine downtown for the inauguration.

ANALOGY: A comparison used to explain or clarify something. Metaphors and similes are common examples of this technique.

> Example: The leftover coffee was like sludge in the carafe.

To describe a camp counselor's job as "spending the whole week herding cats" is to depend upon the listener's understanding that just as it is very challenging to try to get a bunch of cats to all do the same thing when directed, so too is it difficult to get campers to stay together and follow directions.

ANECDOTE*: A short narrative or story about an interesting event, usually presented as if the recounted incident is interesting in isolation or as a subjective description (rather than as part of a larger narrative or a piece of objective data).

> Example: Although they lacked clear evidence that the school was haunted, the students compiled a set of anecdotes detailing the individual creepy occurrences they'd experienced on the premises.

ANTAGONIST: The major character opposing the protagonist; usually the villain.

> Example: The Joker, Batman's archenemy, is my favorite antagonist.

ANTHROPOMORPHISM: The assignment of human attributes, such as emotions or physical characteristics, to nonhuman things. Anthropomorphism is usually applied to animals—unlike personification, which is a more general category that can apply to all types of things (objects, buildings, abstract concepts, etc.).

> Example: Everyone jokes that my cat is a snob because of her regal stance and cold demeanor.

APOSTROPHE: An address to a person (or abstract concept), usually a person who is absent. This device is usually found in plays or poetry, either at the beginning of a speech or as an interjection.

> Examples: O Romeo, Romeo! Wherefore art thou Romeo? (William Shakespeare)
> Still, wond'rous youth! each noble path pursue,
> On deathless glories fix thine ardent view (Phillis Wheatley)

ARGUMENT*: A series of reasons offered to persuade an audience of something (or against something); some literary texts begin with "arguments" that summarize the work's plot or main subject.

> Example: The primary argument of Virginia Woolf's *A Room of One's Own* is that women need physical space and economic independence if they are going to write fiction; to persuade her readers, Woolf introduces a series of examples, surveying literary history to show how money and a place to work helped some writers succeed, while destitution and a lack of solitude thwarted others' endeavors.

ASIDE: A brief comment made in the presence of other characters that seems to be directed not at those other characters but at the audience, or to the speaker him/herself. An aside is usually labeled as such in stage directions.

> Example: PROSPERO. Soft, sir! one word more.
> (Aside) They are both in either's powers; but this swift business
> I must uneasy make, lest too light winning
> Make the prize light.

In this speech from William Shakespeare's *The Tempest*, Prospero addresses Ferdinand ("sir"), then makes a comment directed not at Ferdinand, nor at any other character present in the scene; the aside allows Prospero to inform the audience that when he subsequently seems to turn against Ferdinand's courtship of Miranda, it is not because Prospero actually disapproves of the match, but because Prospero doesn't want "too light winning / [to] Make the prize light."

BLANK VERSE: A poetic form in which the lines have a regular meter (usually iambic pentameter) but don't conform to a consistent rhyme scheme.

> Example: Although a blank verse poem doesn't rhyme,
> Its rhythm helps its readers move along:
> Its meter like a heartbeat underlies
> Thusly each argument the speaker makes.

COMEDY*: The genre of drama (or literature more generally) that is primarily meant to provoke laughter and amusement; a work of literature written in a light or satirical style and having a happy resolution.

> Example: Part of the pleasure of watching a romantic comedy comes from the formula of the genre: I can watch the movie confident that, no matter what obstacles the couple faces, somehow they'll end up together at the end.

DICTION: An author's choice of words, phrasing, and sentence structure. Descriptions of diction often characterize it as being formal, informal, colloquial, or slang.

> Example: Jenny's use of archaic diction in texting her siblings drove them crazy, since they could never remember what words like "forsooth" or "thine" meant.

ELEGY*: A mournful and melancholy poem or song, usually to pay tribute to a deceased person.

> Example: John Milton's "Lycidas" opens with the argument that the deceased title character "must not float upon his wat'ry bier/ Unwept, and welter to the parching wind"; consequently, the elegy details and laments the circumstances and consequences of Lycidas' drowning.

EMPHASIS: An especially forceful expression that gives particular importance to the mentioned person, place, or thing. In writing, this intensified expression can be accomplished in a lot of ways: typographically, with italics or by using capital letters; rhetorically, through repetition or forceful diction; etc.

>   Example: The nerve of some drivers, to speed across a pedestrian walkway when I've clearly already started crossing the street.

FABLE: A story that has a moral, usually involving animals as the main characters.

>   Example: Aesop's fable about the grasshopper and the ant is a great illustration of why you should work hard and prepare for bad times.

FARCE: A satire that borders on the absurd or ridiculous.

>   Example: The play produced a farcical portrait of academia, culminating in a graduation ceremony in which none of the student's advisors could remember her name.

FIGURATIVE LANGUAGE: The use of figures of speech—including metaphors, similes, and elaborate imagery—to convey a meaning beyond the literal definitions of the words used.

>   Example: When you told me "my heart is beating like a drum," I knew that your pulse must have been reflecting your nervousness as you got ready to sing your solo.

FORM: The organization and structure of a piece of literary writing; more general than genre.

>   Example: In form, the work was prose, organized into chapters, paragraphs, and sentences; in its content, however, the work was much more like a poem, since most of its sentences consisted of a series of images connected through metaphor.

FREE VERSE: A poetic form where there are no regular (or specified) line lengths or metrical patterns.

>   Example: It is hard
>   When confronted with a poem in free verse
>   To overstate just how differently
>   Its rhythms develop
>   Than is the case in a poem of more
>   Regular meter.

GENRE: A particular category or style of literature, especially one that is characterized by particular techniques or purposes.

> Example: The conventions of the detective novel, from the cataloguing of clues to the progression of the plot from initial crime through investigation to resolution and justice, make it fairly easy to recognize when a novel belongs, or is responding, to the genre.

HYPERBOLE: A deliberate exaggeration.

> Examples: That test was the worst thing in the world.
> There were a billion people at the concert.
> I'm going to be grounded for ten years when my parents find out where I was last night.

IMAGERY: The use of descriptive or figurative language to create a picture in the mind of the reader.

> Example: He illustrated his point about how rundown the gym was by describing in detail the rusty doors on the lockers, the broken handlebars on the stationary bikes, and the mold growing in the grout of the showers.

INDIRECT SPEECH: Narration that explains what was expressed out loud, often in a conversation, without directly quoting the speakers. (A common subcategory of this term is indirect dialogue, but indirect speech can also be used to present information about what a character has said to him/herself.)

> Example: During breakfast, Janet's father told her that she couldn't borrow the car anymore.

IRONY: An expression of meaning that is the opposite of the literal meaning.

> Example: Here's a soothing little ditty by Megadeth.

Stories can be ironic as well when they end in a way that is the opposite of what you would have expected. A story about an obsessively clean man who is killed by a garbage truck is ironic. O. Henry's classic story "The Gift of the Magi" is a classic example of dramatic irony. The husband sells his watch to buy his wife an ornate hair comb for Christmas, only to find out that she has sold her hair to buy him a watch chain.

MEANING: What a writer conveys or indicates, directly or indirectly, in a particular text.

> Example: "What do I care?" is literally a question that asks, "What do I have invested in the situation?" but the phrase is used most frequently to convey the meaning that "It doesn't matter to me."

METAPHOR*: A technique of comparison in which words describing one kind of thing are used to describe another type of thing, suggesting a direct relationship between the two things. This technique is closely related to simile, but it goes farther than asserting similarity using words such as "like" or "as": in a metaphor, X is not like Y, but X is Y.

> Examples: She was a breath of fresh air in the classroom.
> The new principal was a prison warden; the students were his inmates.
> Johnny is a tiger when it comes to football.

METER: The ordered pattern of syllables in lines of a poem. In poetry, combinations of syllables are called "feet": identifying a poem's meter allows you to describe (a) what kinds of feet appear in the poem and (b) how many feet appear in each line.

> Example: Elizabeth Barrett Browning wrote most of the poems in *Sonnets from the Portuguese* in iambic pentameter: each line has ten syllables organized into five iambic feet (an unstressed syllable followed by a stressed syllable), as in the line "The face of all the world is changed, I think."

MONOLOGUE: A long passage of drama during which only one character speaks (even if there are other, non-speaking characters on stage as well).

> Example: When Rachael began to recite her monologue, her voice was so quiet that even the actors on stage near her had trouble understanding her words; by the end of the speech, though, when the character was supposed to raise a rallying cry for justice, Rachael was so caught up in the part that she found herself practically shouting her lines.

NARRATIVE: The representation of a sequence of events; the telling of a specific story.

> Example: In the final decades of legal slavery in the United States, writers like Harriet Jacobs and Frederick Douglass produced autobiographical narratives detailing their lives as enslaved people and their escapes to freedom.

ONOMATOPOEIA: A word intended to simulate the actual sound of the thing or action it describes.

> Examples: A *buzzing* bee.
> "*Bam!*" The superhero hit the criminal.
> The snake *hissed* at its predator.

OXYMORON: A phrase in which the words are contradictory.

> Examples: He was happy in his pessimism.
> They were intelligently ignorant.

Sometimes an oxymoron is used for comic effect; sometimes it is used to illustrate a paradox.

PAEAN: An expression of joyful praise.

> Example: Gerard Manley Hopkins's "Pied Beauty" begins with the exclamation "Glory be to God for dappled things," and it unfolds as a paean to the natural world in all its multicolored, complicated forms.

PARABLE: A story told to convey a moral message or lesson.

> Example: In the Bible, Jesus tells his disciples the parable of the Good Samaritan to illustrate the moral imperative to help those in need.

PARADOX: A phrase or account that appears to contain contradictory ideas but may in fact contain a basic truth that resolves the contradiction.

> Example: Although he was sentenced to ten years of hard labor, the guilt-ridden criminal looked as though a weight had been lifted from his shoulders.

PARALLELISM: The repetition of sounds, meanings, or sentence structures to reflect an equivalence of meaning or emphasis.

> Example: I don't want your pity. I don't want your money. I don't want your car. I only want your love.

PARODY*: A literary work that imitates the style of another author or era for comic effect, often by exaggerating the style or by applying it to an unexpected or inappropriate subject.

> Example: The hyperbolic diction and formal syntax of Alexander Pope's "The Rape of the Lock", when applied to the poem's plot (the surreptitious snipping of a lock of someone's hair), mark the poem as a parody of how conventional epic poetry describes dramatic battles and tragedies.

PASTORAL: A work that portrays the lives of people in the country, especially shepherds, or of people immersed in nature. This kind of text often idealizes or romanticizes the adventures of rural life.

> Example: Flannery O'Connor's short stories often disrupt conventions of pastoral narrative when characters confront unexpectedly complicated, cruel, or violent aspects of rural experience.

PATHOS: Something that evokes a feeling of pity or sympathy. Think of the word "pathetic." A pathetic person adds an element of pathos to a story.

> Example: And so, the little orphan girl curled up on the cold steps of the church and tried to sleep.

PERSONIFICATION: The assignment of human attributes to something nonhuman.

> Examples: I hope that fortune will smile on me when I take my exam. My car always seems so miserable when I let someone else drive.

PERSPECTIVE: The individual point of view from which a narrator or character observes events or situations.

> Example: Because Emma Donoghue's *Room* is narrated from the perspective of a young child, the reader's understanding of what is happening in the novel depends on how the child uses his limited vocabulary to describe what he experiences, or how he uses imagery to express the implications of specific events.

PLOT: The main events of a literary work, described as an interrelated series of episodes; the storyline of a literary text.

> Example: I can't summarize the plot of the last Hunger Games novel for you—I don't want to give away what happens at the end!

POINT OF VIEW: The vantage point from which a story is presented to a reader; the most common categories of point of view are first person (where the narrator telling the story refers to him/herself as "I") and third person (where the narrator does not appear as an individual in the story, but instead refers to other characters using "he/she/they" pronouns). Point of view is also often called "voice" or "narrative voice."

> Example: In a story like Jamaica Kincaid's *Girl*, the second-person point of view, which addresses the reader as "you," invites the reader to experience a series of commands or pieces of advice in the same style that the character experiences it.

PROTAGONIST: The main character in a literary text; usually the hero.

Example: Jane Eyre, Charlotte Brontë's most famous protagonist, is my favorite heroine in English literature.

RHYME SCHEME: The pattern according to which a poem's rhymes are arranged. This is usually indicated using letters of the alphabet to show which lines rhyme with one another.

Example:

Thy glass will show thee how thy beauties wear,
Thy dial how thy precious minutes waste;
The vacant leaves thy mind's imprint will bear,
Line And of this book this learning mayst thou taste.
(5) The wrinkles which thy glass will truly show,
Of mouthed graves will give thee memory;
Thou by thy dial's shady stealth mayst know
Time's theivish progress to eternity.
Look what thy memory can not contain
(10) Commit to these waste blanks, and thou shalt find
Those children nurs'd, deliver'd from thy brain,
To take a new acquaintance of thy mind.
These offices, so oft as thou wilt look,
Shall profit thee and much enrich thy book.

This sonnet by William Shakespeare is comprised mostly of alternating rhyming lines: it has a rhyme scheme of ABAB CDCD EFEF GG.

RHYTHM: The pattern of sounds (including stressed and unstressed syllables) characteristic of a piece of verse.

Example: The rhythm of an iambic line of verse has been described as sounding like a heartbeat or a horse's gait because of the alternating unstressed and stressed syllables: duh DUH duh DUH duh DUH.

SATIRE*: A literary work that uses techniques like hyperbole, irony, and sarcasm to criticize or ridicule a specific subject.

Example: Jonathan Swift's *A Modest Proposal* satirizes the inhumane policies that perpetuated horrific living conditions in eighteenth-century Ireland by advocating cannibalism as a means of solving the problems of starvation.

SIMILE: A comparison of two items, often using the words "like" or "as" to articulate the items' relationship.

> Examples: I'm as quick as a cricket.
> He's as sly as a fox.
> He was greeted like a rooster in a hen house.

Similes are frequently used in poetry to evoke an idea through an image.

SOLILOQUY: A speech, addressed to the audience, delivered while only one actor is on stage. A soliloquy often allows a character to expound upon a predicament or emotional state.

> Example: The character's self-assured demeanor in talking with his friends was in stark contrast to the tone of his tentative soliloquy, in which he grappled with whether to tell anyone about his parents' divorce.

STAGE DIRECTION: An authorial instruction inserted in parentheses (and printed in italics) within a line of dramatic speech in order to encourage the actor to speak or move in a certain way.

> Example: ALGERNON: *(Stiffly.)* I believe it is customary in good society to take some slight refreshment at five o'clock. Where have you been since last Thursday?
> JACK: *(Sitting down on the sofa.)* In the country.

This brief passage from Oscar Wilde's *The Importance of Being Earnest* demonstrates two common ways stage directions function in dramatic scripts: to direct an actor to articulate a line of dialogue in a certain way—here, stiffly—or to specify how an actor should move physically around the stage.

STANZA: A grouping of the lines of a poem, sometimes determined by rhyme scheme or other formal convention. Just as a piece of prose often contains multiple smaller units called paragraphs, many poems contain multiple stanzas. In a poem with multiple stanzas, white space appears between each set of lines to separate them.

> Example: Roses are red while violets are blue.
> A couplet is a stanza whose lines number two.
>
> Roses are red; smiles are free.
> A tercet is a stanza
> Whose lines number three.
>
> Roses are red.
> They speak of amour.
> A quatrain is a stanza
> Whose lines number four.

STRUCTURE: The organization or overall design of a work of literature: this can include how a plot develops and resolves, how a play is broken into scenes and acts, or how a poem progresses from one kind of imagery in one stanza to another in the next.

> Example: The term "Freytag's pyramid" describes a narrative structure where the plot moves from description of a conflict through a series of increasingly exciting events ("rising action"); the conflict reaches a climax, the plot's "make or break" moment, which is followed by events that depict the resolution of the conflict ("falling action") and the final situation of the characters.

STYLE: The manner of expression that characterizes a particular literary work, or the work of a particular writer, literary group, or period.

> Example: Gertrude Stein's poetic style resonates with the Cubist style developed in painting by artists like Pablo Picasso: Stein's poems often present concrete images or observations, described from multiple distinct points of view, without using punctuation or language to explain how those points of view are related to one another.

SYNTAX: The ordering of words into grammatically meaningful patterns such as phrases, clauses, and sentences. Writers often manipulate syntax by changing traditional word order to emphasize particular words or phrases.

> Example: John Milton's syntax often reworks standard English subject-verb-object constructions, listing the recipients of an action before naming the action itself—sometimes his poetry even sounds like it's been translated from another language, like Latin.

THEME: A dominant idea or central concept in a literary work; an idea or message evoked by many of the work's symbols or elements of the plot, characters, or setting.

> Example: Themes of identity and humanity echo through the scientific experiments, philosophical explorations, and physical conflicts that dominate the pages of Mary Shelley's *Frankenstein* as the creature (and the novel's readers) tries to define who and what he is.

TONE: The attitude of a writer (or narrator) toward a specific subject, event, or audience, as reflected in the literary work's style or manner of expression.

> Example: Marquis' admiration of the other people in his study group was clear from the tone of his email—from his complimentary comments about their work habits to the profusion of exclamation points he used to punctuate his suggestions.

TRAGEDY: A genre of literature or drama that depicts characters facing sorrowful or difficult experiences; a play whose main character may have a "fatal flaw" that leads to disastrous consequences.

> Example: Part of the heartbreak of reading a tragedy is wanting to shout, again and again, for characters to do things differently, to avoid making the stubborn determinations or naïve pronouncements that seem to seal their devastating fates.

VOICE: (See Point of View)

* NOTE: Some of these terms have adjectival forms that can be used in more general senses than the nouns. A poem's tone can be elegiac, for example, even if the poem doesn't necessarily frame itself as an elegy; language described as metaphorical can sometimes include similes and personification.

Parts of Speech

Although you don't need to be able to diagram sentences, sometimes questions ask you about how words function within a text. For example, you might see the question, "What's the main verb of this sentence?" This may already be old hat for you. If so, smile smugly as you review parts of speech:

Be a Grammar Guru
Even though the SAT Subject Test in Literature isn't a grammar exam, it may help to review some basic grammar rules—especially if your skills are a bit rusty. For some extra grammar prep, pick up a copy of *Grammar Smart, 4th Edition*.

> **Noun:** word that names a person, place, thing, or idea
>
> **Verb:** action word or a word that expresses a state of being
>
> **Adverb:** description word that modifies (describes, refers to) a verb, an adjective, or another adverb
>
> **Adjective:** description word that modifies a noun
>
> **Pronoun:** word that takes the place of a noun

In the sentence "The quick, brown fox jumped gracefully over the lazy dog,"

- *quick*, *brown*, and *lazy* are **adjectives** (they modify *fox* and *dog*)
- *fox* is a **noun** and the **subject** of the sentence; *dog* is also a **noun**
- *jumped* is a **verb**
- *gracefully* is an **adverb** (it modifies the verb *jumped*)

Drill 1

The sentences below contain examples of simile, metaphor, and personification/anthropomorphism. Identify the literary device used in each sentence, and place the sentence number in the appropriate column in the chart.

Metaphor	Simile	Personification/Anthropomorphism
_____	_____	_____
_____	_____	_____
_____	_____	_____
_____	_____	_____
_____	_____	_____
_____	_____	_____

1. She moved through the room like a cool summer breeze.
2. The house shivered in the cold winter wind.
3. Marie was as sad as a basset hound when she heard the news.
4. The news that she had won the sweepstakes was a dream come true to Mary Anne.
5. Bunnies often feel dejected when kept in their hutches for too long.
6. The wind sang a song of melancholy as it whistled through the field.
7. Taking standardized tests is torture unless you're prepared.
8. Like a soldier marching into battle, the student body president went to meet with the new principal.
9. That test was no day at the beach.
10. My puppy is too proud to wear a silly collar like that one!

Answers can be found in Part IV.

Drill 2

The sentences below contain examples of onomatopoeia, alliteration, oxymoron, and pathos. Identify the literary device used in each sentence and place the sentence number in the appropriate column in the chart.

Onomatopoeia	Alliteration	Oxymoron	Pathos
_____	_____	_____	_____
_____	_____	_____	_____
_____	_____	_____	_____
_____	_____	_____	_____
_____	_____	_____	_____
_____	_____	_____	_____

1. Yet again they made fun of the poor handicapped boy because he was too short to reach the sink.
2. The announcer's booming voice caught the attention of the excited *American Idol* hopefuls.
3. He was conspicuous by his absence at the new student meeting.
4. Sailing swiftly through the water, they won the race.
5. Napoleon was a giant in his smallness.
6. After waiting all through the night, Joan and David were told that no more petitions would be accepted, and their request for medicine for their sick child would go unheard.
7. "Knock, knock, knock" was tapped out to signal that a club member was at the door.
8. The new attorney on the case was practically pompous.
9. An odd atmosphere descended on the room, perfectly described by Shakespeare's "heavy lightness."

Answers can be found in Part IV.

Drill 3

Read the following poem carefully before you choose your answers.

"Elegy"

Let them bury your big eyes
In the secret earth securely,
Your thin fingers, and your fair,
Line   Soft, indefinite-coloured hair,—
(5)   All of these in some way, surely,
From the secret earth shall rise;
Not for these I sit and stare,
Broken and bereft completely;
Your young flesh that sat so neatly
(10)   On your little bones will sweetly
Blossom in the air.

But your voice…never the rushing
Of a river underground,
Not the rising of the wind
(15)   In the trees before the rain,
Not the woodcock's watery call,
Not the note the white-throat utters,
Not the feet of children pushing
Yellow leaves along the gutters
(20)   In the blue and bitter fall,
Shall content my musing mind
For the beauty of that sound
That in no new way at all
Ever will be heard again.

(25)   Sweetly through the sappy stalk
Of the vigorous weed,
Holding all it held before,
Cherished by the faithful sun,
On and on eternally
(30)   Shall your altered fluid run,
Bud and bloom and go to seed:
But your singing days are done;
But the music of your talk
Never shall the chemistry
(35)   Of the secret earth restore.
All your lovely words are spoken.
Once the ivory box is broken,
Beats the golden bird no more.

(1927)

1. The main verb in the second stanza is

   (A) "rising" (line 14)
   (B) "pushing" (line 18)
   (C) "fall" (line 20)
   (D) "Shall content" (line 21)
   (E) "will be heard" (line 24)

2. The "voice" of the deceased is compared to all of the following EXCEPT

   (A) the sound of an underground stream
   (B) the wind
   (C) the blossom of a flower
   (D) the music of a bird
   (E) the pattering of feet

3. The phrase "cherished by the faithful sun" (line 28) is an example of

   (A) irony
   (B) paradox
   (C) personification
   (D) oxymoron
   (E) poetic license

4. The poem is written in

   (A) a regular meter
   (B) the elegiac tradition
   (C) a consistent rhyme scheme
   (D) an extended allegory
   (E) pathetic empathy

"Elegy" was written by Edna St. Vincent Millay, an American poet and playwright. Answers and explanations can be found in Part IV.

Drill 4

Test yourself: See whether you can define the following terms. Check your answers in the glossary of terms on pages 78–89.

allegory _____

satire _____

parable _____

protagonist _____

stanza _____

parallelism _____

perspective _____

Summary

Did you get all that?

Before moving on, you should be comfortable identifying

- prose
- poetry
- drama
- the literary terms on pages 78–89
- basic parts of speech

Chapter 9
Analyzing Prose

This chapter covers fundamental concepts in literature, such as character, plot, and point of view. These are important components within the prose section of the SAT Subject Test in Literature. By the end of this chapter, you should understand the primary forms of prose as well as some of their key elements, such as character and voice.

WHAT IS PROSE?

Prose is a form of writing that is not organized by strict metrical rhythms. It's how people speak; it's the stuff of novels and speeches, essays and chronicles, comic books and news articles, letters and dissertations. As this list highlights, prose writing is generally divided into two major categories: nonfiction, which presents information about real people, places, and events, and fiction, which features invented scenarios and characters. For the purposes of the SAT Subject Test in Literature, it's not important to distinguish between the two: you'll never be asked to decide whether a passage is fiction or nonfiction. Indeed, as we'll see below, writers of fiction and nonfiction use many of the same techniques to present information to their readers.

One thing fiction and nonfiction have in common: both forms of prose are broken into units called paragraphs. Understanding the movement within and between paragraphs can help clarify what the passage is about—its *plot*, if the passage is telling a story, or its *argument*, if it is trying to persuade readers of an idea.

PROSE PASSAGES: WHAT TO LOOK FOR

To practice analyzing prose, let's look at an example from *Moll Flanders*, by Daniel Defoe.

> My true name is so well known in the records
> or registers at Newgate, and in the Old Bailey, and
> there are some things of such consequence still
> *Line* depending there, relating to my particular conduct,
> (5) that it is not be expected I should set my name or
> the account of my family to this work; perhaps,
> after my death, it may be better known; at present
> it would not be proper, nor not though a general
> pardon should be issued, even without exceptions
> (10) and reserve of persons or crimes.
> It is enough to tell you, that as some of my worst
> comrades, who are out of the way of doing me harm
> (having gone out of the world by the steps and the
> string, as I often expected to go), knew me by the
> (15) name of Moll Flanders, so you may give me leave to
> speak of myself under that name till I dare own who
> I have been, as well as who I am.
> I have been told that in one of neighbour nations,
> whether it be in France or where else I know not,
> (20) they have an order from the king, that when any
> criminal is condemned, either to die, or to the
> galleys, or to be transported, if they leave any
> children, as such are generally unprovided for, by
> the poverty or forfeiture of their parents, so they are

(25) immediately taken into the care of the Government,
and put into a hospital called the House of Orphans,
where they are bred up, clothed, fed, taught, and
when fit to go out, are placed out to trades or
to services, so as to be well able to provide for
(30) themselves by an honest, industrious behaviour.

Had this been the custom in our country, I had
not been left a poor desolate girl without friends,
without clothes, without help or helper in the
world, as was my fate; and by which I was not only
(35) exposed to very great distresses, even before I was
capable either of understanding my case or how to
amend it, but brought into a course of life which
was not only scandalous in itself, but which in its
ordinary course tended to the swift destruction both
(40) of soul and body.

But the case was otherwise here.

(1722)

Time Period

Start by looking at the date of the passage's publication. What do you know about the global and social history of that period? Can you think of any wars, colonizing activity, scientific developments, or social reforms that the passage's writer might be engaging with? Such context can help you identify key *themes* in the passage.

In this example: *Moll Flanders* was first published in 1722. An important historical context for the passage might be the Enlightenment, a period when science, philosophy, politics, and literature underwent significant changes.

General hints: Prose, like poetry and drama, often responds to the formal conventions and thematic preoccupations of its historical context. Many nonfiction prose texts written before the 1800s focus on making theological or scientific arguments through didactic reasoning; in many novels of the period, narrators (like Moll) frame their stories as "real" autobiographies or travelers' accounts. After the development of the scientific method, nonfiction in the nineteenth century tends to rely more on collecting and analyzing sets of data to deduce argumentative claims; fiction, meanwhile, developed a set of conventions for representing the "real" experiences of its characters. In the later part of the nineteenth century, both nonfictional and fictional works often reflect social reform movements addressing issues of race, class, and gender. The twentieth century was

Questions about Narrators, Characters, and Purpose

Pay attention to the interactions or relationships between the narrator of a passage and the other characters. Sometimes on the SAT Subject Test in Literature you may be asked to identify what effect a certain word or description has on your perception of a specific character. It is easier to analyze the "purpose" of specific words or phrases when you view that language in the context of the narrator's overall attitude toward characters or situations. Based on the language mentioned in the question, is the narrator being judgmental or complimentary? Tentative or effusive?

marked by two World Wars, plus a global Depression, an ever-increasing rate of scientific and technological change, and greater social mobility. These major events are reflected in literature's shifting attempts to represent its characters' "real" lives.

Speaker(s)

Who is speaking in the passage? In prose, the "teller" of the story is called the narrator. What do you know about the narrator's position relative to other characters in the passage? Does the narrator seem to recount the story to a specific audience (another character, or the reader him/herself)? Does the narrator seem to have a bird's-eye view of the story, swooping into different characters' experiences and describing those characters' thoughts with perfect accuracy? Or is the narrator only able to describe his/her own experiences, excluding specific claims about other characters' motivations or insights?

In this example: Although the passage's narrator declines to give her "true name," she asks the reader to "give leave" for her to use the name Moll Flanders. Whatever her name, the narrator makes clear that she is talking about her own experience, her own "particular conduct." Moll suggests she is so infamous "that it is not be expected I should set my name or the account of my family to this work"; she seems to be preparing to tell the story of her life to this point, describing retrospectively "a course of life which was not only scandalous in itself, but which in its ordinary course tended to the swift destruction both of soul and body." At the same time, Moll refers to other people's knowledge to lend authority to her own account: she has "been told" about how other countries treat the children of criminals differently, though she herself doesn't know which countries do so.

General hints: Prose passages rely on narration to ground the reader in a specific situation—for that reason, identifying the narrator's *point of view*, or the vantage from which the narrator presents the story to the reader, is crucial to understanding the contents of the passage.

In **first-person** prose (like the opening of *Moll Flanders*), the narrator is a character in the story he/she is telling. It's easy to identify when a passage is narrated in the first person, because the story will be told using I/me pronouns. This kind of *narrative* is often very personal, revealing details about the narrator that may not be known to other characters. Because first-person prose primarily reflects one character's experience, one limitation is that the reader doesn't have firsthand access to other characters' experiences of the story. Sometimes first-person narrators don't tell the truth; sometimes first-person narrators misunderstand, or ignore, what is happening around them.

In **third-person** prose, the narrator's *perspective* is separate from that of the characters in the story. This narrative *voice*, which refers to characters using third-person pronouns (he/him, she/her, they/them), can be restricted to reporting one character's point of view, or the writer may instead use third-person narration to show a "bird's-eye" view of the story from multiple points of view. While first-person narration tends to be highly subjective, a third-person narrator can comment more objectively on the characters and situation of the story.

Most works you'll encounter on the test will be narrated in the first- or third-person, but two other less-common narrative voices could show up. **Second-person** narration describes a sequence of actions as it happens to "you," like a Choose-Your-Own-Adventure story ("You walk into a class. You choose the same desk you always do. You sigh wearily"). Using the "you" pronoun allows this voice to create a special, intense relationship between the reader and the events of the story—the reader seems to become a character in the book, rather than just an observer.

Finally, **first-person plural** narration uses, you guessed it, the first-person plural pronouns, we/us, to describe the experiences of a group of narrators together. ("We looked into the crystal ball. What we saw there scared the bejesus out of every one of us.") Because this perspective tells the story of what has happened to multiple people, often without naming or otherwise distinguishing among those narrators' experiences, this narrative technique evokes a community that has shared specific kinds of experience, inviting the reader to focus on the events the narrative recounts rather than on characters' individual subjective reactions to those events.

Situation

What kind of story is the passage telling about the characters and their interaction? What is happening? What argumentative claims is the narrator making about him/herself, about other characters, or about the natural or social world?

In this example: Moll mentions repeatedly the criminality and destitution of her background: she resists naming herself or her family while she's alive, even if a general pardon is issued "of persons or crimes"; she notes that some of her "worst comrades" have been executed "by the steps and the string" (hanging), a method of death that Moll has "often expected" to experience. In the third and fourth paragraphs, Moll suggests that she is the child of at least one criminal parent—she recalls having been told that in other countries, "when any criminal is condemned," any children left "generally unprovided for" are "immediately taken into the care of the Government," but "the case was otherwise" for Moll herself.

General hints: To assess the situation of the passage, think first about the setting and plot of the passage—the story literally being told about the characters. Where are the characters, and what are they doing?

Analyzing the *form* of the narrative can also be helpful in identifying situation: does the narrative incorporate a lot of dialogue? Is it primarily one character's account? Does it describe a specific landscape or a general social condition?

Do the characters seem to be joking with one another, which might suggest the *genre* of the passage is *comedy*? Do the characters seem to represent abstract concepts (like Vice or Reason) rather than specific individuals, which might suggest the passage is *allegorical*? Having a sense of the genre of the passage can help you eliminate answer choices—in a scientific treatise, the narrator is unlikely to claim that a point is true "because I said so," while in a piece of magical realism, it is not uncommon for supernatural figures and phenomena to appear alongside human characters.

Tone/Voice

Now that you know what is happening, and to whom it is happening, you can analyze *how* the passage conveys what is happening. Does the narrator present information about other characters' inner experiences? Do certain characters' comments change in *tone* over the course of the passage? Are certain characters using *figurative language*—and if so, what are the effects of that *imagery*?

In this example: The passage opens with Moll assuring the reader that there are reasons for her refusing to share certain information. This technique both establishes Moll as an authoritative narrator, in control of the telling of her own story, and also emphasizes the subjectivity of her account—she isn't going to tell us everything, nor does she necessarily want to. The *diction* of the passage is not especially elevated, but the passage's multiple long sentences and complex *syntax* seem to reflect Moll's attempts to provide a rationale for her behavior without getting into the specifics of her family history ("the account of my family").

As the passage progresses, Moll uses the contrast of "one of [the] neighbour nations" with her own context to suggest that she is not solely responsible for the circumstances of her criminality and poverty: the third and fourth paragraphs describe retrospectively and very generally how her abandonment by both parents and government left her to face "very great distresses" and ultimately settle on a destructive "course of life."

General hints: Think about whether the passage's formal components, which you've identified in your analysis of its narrator and plot, affirm or complicate the attitudes or arguments expressed in the narrator's actual language. If dialogue appears, do characters speak with the same levels of formality or informality? Does the narrator's diction or syntax differ drastically from those of the other characters? Does one description or set of images contradict or reframe observations made elsewhere? Does the argument rely on assertions of opinion rather than evidence of facts?

Drill 1

Try reading this prose passage and answering the questions that follow.

> They had walked in single file down the path, and
> even in the open one stayed behind the other. Both
> were dressed in denim trousers and in denim coats
> Line with brass buttons. Both wore black, shapeless hats
> (5) and both carried tight blanket rolls slung over their
> shoulders. The first man was small and quick, dark
> of face, with restless eyes and sharp, strong features.
> Every part of him was defined: small, strong hands,
> slender arms, a thin and bony nose. Behind him
> (10) walked his opposite, a huge man, shapeless of face,
> with large, pale eyes, with wide, sloping shoulders;
> and he walked heavily, dragging his feet a little, the
> way a bear drags his paws. His arms did not swing
> at his sides, but hung loosely.
>
> (1937)

What historical context, if any, does the passage's date suggest to you?

_____

From what/whose point of view is this passage narrated? Whose thoughts or feelings is the narrator expressing?

_____

What kind of information is emphasized in the passage?

_____

Now try using the information you brainstormed above to help you answer some test-style questions about the passage.

How does the diction in the passage contribute to your sense of the two men?

_____

How would you describe the syntax of the passage?

_____

1. The structure of the passage is best described as

   (A) two characters are compared and then contrasted
   (B) each character is introduced and described
   (C) two characters are compared to each other and then each is compared to an animal
   (D) two characters' physical characteristics are described, followed by their clothing
   (E) characters' outward appearances are stated, followed by their inner thoughts

2. The tone of the passage can best be described as

   (A) contemptuous
   (B) dispassionate
   (C) apathetic
   (D) eerie
   (E) enthusiastic

This passage is from John Steinbeck's *Of Mice and Men*. Answers and explanations can be found in Part IV.

Drill 2

Read the following first-person passage and answer the questions that follow.

> Call me Ishmael. Some years ago—never mind
> how long precisely—having little or no money in
> my purse, and nothing particular to interest me on
> Line shore, I thought I would sail about a little and see
> (5) the watery part of the world. It is a way I have of
> driving off the spleen, and regulating the circulation.
> Whenever I find myself growing grim about the
> mouth; whenever it is a damp, drizzly November
> in my soul; whenever I find myself involuntarily
> (10) pausing before coffin warehouses, and bringing
> up the rear of every funeral I meet; and especially
> whenever my hypos get such an upper hand of me,
> that it requires a strong moral principle to prevent
> me from deliberately stepping into the street, and
> (15) methodically knocking people's hats off—then, I
> account it high time to get to sea as soon as I can.
>
> (1851)

What historical context, if any, does the passage's date suggest to you?

_____

From what/whose point of view is this passage narrated?

_____

How does the syntax of the passage change from the first sentence to the final sentence?

_____

How does the changing syntax affect your understanding of Ishmael's personality or history?

_____

Now let's see how this quick analysis helps us answer test-style questions about the passage.

1. The passage is best described as

    (A) allegorical drama
    (B) character introduction
    (C) historical commentary
    (D) interior monologue
    (E) political satire

2. By the end of the passage, Ishmael emerges as

(A) ambitious but generous
(B) crude and inconsiderate
(C) insecure and self-centered
(D) sensitive but self-confident
(E) temperamental but self-aware

3. In line 6, the word "spleen" most nearly means

(A) path
(B) blood
(C) melancholy
(D) internal organ
(E) energy

4. Lines 7-16 ("Whenever I find…as soon as I can.") contain which of the following?

I. Alliteration
II. Hyperbole
III. Parallel structure

(A) None of the above
(B) I only
(C) II only
(D) I and III only
(E) All of the above

This passage is from *Moby Dick*, by Herman Melville. Answers and explanations can be found in Part IV.

Drill 3

Try applying what you've learned so far to the opening of this short story.

> The year was 2081, and everybody was finally
> equal. They weren't only equal before God and the
> law. They were equal every which way. Nobody
> _Line_ was smarter than anybody else. Nobody was better
> (5) looking than anybody else. Nobody was stronger
> or quicker than anybody else. All this equality was
> due to the 211th, 212th, and 213th Amendments to
> the Constitution, and to the unceasing vigilance of
> agents of the U. S. Handicapper General.
> (10)   Some things about living still weren't quite right,
> though. April, for instance, still drove people crazy
> by not being springtime. And it was in that clammy
> month that the H-G men took George and Hazel
> Bergeron's fourteen-year-old son, Harrison, away.
>
>   (1961)

Once again: does the passage's date remind you of any specific historical or social contexts?

_____

From what/whose perspective is the passage narrated?

_____

How would you describe the relationship of the first paragraph to the second paragraph?

_____

How would you describe the diction and syntax of the passage?

_____

1. The narrator's tone can best be described as

    (A) satirical
    (B) harshly critical
    (C) wholly frustrated
    (D) mildly emotional
    (E) excessively casual

2. The effect of the repetition of the phrase "nobody was" is to

   (A) introduce theme
   —(B) underscore a point
   (C) instill a sense of loneliness
   (D) refute a commonly held assumption
   (E) present three contradictory elements

3. In the first paragraph, the author employs which of the following?

   (A) Internal rhymes
   (B) Mimicry of the speech of the lower class
   (C) General comparison
   —(D) Parallel construction
   (E) Introduction of the protagonist

This passage is from "Harrison Bergeron," by Kurt Vonnegut. Answers and explanations can be found in Part IV.

Drill 4

Take a look at the following passage and questions that follow.

My name had lost its ring of familiarity and I
had to be nudged to go and receive my diploma.
All my preparations had fled. I neither marched up
Line to the stage like a conquering Amazon, nor did I
(5) look in the audience for Bailey's nod of approval.
Marguerite Johnson, I heard the name again, my
honors were read, there were noises in the audience
of appreciation, and I took my place on the stage
as rehearsed.
(10) I thought about colors I hated: ecru, puce, lavender,
beige, and black.

(1969)

1. From the passage, it is reasonable to infer that

   (A) the audience was more interested in
       Marguerite's graduation than she was
   (B) Marguerite was surprised that her name was
       called
   (C) the experience of graduating was more
       overwhelming than Marguerite had imagined
   (D) Marguerite was unable to get her diploma
   (E) Marguerite had tried to make a painting of
       the scene before it happened

2. The sentence "I neither marched up to the stage
   like a conquering Amazon, nor did I look in the
   audience for Bailey's nod of approval" (lines 3-5)
   contains an example of

   (A) authorial intrusion
   (B) startling anachronism
   (C) complicated syntax
   (D) anthropomorphism
   (E) classical allusion

This selection is from the autobiography of Maya Angelou, *I Know Why the Caged Bird Sings*. Answers and explanations are in Part IV.

Drill 5

Now test your skill on this passage.

"Try and make a clever woman of her, Lavinia;
I should like her to be a clever woman."

Mrs. Penniman, at this, looked thoughtful a
Line moment. "My dear Austin," she then inquired, "do
(5) you think it is better to be clever than to be good?"

"Good for what?" asked the Doctor. "You are
good for nothing unless you are clever."

From this assertion Mrs. Penniman saw no reason
to dissent; she possibly reflected that her own great
(10) use in the world was owing to her aptitude for
many things.

"Of course I wish Catherine to be good," the
Doctor said next day; "but she won't be any the less
virtuous for not being a fool. I am not afraid of her
(15) being wicked; she will never have the salt of malice
in her character. She is 'as good as good bread,' as
the French say; but six years hence I don't want to
have to compare her to good bread-and-butter."

"Are you afraid she will be insipid? My dear
(20) brother, it is I who supply the butter; so you needn't
fear!" said Mrs. Penniman, who had taken in hand
the child's "accomplishments," overlooking her
at the piano, where Catherine displayed a certain
talent, and going with her to the dancing-class,
(25) where it must be confessed that she made but a
modest figure.

Mrs. Penniman was a tall, thin, fair, rather faded
woman, with a perfectly amiable disposition, a high
standard of gentility, a taste for light literature, and
(30) a certain foolish indirectness and obliquity of
character. She was romantic; she was sentimental;
she had a passion for little secrets and mysteries—a
very innocent passion, for her secrets had hitherto
always been as unpractical as addled eggs.

(1881)

1. The word "overlooking" (line 22) is meant to suggest
that Mrs. Penniman does which of the following?

   (A) Ignores Catherine's talent
   (B) Teaches Catherine how to play the piano
   (C) Supervises Catherine's piano playing
   (D) Discourages Catherine
   (E) Hires Catherine's tutors

2. Which of the following does Mrs. Penniman use metaphorically to talk about her influence on Catherine?

   (A) Addled eggs
   (B) Butter
   (C) Bread
   (D) Salt
   (E) A fool

3. What does the author imply by the terms "it must be confessed that she made but a modest figure" (lines 25-26)?

   (A) Catherine was trim and fit.
   (B) Catherine was unaware of her talent.
   (C) Catherine was unlikely to brag.
   (D) Catherine was a talented dancer.
   (E) Catherine was just an average dancer.

4. The narrative tone in the above piece can best be described as

   (A) melodramatic
   (B) ironic
   (C) sardonic
   (D) didactic
   (E) observant

5. The narrative point of view in the above passage is that of a

   (A) third person
   (B) protagonist
   (C) second person
   (D) sarcastic first person
   (E) detached first person

6. In this context, "addled" (line 34) most nearly means

   (A) confused
   (B) rotten
   (C) scrambled
   (D) burdened
   (E) useful

This passage is from Henry James's *Washington Square*. Answers and explanations can be found in Part IV.

Drill 6

Now put it all together with this passage and accompanying questions.

Their adobe house was the same as two
decades before, four large rooms under a
thatched roof and three square windows facing
Line south with their frames painted sky blue. Lin
(5) stood in the yard facing the front wall while
flipping over a dozen mildewed books he had
left to be sunned on a stack of firewood. Sure
thing, he thought, Shuyu doesn't know how to
take care of books. Maybe I should give them to
(10) my nephews. These books are of no use to me
anymore.
　　Beside him chickens were strutting and geese
waddling. A few little chicks were passing back
and forth through the narrow gaps in the paling
(15) that fenced a small vegetable garden. In the
garden pole beans and long cucumbers hung on
trellises, eggplants curved like ox horns, and
lettuce heads were so robust that they covered up
the furrows. In addition to the poultry, his wife
(20) kept two pigs and a goat for milk. Their sow was
oinking from the pigpen, which was adjacent to
the western end of the vegetable garden. Against
the wall of the pigpen a pile of manure waited
to be carted to their family plot, where it would
(25) go through high-temperature composting in a pit
for two months before being put into the field.
The air reeked of distillers' grains mixed in the
pig feed. Lin disliked the sour smell, which was
the only uncomfortable thing to him here. From
(30) the kitchen, where Shuyu was cooking, came the
coughing of the bellows. In the south, elm and
birch crowns shaded their neighbors' straw and
titled roofs. Now and then a dog barked from
one of these homes.
(35)　　Having turned over all the books, Lin went
out of the front wall, which was three feet high
and topped with thorny jujube branches. In one
hand he held a dog-eared Russian dictionary he
had used in high school. Having nothing to do,
(40) he sat on their grinding stone, thumbing through
the old dictionary. He still remembered some
Russian vocabulary and even tried to form a few
short sentences in his mind with some words.

But he couldn't recall the grammatical rules
(45) for the case changes exactly, so he gave up and
let the book lie on his lap. Its pages fluttered
a little as a breeze blew across. He raised his
eyes to watch the villagers hoeing potatoes in
a distant field, which was so vast that a red flag
(50) was planted in the middle of it as a marker, so
that they could take a break when they reached
the flag. Lin was fascinated by the sight, but he
knew little about farm work.

(1999)

1. The passage as a whole can be said to be a contrast of

   (A) center and periphery
   (B) corruption and honesty
   (C) intellect and physicality
   (D) heaven and earth
   (E) secular and divine

2. Lin's attitude could best be described as

   (A) haughty
   (B) indifferent
   (C) excited
   (D) thoughtful
   (E) enthralled

3. It is reasonable to infer that

   (A) Lin is a professor in the city
   (B) Lin is returning home after a long
   time away
   (C) Lin is on vacation
   (D) Lin is not used to the country
   (E) Lin is blind to the beauty of the country

4. Which of the following is an example of personification?

  (A) "long cucumbers hung on trellises" (lines 16-17)
  (B) "chickens were strutting and geese waddling" (lines 12-13)
  (C) "The air reeked of distillers' grains mixed in the pig feed" (lines 27-28)
  (D) "From the kitchen, where Shuyu was cooking, came the coughing of the bellows" (lines 29-31)
  (E) "Their sow was oinking from the pigpen" (lines 20-21)

5. The lines "Sure thing, he thought, Shuyu doesn't know how to take care of books. Maybe I should give them to my nephews. These books are of no use to me anymore" (lines 7-11)

  I.   are an example of indirect dialogue
  II. signify a shift in the narrator's focus
  III. represent a relinquishing of Lin's pastoral life

  (A) I only
  (B) II only
  (C) III only
  (D) I, II, and III
  (E) I and II

6. The "sour smell" (line 28) refers to

  (A) Shuyu's cooking
  (B) the manure near the pigpen
  (C) the pig feed
  (D) the mildewed books
  (E) the nearby field

7. The passage as a whole is best described as

  (A) a paean to rural life
  (B) an elegy for a lost time
  (C) a detailed description of a place
  (D) an epiphanic moment in a young man's life
  (E) an allegory of a homeward journey

The excerpt is from Ha Jin's *Waiting*. Answers and explanations can be found in Part IV.

Summary

Did you get all that?

Before you move on, make sure you understand

- genre
- plot
- character
- voice
- point of view

Chapter 10
Tackling Poetry

Poetry has a reputation for being unnecessarily complex and hard to understand, but very often the poetry passages are the easiest on the SAT Subject Test in Literature. In this chapter, we'll give you the tools with which you can successfully analyze poetry and identify poetic devices, including form, meter, and theme. We will also discuss classical and modern poetry, and there is a list of useful terms in the chapter as well.

WHAT IS POETRY?

As defined broadly in Chapter 8, poetry is "a rhythmic expression of feelings and ideas." That definition is vague on purpose, because poetry encompasses a broad range of material, from the rhyming messages found on greeting cards to the deliberately difficult *stanzas* of T.S. Eliot. What most poems share, however, is that certain feelings and/or ideas are emphasized through a given poem's patterns of *style* or *rhythm*.

These "patterns" include the poem's organization into lines and stanzas; they also include whether the language in the poem conforms to a specific *rhyme scheme* (a pattern of rhyming lines) or *meter* (a pattern governing how many stressed syllables each line of poetry contains, and in what arrangement). These formal components of the poem affect how the poem's *diction* and *syntax* present specific ideas to the reader.

Sometimes poetry passages can seem intimidating: line breaks can make it difficult to identify the subject or main verb of a sentence, and extended sequences of images don't always immediately seem to fit together. The good news is that poetry passages are usually shorter than prose passages, which leaves you more time to think about the implications of their language.

WHAT TO LOOK FOR

To practice analyzing poetry, let's look at an example from *Sonnets from the Portuguese*, a collection by Elizabeth Barrett Browning.

> When our two souls stand up erect and strong, A
> Face to face, silent, drawing nigh and nigher, B
> Until the lengthening wings break into fire B
> At either curved point, — what bitter wrong A
> Can the earth do to us, that we should not long A
> Be here contented? Think. In mounting higher, B
> The angels would press on us, and aspire B
> To drop some golden orb of perfect song A
> Into our deep, dear silence. Let us stay C
> Rather on earth, Beloved, — where the unfit D
> Contrarious moods of men recoil away C
> And isolate pure spirits, and permit D
> A place to stand and love in for a day, C
> With darkness and the death-hour rounding it. D
>
> (1850)

It's All in the Form
A poem's form is its physical *structure*, including line length, rhythm, rhyme, and repetition.

Time Period

As you did with the prose example, start by looking at the date of the passage's publication. What do you know about the global and social history of that period? Can you think of any wars, colonizing activity, scientific developments, or social reforms that the passage's writer might be engaging with? Such context can help you identify key themes in the passage.

In this example: *Sonnets from the Portuguese* was first published in 1850. You may remember that the mid-nineteenth-century was a time of rampant industrialization and urbanization. This sonnet doesn't mention industry, pollution, or city congestion, but its references to "pure spirits," the "golden orb," and the earth's potential to effect "bitter wrong" echo the *imagery* and tensions of slightly earlier romantic verse. ("Romantic" here doesn't mean sappy—it refers to an artistic movement, dominant in the early nineteenth century, that focused on the intensity of individual feelings and the power of individual experiences of nature.) You may also remember that in the nineteenth century, women began advocating for their rights to earn income, own property, and divorce their spouses, among other things. Browning's poem reflects these shifts in conventional gender hierarchies by asserting the equality of both the speaker and the beloved, whose "two souls stand up erect and strong, / Face to face," instead of reiterating the gender dynamics of classical love poetry—where the (male) lover usually asserts the power of his poetry by using verse to catalogue the singular virtues of his (female) beloved.

General hints: Poetry, like prose and drama, often responds to the formal conventions and thematic preoccupations of its historical context. Many poems written before the 1800s emphasize themes of religion or mythology, romantic love, or the fleeting nature of worldly beauty, and they often maintain definite formal structures and rhyme schemes. Poems from the nineteenth century tend to focus more on the balance between intellect and emotion, nature and industry; in the later part of the century, literary works often reflect social reform movements addressing issues of race, class, and gender. The twentieth century was marked by two World Wars, plus a global Depression, an ever-increasing rate of scientific and technological change, and greater social mobility. These major events are reflected in literature's shifting attempts to represent its characters' experiences. In these later centuries, poems that conform to traditional metrical or formal structures often do so to comment on the thematic or political implications of those conventions.

Speaker(s)

Who is speaking in the passage? Is the speaker addressing a specific person (or abstract concept), or does the speaker seem simply to be describing an experience or emotional situation? Is the speaker reflecting on a past experience? Musing on a philosophical or theological conundrum? Advancing an argumentative claim?

In this example: Throughout the poem, Browning's speaker addresses a person who is "Beloved." Rather than summarizing their past relationship, the speaker looks forward to the future, when the lovers' souls stand up together, and speculates about the best outcome of that communion.

General hints: A poem's title, if given, may help you identify the speaker, or define the relationship between the poem's speaker and the person or thing the speaker is addressing. *Elegies* and love poems frequently deal with real people; other poems, like odes or *paeans*, are more likely to address *personified* abstractions or even parts of the speaker's self. In trying to articulate the relationship of speaker to subject, look out for instances of *apostrophe*, when a poem's speaker suddenly addresses a new (often absent and/or nonhuman) figure like nature, morality, beauty, or death.

Consider, too, whether the speaker is integrating someone else's language into his or her address. Does the poem directly quote another writer's work, or does the speaker attribute certain statements to another source?

Situation

While prose and drama represent specific stories about (usually) named characters, sometimes poetry doesn't have an obvious *plot*, focusing instead on using figurative language and/or *allusion* to describe a complex situation faced by the poem's speaker.

What seems to be the occasion for the speaker's articulation of the ideas in the poem? Is the speaker in love? In mourning? Satirizing a problematic social institution?

In this example: The speaker asks the beloved a question, exhorts the beloved to "Think" about the available options, and suggests that staying on earth will actually be preferable to what initially seems like the ideal outcome—ascending to heaven with their angelic souls. In heaven, the speaker argues, "angels would press on us, and aspire / To drop some golden orb of perfect song / Into our deep, dear silence": recognizing the value of their relationship, the angels would want to fill the lovers' silence with song. On earth, however, the "unfit / Contrarious moods of men" will avoid the lovers' "pure spirits." Even though their solitude will have "darkness and the death-hour rounding it," the speaker suggests, having "A place to stand and love in for a day" will be worth it.

The poem's rhyme scheme can be represented as ABBA ABBA CDCDCD. That notation makes clear that the first, fourth, fifth, and eighth lines all rhyme; the second, third, sixth, and seventh lines all rhyme; etc. This symmetrical rhyme scheme, along with the poem's regular meter (iambic pentameter), reflects formally the marriage of the lovers' well-matched souls. It also, by conforming to the conventions of traditional sonnet form, actually positions the speaker's utterance in opposition to the "golden orb of perfect song" that the angels might seek to impose on the lovers.

General hints: To assess the situation of a poem, first try to articulate the poem's occasion. Is it an *elegy*, written to mourn the loss of a loved one or a national hero? Is it a love poem? Is the speaker instead expressing ecstatic joy about something, which might suggest that the poem is a paean? Having a sense of the genre of the passage can help you eliminate answer choices—a *pastoral* poem is unlikely to mount a scathing critique of lazy shepherds, while a *satirical* poem is unlikely to offer sincere praise to its subject.

Analyzing the *form* of the poem can also be helpful in identifying the situation of the speaker or the *tone* of the speaker's claims. What is the rhyme scheme? Is the meter (the beat of the poems' lines) uniform and steady, or is it more erratic? A regular meter can sound soothing and stable, while unmetered poetry can sound more chaotic or colloquial.

Tone/Voice

Now that you know what is happening, and to whom it is happening, you can analyze how the language of the passage conveys what is happening. If you've identified a specific occasion for the poem, do you notice the speaker challenging expected components of that genre in any way? Does the speaker's use of imagery align with a particular argumentative claim?

In this example: The poem begins with imagery that suggests the lovers are already essentially divine: their souls draw "nigher and nigher / Until the lengthening wings break into fire / At either curved point," suggesting that they have wings like the angels. By the end of the poem, however, the speaker is claiming a preference for mortal experience, where the curved fiery wings are exchanged for a different curvature, "A place to stand and love in for a day, / With darkness and the death-hour rounding it."

Although the meter and rhyme scheme of the poem are in many ways very conventional, the diction of the poem is fairly simple, and the syntax fairly straightforward. Amidst the series of extended images evoking life and death, angelic immortality and isolated souls, the short sentence "Think." stands out as a command for both reader and beloved to obey.

General hints: Think about whether the poem's formal components, which you've identified in your analysis of its speaker and occasion, affirm or complicate the attitudes or arguments expressed in the poem's actual language. How do the poem's sonic features (like *alliteration* or *onomatopoeia*) affect the tone of the lines? Does one set of images complicate the claims made by another set of images? Does the poem use *paradoxical* assertions or *irony* to foreground the speaker's position as an individual?

Poem-Cracking Techniques
To find the *meaning* of a poem, take a look at the date it was written and the language it uses. These elements will often help you understand the issues the poem is addressing.

Drill 1

Try out some questions about the following anonymous poem.

"A Pilgrim's Solace"

Stay, O sweet, and do not rise!
The light that shines comes from thine eyes;
The day breaks not: it is my heart,
Because that you and I must part.
    Stay! Or else my joys will die
    And perish in their infancy.
                            (1612)

What historical context, if any, does the poem's date suggest to you?

_____

What do we know about the poem's speaker? Is the speaker addressing any other characters?

_____

Does the poem have a noticeable rhyme scheme or regular meter?

_____

What kinds of figurative language does the speaker use?

_____

Now use this information to answer these questions.

1. All of the following statements about "do not rise"
    in line 1 are true EXCEPT:

    (A) It is a command.
    (B) The speaker addresses it to someone dear to him.
    (C) It combines with "light" and "day" to suggest the idea
        of morning.
    (D) It hints that the poem will play with expectations.
    (E) Its primary purpose is to conjure the idea of warm
        bread baking in the morning.

2. Which of the following can be inferred from the poem?

    (A) The sun is setting.
    (B) The speaker and the addressee are illicit lovers.
    (C) The speaker is about to depart on a long journey.
    (D) The speaker and the addressee have a child.
    (E) The addressee makes the speaker happy.

Answers and explanations can be found in Part IV.

Drill 2

Let's take a look at some modern poetry.

"Brass Spittoons"*

Clean the spittoons, boy.
    Detroit,
    Chicago,
    Atlantic City,
    Palm Beach.
Clean the spittoons.
The steam in hotel kitchens,
And the smoke in hotel lobbies,
And the slime in hotel spittoons:
Part of my life.

    Hey, boy!
    A nickel,
    A dime,
    A dollar,
Two dollars a day.
    Hey, boy!
    A nickel,
    A dime,
    A dollar,
    Two dollars
Buys shoes for the baby.
House rent to pay.
God on Sunday.
    My God!

Babies and church
and women and Sunday
all mixed up with dimes and
dollars and clean spittoons
and house rent to pay.
    Hey, boy!

A bright bowl of brass is beautiful to the Lord.
Bright polished brass like the cymbals
Of King David's dancers,
Like the wine cups of Solomon.
    Hey, boy!
A clean spittoon on the altar of the Lord.
A clean bright spittoon all newly polished,—
At least I can offer that.
    Com'mere boy!

(1927)

* a spittoon is a receptacle for spit (usually in a public place)

So what do you notice right off the bat? Well, there are names of cities. (Urban themes!) There is steam, smoke, and slime. (Dirty cities!) Someone is calling for a "boy." (Power!) Money is changing hands. (Commerce!) Then there's all this religious stuff. (Lofty themes! Big thoughts!)

See? We already know a little bit about what the poem is about. But let's look closer. See whether you can find some of the literary techniques you learned about in Chapter 8. Make sure you write down the answers in the space provided.

What historical context, if any, does this poem's date suggest to you?

_____

_____

_____

What do we know about this poem's speaker? What do we know about the poem's situation or setting?

_____

_____

_____

How would you describe the poem's diction? Its syntax?

_____

_____

_____

What kinds of language get repeated in the poem?

_____

_____

_____

How does the use of repetition and lists affect our understanding of the speaker's attitude toward his subject?

_____

_____

_____

Now let's see how that information helps us answer some test-style questions about the poem.

1. The speaker of the poem is most likely

    (A) someone who has only recently joined the workforce
    (B) regularly recognized by his employer for his strong work ethic
    (C) a poet in his spare time
    (D) somewhat disenchanted with his job
    (E) someone who has studied to be a minister

2. The repeated use of "boy" (lines 1, 11, 16, 30, 35, and 39) functions to

    I. Contrast strikingly against the speaker's adult concerns
    II. Suggest that the speaker refuses to grow up
    III. Echo the disruptive nature of the phrase in the speaker's life

    (A) I only
    (B) II only
    (C) III only
    (D) I and III only
    (E) II and III only

3. The use of alliteration in line 31 serves to develop a contrast between

    (A) clean spittoons and dirty ones
    (B) hotel lobbies and hotel ballrooms
    (C) elevated language and the humble thing it describes
    (D) the use of the term "boy" and the responsibilities of a man
    (E) weekdays and Sundays

4. The poem can best be described as

    (A) an idealized pastoral scene
    (B) an eloquent description of place
    (C) a religious allegory
    (D) a didactic narrative
    (E) a realistic portrait

5. A main theme of the poem overall can be effectively paraphrased as

    (A) poverty is arduous
    (B) thriftiness is a virtue
    (C) cleanliness is next to godliness
    (D) what matters is not what we do, but how we do it
    (E) good things come to those who wait

"Brass Spittoons" was written by Langston Hughes. Answers and explanations can be found in Part IV.

Drill 3

Now try the techniques on this poem.

"There Is No Frigate Like a Book"

There is no frigate like a book
    To take us lands away,
Nor any coursers like a page
    Of prancing poetry.
This traverse may the poorest take
    Without oppress of toll;
How frugal is the chariot
    That bears a human soul!

(1890)

One more time: can you think of any historical or social contexts that would apply to the date of this poem?

_____
_____
_____

What argument is the speaker making? Is the speaker addressing any other characters?

_____
_____
_____

What kinds of images does the speaker use to build the argument?

_____
_____
_____

How would you describe the rhythm and/or meter of the poem?

_____
_____
_____

Be More Specific
Don't forget to do specific questions first.

1. The poem implies that

   (A) boats are unlike books
   (B) it is better to have a vehicle for the body than for the mind
   (C) there are more books than boats
   (D) books are excellent ways to experience the world
   (E) the author values the practical over the frivolous

2. In line 3, "coursers" most nearly means

   (A) swift horses
   (B) slow skiffs
   (C) textbooks
   (D) ancient chariots
   (E) poetic devices

3. The diction of the poem is characterized by

   (A) an abundance of description
   (B) lofty word choice
   (C) forceful actions
   (D) humorous wordplay
   (E) awkward contrasts

4. Which of the following does the poem imply?

   (A) The poor are less likely to travel than the rich.
   (B) Saved money should be put toward travel.
   (C) Literature is an inexpensive means of escape.
   (D) Literature should be free.
   (E) Literature can touch a person's soul.

5. It is reasonable to infer that

   (A) the speaker prefers action to passivity
   (B) the speaker thinks there is great power in the written word
   (C) the speaker enjoys travel narratives
   (D) the speaker has an active fantasy life
   (E) the speaker values frugality as a virtue

6. In line 5, "This traverse" refers metaphorically to

   (A) the journey across the river of life
   (B) the path toward wisdom
   (C) getting lost in a book
   (D) the process of education
   (E) the inevitability of old age

7. The speaker's tone is best described as

   (A) cheerfully lecturing
   (B) forcefully instructive
   (C) tirelessly proactive
   (D) gently persuasive
   (E) selfishly sincere

"There Is No Frigate Like a Book" was written by Emily Dickinson (1830–1886). Answers and explanations can be found in Part IV.

Drill 4

Now try the techniques out on this next poem. Instead of writing down answers to questions, think about poetic devices like alliteration, rhythm, personification, and theme while you're reading. Don't forget to do the specific questions first.

"The Dying Christian to His Soul"

Vital spark of heav'nly flame!
Quit, O quit this mortal frame:
Trembling, hoping, ling'ring, flying,
Line O the pain, the bliss of dying!
(5) Cease, fond Nature, cease thy strife,
And let me languish into life.

Hark! they whisper; angels say,
Sister Spirit, come away!
What is this absorbs me quite?
(10) Steals my senses, shuts my sight,
Drowns my spirits, draws my breath?
Tell me, my soul, can this be death?

The world recedes; it disappears!
Heav'n opens on my eyes! my ears
(15) With sounds seraphic ring!
Lend, lend your wings! I mount! I fly!
O Grave! where is thy victory?
O Death! where is thy sting?

(1712)

Hint:
Try answering the specific questions first. And remember to look at the date!

1. The author of the poem uses all of the following EXCEPT

   (A) expressive punctuation
   (B) a particular rhyme scheme
   (C) regular meter
   (D) adjectives
   (E) Dickensian allusion

2. The question "O Death! where is thy sting?" can best be described as

   (A) harshly rhetorical
   (B) dubiously questioning
   (C) gently taunting
   (D) gravely earnest
   (E) paradoxical

3. Which of the following is NOT an active verb?

   (A) "Quit" (line 2)
   (B) "draws" (line 11)
   (C) "Tell" (line 12)
   (D) "sounds" (line 15)
   (E) "ring" (line 15)

4. The three stanzas differ in that

   (A) the first is directed at nature, the second at the soul, and the third at angels
   (B) the first speaks of dying, the second speaks of the loss of sense, and the third speaks of life after death
   (C) the first stanza describes death as purely painful, the second describes the loss of sense, and the third describes angels
   (D) the speaker of the first stanza is mortal, the speaker of the second is angelic, and the speaker of the third is death
   (E) the first stanza welcomes death, the second stanza taunts it, and the third stanza reluctantly accepts it

5. By "frame" (line 2), the author most likely means

   (A) a picture of the world
   (B) a previously held image of death
   (C) a cage for the soul
   (D) a metaphorical skeleton
   (E) the mortal body

6. The overall theme of the poem is best stated as

   (A) death is sublime even though it is painful
   (B) death is the victory of heaven over the soul
   (C) death can be resisted but it always eventually wins
   (D) even if one suffers in this life, the next life will be better
   (E) pain is only temporary; death is eternal

7. The style of the poem can best be described as

   (A) ornately romantic
   (B) playfully suggestive
   (C) harshly critical
   (D) elaborately descriptive
   (E) emotionally cryptic

8. The questions in the last two lines serve mainly
   to emphasize

   (A) the speaker's surprise at how little
       death hurts
   (B) the mental ecstasy of death overshadowing
       physical pain
   (C) the battle that is fought between the body
       and the soul
   (D) the speaker's antagonistic relationship
       with death
   (E) the transient nature of death

This poem is by Alexander Pope, who lived from 1688–1744. Answers and explanations can be found in Part IV.

Drill 5

Let's try a more modern poem.

"Madman's Song"

Better to see your cheek grown hollow,
Better to see your temple worn,
Than to forget to follow, follow,
After the sound of a silver horn.

Line
(5) Better to bind your brow with willow
And follow, follow until you die,
Than to sleep with your head on a golden pillow,
Nor lift it up when the hunt goes by.

Better to see your cheek grown sallow
(10) And your hair grown gray, so soon, so soon,
Than to forget to hallo, hallo,
After the milk-white hounds of the moon.

(1921)

1. What is the effect of using "silver" to describe the "horn" (line 4)?

   (A) To imply that the horn is not as valuable as a golden horn
   (B) To foreshadow any item that may be used in the "hunt" (line 8)
   (C) To be alliterative with the word "sound"
   (D) To indicate that the image would be bright
   (E) To symbolize the beauty of wealth

2. Given in context, the word "hallo" (line 11) is probably meant to convey which of the following?

   (A) A form of greeting
   (B) Another form of the word "hollow" (line 1)
   (C) An echo
   (D) A sound that hounds might make such as baying at the moon
   (E) A variation on the word "halo"

3. The attitude of the author toward the reader is best described as

   (A) openly hostile
   (B) gently insistent
   (C) didactic
   (D) ambivalent
   (E) disgusted

4. The author is most likely addressing the poem to someone

   (A) who has lost touch with what is important
   (B) who is ashamed of her background
   (C) who has become very wealthy
   (D) who is about to die
   (E) who is vain

5. In this poem, the images are meant to convey which of the following?

   I. Someone who has been committed to an insane asylum
   II. Someone who has lost passion for life
   III. Someone who has been filled with passion

   (A) I only
   (B) II only
   (C) II and III only
   (D) III only
   (E) I, II, and III

6. The repetition in the poem most likely

   (A) helps the rhyme scheme
   (B) emphasizes the main theme
   (C) chastises the reader
   (D) reveals the speaker's anger
   (E) contrasts with the laziness of the person addressed

"Madman's Song" was written by William Rose Benét. Answers and explanations can be found in Part IV.

Drill 6

"Elegy on the Year 1788"

For lords or kings I dinna mourn,
E'en let them die—for that they're born:
But oh! prodigious to reflec'!

Line A Towmont, sirs, is gane to wreck!
(5) O Eighty-eight, in thy sma' space,
What dire events hae taken place!
Of what enjoyments thou hast reft us!
In what a pickle thou has left us!

The Spanish empire's tint a head,
(10) And my auld teethless, Bawtie's dead:
The tulyie's teugh 'tween Pitt and Fox,
And 'tween our Maggie's twa wee cocks;
The tane is game, a bluidy devil,
But to the hen-birds unco civil;
(15) The tither's something dour o' treadin,
But better stuff ne'er claw'd a middin.

Ye ministers, come mount the poupit,
An' cry till ye be hearse an' roupit,
For Eighty-eight, he wished you weel,
(20) An' gied ye a' baith gear an' meal;
E'en monc a plack, and mony a peck,
Ye ken yoursels, for little feck!

Ye bonie lasses, dight your e'en,
For some o' you hae tint a frien';
(25) In Eighty-eight, ye ken, was taen,
What ye'll ne'er hae to gie again.

Observe the very nowt an' sheep,
How dowff an' daviely they creep;
Nay, even the yirth itsel' does cry,
(30) For E'nburgh wells are grutten dry

O Eighty-nine, thou's but a bairn,
An' no owre auld, I hope, to learn!
Thou beardless boy, I pray tak care,
Thou now hast got thy Daddy's chair;
(35) Nae handcuff'd, mizl'd, hap-shackl'd Regent,
But, like himsel, a full free agent,
Be sure ye follow out the plan
Nae waur than he did, honest man!
As muckle better as you can.

(1789)

1. Which of the following best restates the meaning of lines 7-8?

   (A) Oh what joy you have left us! Oh what pain you have given us!
   (B) Of what enjoyments you have robbed us! In what a state you have left us!
   (C) Oh what happiness you have promised us! What bounty you have provided us!
   (D) Oh what pleasure you have given us! Oh what memories you have left us!
   (E) Oh what disasters have occurred in such a short length of time!

2. What desire does the speaker express in the last stanza?

   (A) That success will continue to grow into the next year
   (B) That his son will grow up to be an honest and successful man
   (C) That the new year will be no worse, and perhaps better, than the last year
   (D) That he will keep his resolutions
   (E) That he will finally be released from prison and will live as an honest man

3. The speaker's tone in the passage is best described as

   (A) nostalgic
   (B) apathetic
   (C) flirtatious
   (D) anticipatory
   (E) circumspect

4. The poet directly addresses all of the following EXCEPT

   (A) the Spanish empire
   (B) ministers
   (C) 1788
   (D) pretty girls
   (E) 1789

5. Why does line 2, "E'en let them die—for that they're born:" contain contractions?

   (A) The poet was limited in the number of characters he could use in his published texts.
   (B) The poet wanted the second line to rhyme with the first.
   (C) The poet wanted the line to fit the poem's meter.
   (D) The poet was known for his creative use of punctuation.
   (E) The poet wanted to make the vocal delivery of the poem more conversational, since it was intended to be read aloud.

6. To whom does "himsel" refer in line 36?

   (A) The plan
   (B) The free agent
   (C) Regent
   (D) The beardless boy
   (E) Eighty-eight

7. Which stylistic device does the poet NOT utilize?

   (A) Alliteration
   (B) Meter and rhyme
   (C) Foreign words and phrases
   (D) Colloquialisms
   (E) Personification

This poem was written by the Scottish poet Robert Burns. Answers and explanations can be found in Part IV.

Summary

Did you get all that?

Make sure you remember the following before moving on:

- Rhyme scheme is the manner in which lines rhyme with other lines.
- Meter is the beat of a poem—the syllable count.
- Identifying the perspective and situation of a poem's speaker is often key to understanding the poem's major themes, and to answering general questions.

Chapter 11
Diving Into Drama

Drama appears on the SAT Subject Test in Literature about half of the time, and we want you to be prepared in case it rears its head. In this chapter, we list some drama terms you should know and give you strategies for approaching questions on this specific genre.

A Little Drama...
Drama makes up 0–20
percent of the test. You'll
see one passage at most,
and many tests don't have
any drama at all!

WHAT IS DRAMA?

Drama is a form of literature that tells a story through the representation of dialogue and action; it is usually meant to be performed, on a stage or on screen, by actors who assume the roles of specific characters. Remember that, before people could go to the movies or watch stories unfold on television programs, plays were a primary form of public entertainment and instruction; even now, drama allows audiences to watch actors perform a story's unfolding.

Each new piece of dialogue in a drama passage will begin with the name of the speaker (in capital letters), followed by a colon and the contents of the speech itself. Whenever the speaker changes, his or her name will begin on a new line. *Stage directions*, or instructions that tell the actor how to move or speak, will be inserted in parentheses; they are usually written in present tense and printed in italics.

If drama appears on the test at all, it will only be one passage. Luckily, while the layout of a drama passage may be visually different from that of a prose or poetry passage, the basic elements of drama are similar to those of prose and poetry.

WHAT TO LOOK FOR

To practice analyzing drama, let's look at an example from *Trifles*, by Susan Glaspell.

(*The men go outside.*)

MRS. HALE (*Resentfully*): I don't know as there's anything so strange, our takin' up our time with little things while we're waiting for them to get the evidence. (*She sits down at the big table smoothing out a block with decision.*) I don't see as it's anything to laugh about.

MRS. PETERS (*Apologetically*): Of course they've got awful important things on their minds.

(*Pulls up a chair and joins* MRS. HALE *at the table.*)

MRS. HALE (*Examining another block*): Mrs. Peters, look at this one. Here, this is the one she was working on, and look at the sewing! All the rest of it has been so nice and even. And look at this! It's all over the place! Why, it looks as if she didn't know what she was about!

(*After she has said this they look at each other, then start to glance back at the door. After an instant* MRS. HALE *has pulled at a knot and ripped the sewing.*)

MRS. PETERS: Oh, what are you doing, Mrs. Hale?

MRS. HALE (*Mildly*): Just pulling out a stitch or two that's not sewed very good. (*Threading a needle.*) Bad sewing always made me fidgety.

MRS. PETERS (*Nervously*): I don't think we ought to touch things.

MRS. HALE: I'll just finish up this end.

(1916)

Time Period

As you do when looking at prose and poetry, start by looking at the date of the passage's publication. What do you know about the global and social history of that period? Can you think of any wars, colonizing activity, scientific developments, or social reforms that the passage's writer might be engaging with? Such context can help you identify key themes in the passage.

In this example: *Trifles* was first published in 1916. Given that Mrs. Hale comments resentfully on how the men trivialize the women's activity—"I don't see as it's anything to laugh about"—you might remember that the early twentieth century was a crucial period for the women's suffrage movements in both Britain and the United States. (The passage doesn't mention anything overtly military, but another important historical context for a text from this period might be World War I, which began in 1914.)

General hints: Like poetry and prose, drama often responds to the formal conventions and thematic preoccupations of its historical context. Drama written before the 1800s often represents or reworks specific mythological or historical events or relationships—Shakespeare's *Macbeth*, for example, retells the story of an early Scottish king. In the nineteenth century, the focus tends to be more on the balance between intellect and emotion, nature and industry; in the later part of the century, literary works often reflect social reform movements addressing issues of race, class, and gender. The twentieth century was marked by two World Wars, plus a global Depression, an ever-increasing rate of scientific and technological change, and greater social mobility. These major events are reflected in literature's shifting attempts to represent the "real" lives of its characters. Bear in mind that several recent passages on the SAT Subject Test in Literature have come from Anglophone literatures beyond British or American contexts (for example, from South African drama). Using your knowledge of world history can help you consider how a given passage may be engaging with the legacies of colonialism and geopolitical conflict.

Speaker(s)

Who is speaking in the passage? What clues do those characters' speeches give you about their relationships to one another? Are characters having an argument about something? Declaring their undying love for one another? Meeting for the first time?

In this example: Two characters are speaking—Mrs. Peters and Mrs. Hale—though we also know that there are other characters nearby, since the stage direction at the beginning says that "the men" have just gone "outside." The women's dialogue gives hints about the nature of their relationship—Mrs. Hale is more assertive, Mrs. Peters more tentative; they are not close enough to call each other by their first names. Their dialogue also positions the women in relation to other, absent characters: the men outside are referred to as "them," and Mrs. Hale's comment about the sewing suggests that they have been discussing another woman (unnamed in the passage), because the sewing "looks as if she didn't know what she was about!"

General hints: Because plays can't depend on a narrator's description to ground the audience in a setting or situation, the majority of text in a drama passage will represent speech and/or action—the passage will transcribe what an audience might hear or see happening on stage. The format of the drama passage means that each new speaker will be named for you, which makes identifying the source of a particular utterance easy—what is sometimes more complicated is teasing out the details, spoken or unspoken, of the characters' interrelationships, or identifying the differences and similarities in their approaches to the situation at hand.

Situation

What kind of story is the passage telling about the characters and their interaction? What is happening?

In this example: The plot of this passage is that while Mrs. Peters and Mrs. Hale are "waiting" for the men "to get the evidence," they are looking at "blocks" of sewing. The women seem to have an unspoken common understanding about the unnamed woman whose sewing they're examining (Mrs. Hale suggests that the sewing seems to reveal something about that woman's state of mind, and Mrs. Hale and Mrs. Peters "look at each other, then start to glance back at the door"), but when Mrs. Hale begins to redo some of the sewing, it makes Mrs. Peters upset.

General hints: To assess the situation of the passage, think first about the *setting* and *plot* of the passage—the story literally being told about the characters' interaction. Where are the characters, and what are they doing?

Analyzing the *form* of the dialogue can also be helpful in identifying situation: does dialogue appear in the form of verse, with rhyme schemes and/or line breaks, or in the form of prose sentences? (Playwrights like William Shakespeare sometimes put certain dialogue in verse in order to emphasize a concept or suggest that the speaker is of high socioeconomic status.)

Do the characters seem to be joking with each other, which might suggest the *genre* of the play is a comedy? Or do they seem to be caught in a downward spiral, which might suggest instead that the play is a *tragedy*? Having a sense of the genre of the passage can help you eliminate answer choices—in a comedy, characters are unlikely to meet genuinely horrific ends, while a tragedy is unlikely to end with a happy wedding.

Tone/Voice

As in poetry and prose, this category looks at *how* information is conveyed through the dialogue of the passage. Now that you know what is happening, and to whom it is happening, you can analyze *how* the passage conveys what is happening. Does one character break off from conversation to reflect on a conflict or confusion alone? Do certain characters' comments change in tone over the course of the passage? Are certain characters using figurative language—and if so, what are the effects of that imagery?

In this example: Both women speak with colloquial diction throughout the passage. Mrs. Peters' first comment is made "apologetically"—and the content of the speech suggests that her comment is apologizing for the men's behavior, because "they've got awful important things on their minds." By the end of the passage, however, in response to Mrs. Hale's starting to rip out the sewing and redo it, Mrs. Peters' language is more alarmed than apologetic: she doesn't think the women should be touching things. Mrs. Hale, on the other hand, starts out defending the women's "takin' up our time with little things" while the men are outside; she then becomes agitated by the state of the sewing she's examining ("Bad sewing always made me fidgety").

General hints: In many drama passages, you will encounter speeches that are much longer than those here. While dialogue uses interaction between characters to develop an audience's sense of the characters' relationships or social situations, a *monologue* (an extended speech made by one person) allows one character to address or try to persuade other characters of something; a *soliloquy* (a speech delivered by one character who is on stage alone), like Hamlet's "To be or not to be" speech, presents in words an individual character's internal struggles or thought processes.

The diction, syntax, and delivery of all these kinds of expression can shape how you understand the motivations or priorities of specific speakers. A character who often speaks in *asides* (revealing information to the audience but not to his/her fellow characters) can seem conniving, while a character who is constantly interrupting others and speaks only in extended monologues might come across as egocentric.

Drill 1

You can apply the same techniques you've practiced in the chapters on prose and poetry to help you analyze drama. Try reading this dramatic passage and answering some questions about it. Do the specific questions first, followed by the general questions.

> ELIZA (*overwhelmed*): Ah-ah-ow-oo!
>
> HIGGINS: There! That's all you'll get out of Eliza.
> Ah-ah-ow-oo! No use explaining. As a military
> *Line* man you ought to know that. Give her orders: that's
> (5) what she wants. Eliza: you are to live here for the
> next six months, learning how to speak beautifully,
> like a lady in a florist's shop. If you're good and
> do whatever you're told, you shall sleep in a
> proper bedroom, and have lots to eat, and money
> (10) to buy chocolates and take rides in taxis. If you're
> naughty and idle, you will sleep in the back kitchen
> among the black beetles, and be walloped by Mrs.
> Pearce with a broomstick. At the end of six months
> you shall go to Buckingham Palace in a carriage,
> (15) beautifully dressed. If the King finds out you're not
> a lady, you will be taken to the Tower of London,
> where your head will be cut off as a warning to
> other presumptuous flower girls. If you are not
> found out, you shall have a present of seven and six
> (20) pence to start life with as a lady in a shop. If you
> refuse this offer you will be a most ungrateful and
> wicked girl, and the angels will weep for you.
>
> (1914)

What historical or social contexts, if any, does the play's date suggest to you?

_____

_____

What does the dialogue reveal to you about the relationship between the characters?

_____

_____

Use What You Learned
Keep in mind that the techniques you learned for poetry and prose passages work with the drama questions as well!

How does Higgins' language change over the course of his monologue? Who does he seem to be addressing?

_____

_____

What do you learn about Eliza's situation from reading this passage?

_____

_____

1. The central contrasts in the passage are expressed in all of the following pairs EXCEPT

    (A) "A lady in a florist's shop"..."flower girls"
    (B) "Buckingham Palace"..."the Tower of London"
    (C) "Mrs. Pearce"..."the King"
    (D) "proper bedroom"..."the back kitchen"
    (E) "good and do whatever you're told"... "naughty and idle"

2. From his speech, it seems clear that Higgins views Eliza as

    (A) a naïve child
    (B) an obedient servant
    (C) a potential wife
    (D) a futile project
    (E) a tenacious competitor

3. According to Higgins, all of the following are characteristic of a "lady" EXCEPT

    (A) articulate speech
    (B) employment in a florist's shop
    (C) private transportation
    (D) fine clothing
    (E) the leisure not to work

Remember:
Don't forget to circle EXCEPT and mark a T or an F next to each answer choice.

4. The first four lines of Higgins' speech imply

   (A) the discipline developed in a military background like Eliza's
   (B) Higgins' prejudice about people of different social classes
   (C) Higgins' long familiarity with Eliza and her character
   (D) the insight Higgins has into what motivates women
   (E) Eliza's preference for direction over explanation

5. Higgins's speech can best be described as

   (A) condescending
   (B) didactic
   (C) instructive
   (D) explicatory
   (E) apathetic

6. From the passage, Higgins may accurately be described as all of the following EXCEPT

   (A) presumptuous
   (B) generous
   (C) arrogant
   (D) self-important
   (E) determined

This excerpt is from *Pygmalion* by George Bernard Shaw. Answers and explanations can be found in Part IV.

Drill 2

SIR EDWARD TRENCHARD: Good morning, Coyle, good morning. (*With affected ease.*) There is a chair, Coyle. (*They sit.*) So you see those infernal tradespeople are pretty troublesome.

Line

(5) COYLE: My agent's letter this morning announces that Walter and Brass have got judgment and execution on their amount for repairing your town house last season. (*Refers to papers.*) Boquet and Barker announce their intention of taking this

(10) same course with the wine account. Handmarth is preparing for a settlement of his heavy demand for the stables. Then there is Temper for pictures and other things and Miss Florence Trenchard's account with Madame Pompon, and—

(15) SIR EDWARD: Confound it, why harass me with details, these infernal particulars? Have you made out the total?

COYLE: Four thousand, eight hundred and thirty pounds, nine shillings and sixpence.

(20) SIR EDWARD: Well, of course we must find means of settling this extortion.

COYLE: Yes, Sir Edward, if possible.

SIR EDWARD: If possible?

COYLE: I, as your agent, must stoop to detail, you

(25) must allow me to repeat, if possible.

SIR EDWARD: Why, you don't say there will be any difficulty in raising the money?

COYLE: What means would you suggest, Sir Edward?

SIR EDWARD: That, sir, is your business.

(30) COYLE: A foretaste in the interest on the Fanhille & Ellenthrope mortgages, you are aware both are in the arrears, the mortgagees in fact, write here to announce their intentions to foreclose. (*Shows papers.*)

SIR EDWARD: Curse your impudence, pay them off.

(35) COYLE: How, Sir Edward?

SIR EDWARD: Confound it, sir, which of us is the agent? Am I to find you brains for your own business?

COYLE: No, Sir Edward, I can furnish the brains, but what I ask of you is to furnish the money.

(40) SIR EDWARD: There must be money somewhere, I came into possession of one of the finest properties

in Hampshire only twenty-six years ago, and now you mean to tell me I cannot raise 4,000 pounds?

COYLE: The fact is distressing, Sir Edward, but so
(45) it is.

SIR EDWARD: There's the Ravensdale property unencumbered.

COYLE: There, Sir Edward, you are under a mistake. The Ravensdale property is deeply
(50) encumbered, to nearly its full value.

SIR EDWARD (*Springing up.*): Good heavens.

COYLE: I have found among my father's papers a mortgage of that very property to him.

SIR EDWARD: To your father! My father's agent?
(55) Sir, do you know that if this be true I am something like a beggar, and your father something like a thief.

COYLE: I see the first plainly, Sir Edward, but not the second.

SIR EDWARD: Do you forget, sir, that your father
(60) was a charity boy, fed, clothed by my father?

COYLE: Well, Sir Edward?

SIR EDWARD: And do you mean to tell me, sir, that your father repaid that kindness by robbing his benefactor?

(65) COYLE: Certainly not, but by advancing money to that benefactor when he wanted it, and by taking the security of one of his benefactor's estates, as any prudent man would under the circumstances.

SIR EDWARD: Why, then, sir, the benefactor's
(70) property is yours.

COYLE: I see one means, at least, of keeping the Ravensdale estate in the family.

SIR EDWARD: What is it?

COYLE: By marrying your daughter to the mortgagee.

(75) SIR EDWARD: To you?

COYLE: I am prepared to settle the estate on Miss Trenchard the day she becomes Mrs. Richard Coyle.

SIR EDWARD (*Springing up.*): You insolent scoundrel, how dare you insult me in my own
(80) house, sir. Leave it, sir, or I will have you kicked out by my servants.

COYLE: I never take an angry man at his word, Sir Edward. Give a few moments reflection to my offer, you can have me kicked out afterwards.

(85) SIR EDWARD: (*Pacing stage.*): A beggar, Sir
Edward Trenchard a beggar, see my children
reduced to labor for their bread, to misery perhaps;
but the alternative, Florence detests him, still the
match would save her, at least, from ruin. He might
(90) take the family name, I might retrench, retire, to the
continent for a few years. Florence's health might
serve as a pretence. Repugnant as the alternative is,
yet it deserves consideration.

COYLE: (*Who has watched.*): Now, Sir Edward,
(95) shall I ring for the servants to kick me out?

(1858)

For the last time: does the play's date suggest that specific historical or social contexts might be relevant?

_____

_____

What new information changes the relationship between Coyle and Sir Edward over the course of the passage?

_____

_____

How would you describe the tone of the characters' dialogue?

_____

_____

1. The phrase "judgment and execution" (lines 6-7) most likely means

    (A) a sentence and the death penalty
    (B) the moral high ground
    (C) an official breakup of a partnership
    (D) a judge's decision and a court order
    (E) a search and seizure of property

2. Coyle and Sir Edward's relationship is that of

    (A) money manager and client
    (B) lawyer and defendant
    (C) servant and master
    (D) benefactor and recipient
    (E) uncle and nephew

3. The word "security" (line 67) most nearly means

   (A) collateral
   (B) agreement
   (C) assurance
   (D) welfare
   (E) prize

4. Which of Sir Edward's choices of words makes it clear that he considers the bills from his creditors to be unfair?

   (A) "infernal" (line 16)
   (B) "Confound" (line 15)
   (C) "extortion" (line 21)
   (D) "impudence" (line 34)
   (E) "unencumbered" (line 47)

5. What is the deal Coyle wants to strike with Sir Edward?

   (A) He will pay off the creditors in exchange for allowing him to marry Sir Edward's daughter.
   (B) He will keep Ravensdale in the family if he is allowed to marry Sir Edward's daughter.
   (C) He will arrange the marriage of Sir Edward's daughter to the current residents of Ravensdale.
   (D) He will marry Sir Edward's daughter to prevent her at least from financial ruin.
   (E) Because Sir Edward is without money, Sir Edward will have to sanction the love affair between Coyle and his daughter.

6. Sir Edward's final lines, "A beggar, Sir Edward Trenchard a beggar, see my children reduced to labor for their bread, to misery perhaps; but the alternative, Florence detests him, still the match would save her, at least, from ruin. He might take the family name, I might retrench, retire, to the continent for a few years. Florence's health might serve as a pretence. Repugnant as the alternative is, yet it deserves consideration" (lines 85-93), are an example of

(A) a monologue expressing doubt
(B) a character dissolving into madness
(C) a character addressing the audience
(D) a character voicing both sides of an argument to himself
(E) a speech explaining a plot point to the audience

The excerpt you just read is from *Our American Cousin* by Tom Taylor. Answers and explanations can be found in Part IV.

Drill 3

MARINA: If I should tell my history, it would seem
Like lies disdain'd in the reporting.

PERICLES: Prithee, speak:

Line Falseness cannot come from thee; for thou look'st

(5) Modest as Justice, and thou seem'st a palace
For the crown'd Truth to dwell in: I will believe thee,
And make my senses credit thy relation
To points that seem impossible; for thou look'st
Like one I loved indeed. What were thy friends?

(10) Didst thou not say, when I did push thee back—

Which was when I perceived thee—that thou camest
From good descending?

MARINA: So indeed I did.
My name is Marina.

(15) PERICLES: O, I am mock'd,
And thou by some incensed god sent hither
To make the world to laugh at me.

MARINA: Patience, good sir,
Or here I'll cease.

(20) PERICLES: Nay, I'll be patient.
Thou little know'st how thou dost startle me,
To call thyself Marina.

MARINA: The name
Was given me by one that had some power,

(25) My father, and a king.

PERICLES: How! a king's daughter?
And call'd Marina?

MARINA: You said you would believe me;
But, not to be a troubler of your peace,

(30) I will end here.

PERICLES: But are you flesh and blood?
Have you a working pulse? and are no fairy?
Motion! Well; speak on. Where were you born?
And wherefore call'd Marina?

(35) MARINA: Call'd Marina
For I was born at sea.

PERICLES: At sea! what mother?

MARINA: My mother was the daughter of a king;
Who died the minute I was born,

(40) As my good nurse Lychorida hath oft
Deliver'd weeping.

PERICLES: O, stop there a little!
(Aside)
This is the rarest dream that e'er dull sleep
Did mock sad fools withal: this cannot be:
(45) My daughter's buried. Well: where were you bred?
I'll hear you more, to the bottom of your story,
And never interrupt you.

...How came you in these parts? where were you bred?

MARINA: The king my father did in Tarsus leave me;
(50) Till cruel Cleon, with his wicked wife,
Did seek to murder me: and having woo'd
A villain to attempt it, who having drawn to do't,
A crew of pirates came and rescued me;
Brought me to Mytilene. But, good sir,
(55) Whither will you have me? Why do you weep?
It may be,
You think me an impostor: no, good faith;
I am the daughter to King Pericles,
If good King Pericles be.

(60) PERICLES: Ho, Helicanus!

HELICANUS: Calls my lord?...

PERICLES: O Helicanus, strike me, honour'd sir;
Give me a gash, put me to present pain;
Lest this great sea of joys rushing upon me
(65) O'erbear the shores of my mortality,
And drown me with their sweetness. O, come hither,
Thou that beget'st him that did thee beget;
Thou that wast born at sea, buried at Tarsus,
And found at sea again! O Helicanus,
(70) Down on thy knees, thank the holy gods as loud
As thunder threatens us: this is Marina.
What was thy mother's name? tell me but that,
For truth can never be confirm'd enough,
Though doubts did ever sleep.

(75) MARINA: First, sir, I pray,
What is your title?

PERICLES: I am Pericles of Tyre: but tell me now
My drown'd queen's name, as in the rest you said
Thou hast been godlike perfect,
(80) The heir of kingdoms and another like
To Pericles thy father.

MARINA: Is it no more to be your daughter than
To say my mother's name was Thaisa?
Thaisa was my mother, who did end
(85) The minute I began.

PERICLES: Now, blessing on thee! rise; thou art
my child.
Give me fresh garments. Mine own, Helicanus;
She is not dead at Tarsus, as she should have been,
(90) By savage Cleon: she shall tell thee all;
When thou shalt kneel, and justify in knowledge
She is thy very princess…

(c. 1608)

1. In context, what does "end" (line 84) most
   nearly mean?

   (A) Finish
   (B) Arrest
   (C) Die
   (D) Fail
   (E) Conclude

2. Why does Pericles ask Helicanus to strike him
   (line 62)?

   (A) To prevent him from dying of happiness
   (B) To stop him from striking Marina
   (C) To prevent him from drowning
   (D) To relieve his present pain
   (E) To awaken him from this dream

3. Which of the following most accurately describes
   the character of Marina?

   (A) An impostor
   (B) The daughter of Pericles
   (C) The deceased daughter of a king
   (D) A pirate's hostage
   (E) A fairy

4. It can be inferred from the questions Pericles
   asks that

   (A) he is old and confused
   (B) he is trying to interrupt the talkative girl
   (C) he mistrusts Marina
   (D) he finds her story incredible
   (E) he is required to confirm her story

5. The tone of lines 15-17 can best be described as

    (A) disquieted
    (B) jovial
    (C) irate
    (D) satirical
    (E) impatient

6. The purpose of this dialogue is most likely to

    I. introduce characters to the audience
    II. build tension
    III. surprise the audience with new information

    (A) I only
    (B) I and II
    (C) I and III
    (D) II and III
    (E) All of the above

This scene is from the final act of *Pericles, Prince of Tyre* by William Shakespeare. Answers and explanations can be found in Part IV.

Summary

Did you get all that?

Make sure you can define the following terms:

- aside
- comedy
- farce
- form
- genre
- monologue
- soliloquy
- stage directions
- tragedy

Part IV
Drill
Answers and
Explanations

CHAPTER 7 DRILLS

Drill 1

Answers will vary, but here are some possibilities.

1. What does the author mean in lines 3–4?

2. What's the big literary device the author uses in lines 7–10?

3. How does the author sound in lines 11–15?

4. What image does the "distant shadow" conjure up?

5. How would you describe the narrator in lines 27–30?

6. What does the response in line 30 tell us about the birds?

Drill 2

What are the six steps for tackling questions?

1. Look at the date.

2. Read the passage.

3. Decide which question to do first and put the question in your own words.

4. Go back to the passage to find the answer.

5. Translate the answer into your own words.

6. Use POE.

What are the three kinds of questions on the SAT Subject Test in Literature?

1. specific

2. general

3. trap

What are the two kinds of trap questions on the SAT Subject Test in Literature?

1. NOT/LEAST/EXCEPT

2. Roman numeral

CHAPTER 8 DRILLS

Drill 1

Metaphor	Simile	Personification/Anthropomorphism
4	1	2
7	3	5
9	8	6
		10

Drill 2

Onomatopoeia	Alliteration	Oxymoron	Pathos
2	4	3	1
7	8	5	6
		9	

Drill 3

1. **D** The sentence, when pared down, is "None of these things shall content my musing mind," so the correct answer is (D). None of the other answer choices contain the main verb.

2. **C** The poem uses the word "blossom" (line 11), but not in comparison to the voice (C), so (C) is the correct answer for this "EXCEPT" question. The voice is compared to a stream (lines 12–13) (A). The voice is compared to the wind (line 14) (B) and woodcock music (line 16) (D). The voice is compared to children's feet in line 18 (E).

3. **C** The author is calling the sun "faithful"—a human characteristic, so this is an example of personification (C). It is not ironic or paradoxical (A), (B). There is no contradiction, so it is not an oxymoron (D). Poetic license (E) is when a writer ignores conventional form or fact to achieve a desired effect. This is not the case here.

4. **B** The title of the poem is "Elegy," so we can assume it's written as an elegy (B). The meter is not regular throughout the poem (A), and the rhyme scheme varies (C). There is no extended allegory (D), and the author is not asking for empathy (E).

CHAPTER 9 DRILLS

Drill 1

1. **A** The characters' similarities are described, followed by their differences (A). The characters are not introduced separately (B). Only the second character is compared to an animal (C). The faces are not described until after their clothes are described (D). There are no inner thoughts (E).

   General Takeaway: Structure questions often have relatively long answer choices; while POE can be very effective, these questions may be more time-consuming than others.

2. **B** The passage provides a straightforward description of the two men and few, if any, words within the passage carry much emotional charge, so (A) and (E) (which are positive and negative words, respectively) can both be eliminated. Choice (D) can also be eliminated, as language is matter-of-fact and does not suggest the details provided are weird or uncanny. While (B) and (C) might appear to be very similar words, the former has the sense of "not affected by personal or emotional involvement" while the latter means "having little or no interest or concern." Since the narrator is bothering to describe the men, the tone might be neutral or unemotional, but it is unlikely to be reflective of little or no interest, so between (B) and (C), (B) is the better answer.

   General Takeaway: In tone questions, it is often possible to eliminate one or more answer choices simply by deciding whether the tone is positive, negative, or neutral. If you've eliminated some answer choices, one of the remaining must be right, even if you don't know exactly what the remaining choices are saying or how best to distinguish between them. In that case, just pick one of the remaining choices and move on.

Drill 2

1. **B** The character Ishmael is introducing himself through first-person narration (B). We don't really have enough of a story to see whether it's an allegory, and no dialogue or stage direction cues to suggest that it's drama (A). While the date of the passage is old enough to be historical, again, there's nothing to suggest that the period in which the piece is set is even further in the past (C). The first-person narrative voice suggests that the speaker is addressing someone other than himself (D). Even if one is not well-versed in the politics of the nineteenth century, the absence of any political references should make it safe to eliminate (E).

   General Takeaway: Don't be afraid to pick a straightforward answer when the passage supports it. Complicated or abstract phrasing and lots of terminology may sound like the sort of answer a literature test might demand, but sometimes the nice or sophisticated answer choices are just there as distraction.

2. **E** Much of the passage, but particularly the last sentence, suggests a moody man who knows himself well enough to get out to sea when the dark moods strike him (E). While Ishmael acknowledges that he sails when he has "little to no money in his purse," it is less for the money than to adjust his moods—we see little evidence of ambition and none of generosity here (A). While "methodically knocking people's hats off" might be construed as inconsiderate (B), Ishmael points out that he avoids doing that. Since the topic of the entire passage seems to be Ishmael's potential mood swings and how they send him to sea, one might see him as self-centered, but there's no evidence of insecurity (C). He is sensitive to his own moods, and he does seem to have some sense that his methods work, but (D) is still not as strong an answer as (E).

   General Takeaway: Even if one answer catches your eye, make sure to check all five answers; the one you noticed could turn out to be the second-best answer.

3. C For the narrator, sailing is the way he gets rid of his melancholy ("growing grim about the mouth... a damp, drizzly November in my soul") (C). An old-fashioned meaning of spleen is "melancholy." Spleen does not mean "path" (A), nor does it refer to the circulation of blood (B). Although a spleen is an organ, the word does not refer to a body part in this context, (D). There is no evidence that the narrator needs to drive off excess energy (E).

General Takeaway: To answer vocab-in-context questions, it's crucial to refer to the passage to determine how the word or phrase is used in that particular instance.

4. E Alliteration (I) can be found in the phrase "growing grim"; hyperbole (II) in "bringing up the rear of every funeral I meet" and "it requires a strong moral principle to prevent me…"; parallel structure (III) in the repetition of, "Whenever I find myself…" Therefore, the correct answer is (E).

General Takeaway: Even in questions that don't ask about hyperbole, it's worth paying attention to extreme language such as "every," "always," or "never." If it's hard to imagine that the claim made with extreme language could be literally true, then you've either got an instance of figurative language or a claim that will be difficult to support.

Drill 3

1. A The narrator is making fun of the notion that everyone is equal (A). He is not harsh (B), nor is he frustrated (C). There is no emotion in the narration (D), and the narration is not too casual (E).

2. B The author uses repetition to underscore his point that everyone is equal (B). The repetition does not introduce a theme (A). The repetition is not intended to make the reader lonely (C). There is no commonly held assumption that is refuted (D). The three elements introduced are not contradictory (E).

3. D The repetition of the subject "nobody" is an example of parallelism (D). There is no internal rhyme (A), and he does not mimic lower-class speech (B). The comparison is not general (C). The protagonist is not mentioned in the first passage (E).

Drill 4

1. C Marguerite doesn't recognize her own name because she is so overwhelmed by the experience, which is challenging despite her "preparations" (line 3) (C). There is nothing to tell us that she is uninterested in her own graduation (A). Having made "preparations," she cannot have been surprised (B), but since her honors were read and she took a place on the stage, it is unlikely that she was unable to get her diploma (D). Despite the mention of colors, there is nothing to suggest that Marguerite's preparations for the day included making a painting of how she imagined the scene (E).

2. E The sentence refers to an Amazon, which, back in 1969, was not a giant online bookseller. When you see a potentially unfamiliar proper name in a passage, especially when it's being used in a comparison, it's probably a reference to the Bible or classical literature. This is a classical allusion (E) to the race of female warriors. The author is not intruding here (A). There is no anachronism (B). The syntax is interesting, but not complicated (C). There is no evidence of anthropomorphism here (D).

Drill 5

1. **C** Mrs. Penniman is in charge of Catherine's lessons, so "supervising" is a good synonym (C). She does not ignore her talent (A), nor does she teach Catherine herself (B). She encourages Catherine (D). We don't know who hires Catherine's tutors (E).

2. **B** "It is I who supply the butter," says Mrs. Penniman (B). Secrets are compared to addled eggs (A). "Bread" is compared to goodness, not Mrs. Penniman's influence (C). "The salt of malice" is a phrase and is not being used as a symbol (D). Mrs. Penniman's influence is not compared to a fool's (E).

3. **E** In contrast to her piano talent, Catherine was just fair as a dancer (E). There is no mention of Catherine's appearance (A). We don't know whether she is aware of her talent (B) or whether it is in her character to brag (C). She was not a talented dancer (D).

4. **E** The narration is observant of Catherine's qualities and Mrs. Penniman's thoughts (E). It is not melodramatic (A), nor is there any evidence of irony (B). It is not sardonic (meanly satiric) (C), nor is it particularly didactic (designed to instruct) (D).

5. **A** The point of view is of an omniscient narrator (A). We don't know who the protagonist is (B). There is no use of the second-person "you" (C) or of first-person "I" (D) and (E).

6. **B** In this passage secrets are compared to "addled eggs." Mrs. Penniman's little secrets are called an "innocent passion" (line 33) and portrayed as useless, like rotten eggs (B). They are definitely not important or useful (E). Eggs cannot be "confused" (A). Choice (C) is a distractor that wants you to be thinking about the "eggs" part of "addled eggs." Don't fall for it. Don't confuse "addled" with "saddled" (D). The correct answer is (B).

Drill 6

1. **C** Lin is thumbing through a book while everyone else is working, so the contrast is between intellect and physicality (C). This is highlighted when Lin sits down on the very surface where work is done (grinding stone) and flips through his Russian dictionary (lines 38–40). There is nothing exactly central or peripheral (A). There is no mention of anyone corrupt or honest (B). There is no mention of heaven (D), so secular and divine are not mentioned either (E).

2. **D** Throughout the passage, Lin is observing and assessing his surroundings, so (D) is the best answer. He is not "haughty" (A), nor is he indifferent to his surroundings (B) or excited (C). "Enthralled" is too strong a word for the curiosity he feels (E).

3. **B** The fact that the house is the same as it was twenty years ago and the books are mildewed suggests that Lin has been away a long time (B). We do not know his profession (A) or the purpose for his visit (C). He is comfortable, so he is used to the country (D), and it is not clear that the landscape is beautiful (E).

4. **D** Bellows do not cough, so this is an example of personification (D). Cucumbers can hang (A), chickens strut, and geese waddle (B). Air can reek (C), and sows can oink (E).

5. **A** The character is speaking to himself without quotes, so Statement I is true. The narrator continues speaking about the books, so there is no shift, so Statement II is false. We do not know whether Lin is relinquishing his pastoral life, so Statement III is not true.

6.　C　The "distillers' grains mixed in the pig feed" cause the sour smell (C), not the cooking (A), nor the manure (B). The mildewed books do not smell (D), nor does the field (E).

7.　C　The passage describes Lin's home in detail (C). It is not a paean (hymn of praise) (A) or an elegy for a previous time (B). The character does not experience an epiphany (D). There is no evident allegory (E).

CHAPTER 10 DRILLS

Drill 1

1.　E　The words are a command and are spoken to someone who is addressed as "O, Sweet," so (A) and (B) are true. "Rise," "light" and "day" (as well as the phrase "day break(s)") are all words that might be associated with morning or the beginning of the day, so (C) is true. While words within the first three lines are associated with morning, the particulars of their use do not conform to the norms of morning: the lover is told not to rise, the light comes not from a sunrise but from eyes, and while "day breaks" sounds like a word for "dawn," the full phrase "day breaks not" denies that dawn has come, so (D) is true. While bread does rise and some people eat bread in the morning, the evidence in support of the other four statements contradicts the claim that the word is used primarily to evoke the idea of bread.

General Takeaway: Begin with the answer choices that are easiest to assess. This makes it easier to focus on the ones that remain.

2.　E　The language of the poem evokes the idea of the sun rising, rather than setting, so there's no evidence to support (A). While the speaker and addressee may be illicit lovers, they might just as well be happily married, so there's no evidence to support (B). The word "pilgrim" could suggest that a long journey is being undertaken, but there's no clear indication that a literal pilgrimage is involved or which of the two would be journeying, so (C) is not well supported. While "infancy" appears in the last line, it is used figuratively to describe the state of the speaker's joy and does not refer to an actual infant, so (D) is not supported. As the speaker's heart is breaking because the two must part and the addressee's failure to stay will kill joy, their time together must make the speaker happy. Choice (E) is well supported by the evidence in the passage.

General Takeaway: While correct answers may require some interpretation of the information in the passage, the correct answer will always be one that is supported by words or phrases you can point to in the passage.

Drill 2

1.　D　The speaker's repeated reference to spittoons among the other obligations of his life (as in the lines "Babies and church / and women and Sunday / all mixed up with dimes and / dollars and clean spittoons") suggests that the speaker has been working for a while, so eliminate (A). The only language that appears to be attributable to the speaker's boss is variations on the order to "Clean the spittoons, boy," so the poem does not suggest that the speaker is regularly applauded by his employer (B). The poem contains no evidence that the speaker considers himself a poet in his spare time (C). Although the second half of the poem features several mentions of Biblical figures and ecclesiastical objects, the speaker gives no insight into what he was doing before he began cleaning spittoons—so we can eliminate (E) as well. Choice (D) best reflects the speaker's familiarity with the details of his job and the speaker's disenchantment as he describes "the slime in hotel spittoons: / Part of my life."

General Takeaway: When analyzing what the passage reveals about the speaker, make sure you can support your answer with specific details from the passage.

2. **D** With Roman numeral questions, start by assessing the numbered statements to see which, if any, are not supported. The repetition of "boy" in the poem contrasts with the speaker's preoccupations with "shoes for the baby" and "House rent to pay," so Statement I is supported. That means that (B), (C) and (E) can be eliminated. Neither of the remaining choices includes Statement II, so skip to assessing Statement III. The final lines of the poem—which juxtapose the speaker's humble assertion that "At least" he can offer God a clean spittoon with the command "Com'mere boy!"—emphasize that the impersonal and demeaning demands for the speaker's attention do intrude into his private musings and his disrupt his attempts to make sense of the world. Since Statement III is supported, eliminate (A). Choice (D) is the correct answer.

General Takeaway: When you're dealing with a Roman numeral question, every time you assess a statement, eliminate any answer choices you can based on that assessment. Compare the remaining answer choices to determine which statement, if any, you need to assess next.

3. **C** Choice (B) is a trap answer: while hotel lobbies and kitchens are contrasted in the poem, there's no mention of hotel ballrooms. The other answers do identify contrasts that appear within the poem, so the trick to choosing the best answer is to think about which one can be connected to line 31 and the alliteration within it. Alliteration is a poetic device, so it is "elevated" or poetic language. "A bright bowl of brass" describes a spittoon; the speaker links it through association with grander things, but ultimately the lovely phrase describes a receptacle into which lots of people spit. Choices (A), (D), and (E) name contrasts that appear in the poem but are not connected directly to the line the question references.

General Takeaway: make sure to consider exactly what the question is asking, as second-best or trap answers may seem appealing at first glance.

4. **E** The details are not idealized, so eliminate (A). The poem focuses more on the speaker's experience than on the description of a particular place, especially as the list of cities suggests the action of the poem might occur in any large city, so eliminate (B). While religious references are made, the poem is not an allegory, so eliminate (C). The poem describes some of the limitations and preoccupations in the speaker's life; it does not tell a story, nor is it primarily intended to instruct, so eliminate (D). The poem includes gritty, rather than idealized, details and could be said to offer a snapshot of the speaker's life, so (E) is the best-supported answer.

General Takeaway: Even if you don't recognize every term or word in an answer—like pastoral or didactic— you can still evaluate the appropriateness of the words you do recognize, which often can help eliminate answers even when you're not sure what every word means.

5. **A** While the speaker clearly has to be thrifty by necessity, the poem does not suggest that his thriftiness is a source of joy, let alone virtue, nor does this theme seem to address all sections of the poem, so eliminate (B). While the speaker mentions the cleanliness of the brass spittoons multiple times and considers a shining spittoon as a tribute to God, this theme also does not apply to all parts of the poem particularly well, so eliminate (C). The speaker does not seem to be waiting for anything specific, nor does he acquire anything special for sticking it out at his job, so eliminate (E). The repetition of details about the speaker's job suggests that the poem does put some emphasis on "what we do" as well as "how we do it," so

eliminate (D). Among these choices, while (A) may not be tremendously appealing, it is the best answer because it accounts for more of the details of the poem overall than the other answer choices do.

General Takeway: You may not love the best answer, but if it's better than the rest, choose it and move on.

Drill 3

1. **D** Books are great for learning about other cultures—better than boats and horses, according to the speaker (D). The speaker is comparing boats to books, so (A) is not correct. The speaker prefers books for the mind rather than boats or horses for the body (B). There is no mention of the number of books or boats (C). There is no evidence that the speaker values the practical or doesn't value the frivolous (E).

2. **A** We know from the fact that they are "prancing" that coursers are probably horses (A). "Skiffs" don't prance (B). "Textbooks" are not mentioned in the poem (C). "Ancient chariots" cannot prance (D). The coursers are things that carry people, so they can't be "poetic devices" (E).

3. **B** The words in the poem are pretty high falutin': "coursers," "frigates" (B). There are not a lot of description words (A) or forceful actions (C). There is no humorous wordplay (D). The contrasts are not awkward (E).

4. **C** Even the poorest can take a journey into a book without having to pay for it (C). There is no mention of which economic group travels more (A). There is no suggestion of how to spend money (B). There is no discussion of how much books should cost (D). The speaker doesn't go so far as to talk about readers' souls (E).

5. **B** The speaker thinks reading is better than traveling, so the written word must have great power (B). There is no discussion of action versus passivity (A). We don't know what kinds of books the speaker likes to read (C). We don't know for sure that the speaker likes to fantasize (D). There is no mention of virtue (E).

6. **C** The poem is about how nothing is quite like the adventure of reading (C). The poem is not about the journey of life (A), nor is it about wisdom (B). There is nothing in the poem about education (D) or about the aging process (E).

7. **D** The speaker is trying to gently convince us about how great it is to read (D). There is not a lecture (A), nor is the speaker forceful (B). The speaker is not proactive (C), nor is she selfish (E).

Drill 4

1. **E** The author employs the first four of the listed techniques, but nowhere makes any Dickensian allusion (E). There is expressive use of punctuation marks, especially exclamation points, throughout the poem (A). The rhyme scheme is regular: AA, BB, CC, DD, EE, FF, and so on. (B), and each of the lines has roughly the same number of syllables (7), making the meter regular (C). There are adjectives, such as "fond" and "seraphic" (D).

2. **C** The speaker is mocking death by saying that he's heard so much about its sting and questioning where it is (C). The question is not harsh (A). The question is not curious or doubtful (B). The question is not earnest—the speaker is not really looking for death's sting (D). There is no paradox in the question (E).

3. D   "Sounds," in this case, is a noun, not a verb (D). All of the other answers are active verbs (A), (B), (C), and (E).

4. A   In the first stanza the speaker talks to nature; in the second, he talks to his soul, and in the third, he asks the angels to lend him their wings (A). He does not talk about life after death (although he can see heaven, he does not talk about what life will be like there) (B). The first stanza says that death is blissful as well as painful (C). The speaker is the same throughout the poem (D). The second stanza does not taunt death, and the third stanza is not reluctant (E).

5. E   The speaker is asking death to take him from his body (E). "Frame" is not a picture of the world (A) or any previously held image (B). The "frame" is a metaphor for the mortal body; the "frame" is *not* a metaphor for another metaphor, so answers (C) and (D) are incorrect.

6. A   As stated in line 4, death may be "painful," but it is also "sublime" (A). Death has no victory ("where is thy victory?") (B). He does not talk of resisting death (C). There is no notion that the next life will be better (D). There is no talk of the eternity of death (E).

7. D   The descriptions of death's symptoms and how death affects his body are elaborate (D). Romance is not a theme in the poem (A). The poem is not playful (B), nor is it harshly critical (C). The poem is emotionally expressive, not cryptic (hard to understand) (E).

8. B   The last lines underscore that death is less about physical pain and more about mental bliss (B). Death does hurt (A). There is no battle being fought (C). The speaker does not have an antagonistic relationship with death (D). Death is not transient (E).

Drill 5

1. C   "Silver" and "sound" are alliterative (C). There is no comparison between silver and gold (A). "Silver" does not foreshadow the hunt (B). Silver is not necessarily bright (D). The horn is not about wealth, nor are we told it's beautiful (E).

2. D   Like the hounds howling at the moon, the sounds are onomatopoetic (D). No one is greeting anyone in the poem (A). There is no suggestion that the speaker means to use the word "hollow" (B). There is no evidence that there is a physical spot to echo back (no cave or canyon) (C). The word "halo" does not make sense in this context (E).

3. B   The speaker is persuading the reader gently but firmly (B). The speaker is not "hostile" (A). The speaker is not trying to teach a lesson (C). The poem stretches across three stanzas; clearly, the speaker is not ambivalent (D). There is no evidence of disgust in the poem (E).

4. A   The poem is about someone who has gotten so caught up in his or her empty life that he or she has forgotten what is really important (A). There is no evidence of shame in the poem (B). The wealth is simply a metaphor. Plus, we don't know whether perhaps the person was wealthy all of his or her life (C). There is no suggestion in the poem that the addressee is about to die (D). Vanity is not mentioned in the poem (E).

5. B   In the poem, the speaker addresses someone who has lost touch with what is important in life, so Statement II is true. The madman's song does not mean that he or she was committed to an asylum, so Statement I is not true. The person to whom the poem is addressed is someone who has lost passion, not someone who is filled with it, so Statement III is not true.

6. B   The repetition in the poem is of the passionate actions—following, hallo-ing, and so on—so it mimics the poem's theme of finding passion (B). It does not necessarily help the rhyme scheme (A). The reader is not punished (C). There is no anger in the poem (D). The person addressed is not lazy, but rather passionless (E).

Drill 6

1. B   In lines 5–6, the speaker proclaims that dire events took place in a short span of time (the previous year, 1788). He goes on to say in lines 7–8 that any previous joys have been taken away, and the people have been left in a difficult situation. Therefore, the best answer is (B). Joy has not been left with them, but rather the opposite: it has been taken away. So, eliminate (A). The year has not given them happiness, no promises have been made, and no evidence of bounty is indicated in these lines, so (C) is not correct. Choice (D) is also incorrect, as the year has not given them pleasures, and the poem makes no mention of memories. While (E) correctly interprets lines 5–6, it is not the best answer overall.

2. C   The speaker personifies the year 1789 as a child who is not yet too old to learn from the mistakes of the past. He cautions 1789 to take care now that it is in the position of taking over, like a prince taking over his father's throne. The year 1789 is not a regent (a stand-in for the ruler) but a free agent (in charge). It needs to follow "the plan" no worse, and hopefully better, than the previous year did (C). The speaker is neither discussing himself nor any literal person. Instead, he is personifying the year 1789, so eliminate (A), (B), (D), and (E).

3. E   Throughout the poem, the speaker considers the events of the previous year and encourages both ministers and young ladies to recognize the events of the previous year for what they were—largely negative and filled with problems. However, he considers the possibility that the new year will be, at least, no worse and possibly better than the one before. Thus, his tone is circumspect (E). He is not nostalgic (A). He is clearly not apathetic (B), which you can conclude from all the exclamation points. Nor is he flirting (C) with anyone. While the last stanza can be considered anticipatory (D), that cannot be said of the other stanzas, leaving (E) as the best choice.

4. A   The speaker directly addresses the ministers (line 17), 1788 (line 5), pretty girls/"bonie lasses" (line 23), and 1789 (line 31). He refers to the Spanish empire (A) in line 9; however, this is not a direct address. Therefore, the correct answer is choice (A).

5. C   The poem is mainly written in iambic tetrameter: four accented syllables in each eight-syllable line, with an unaccented syllable followed by an accented syllable. The use of contractions allows the poet to maintain this meter (C). The contractions do not affect the rhyme scheme of the poem, so we can eliminate choice (B). It's important to remember that the test does not require outside knowledge; therefore, you know that (A), (D), and (E) cannot be correct.

6. E   The word "himsel" is referring to the "Daddy" (line 34), who represents the father of 1789. Thus, the answer is choice (E). "The plan" (A) is a direction for the new year to follow rather than a personification of the year. (Also, keep in mind that an antecedent typically precedes the pronoun that replaces it.) "Regent" (C) is used to illustrate what the new year is not. The "free agent" (B) and "beardless boy" (D) are 1789 personified.

7. C   Alliteration (A) is used throughout the poem, such as in line 11. The poem has a definite meter and rhyme (B). Furthermore, the Scottish dialect is a dead giveaway that colloquial language (D) is being used. The poem itself is an example of personification (E) since the speaker gives 1788, as well as 1789, human

characteristics. The only remaining choice is (C), foreign words and phrases. The poem is in English, but it contains many words that are difficult to understand, so reading it may seem a lot like reading Shakespeare. Therefore, the answer is (C).

CHAPTER 11 DRILLS

Drill 1

1. **C** Mrs. Pearce never is contrasted with the king (C). Eliza was a flower girl—Higgins is hoping to make her into a lady in a florist's shop (A). If she's good, she goes to the palace; if she's bad, she goes to jail in the Tower of London (B). Again, good = proper bedroom, and bad = kitchen (D). Goodness is contrasted with naughtiness (E).

    General Takeaway: It's alarmingly easy even for seasoned test takers to overlook the word in all caps that indicates a NOT/LEAST/EXCEPT question. As you read the question, circle that word to remind you not to grab the first true statement you see.

2. **A** Higgins treats Eliza like a child with his patronizing tone, warning her of what will happen if she is "naughty and idle" or a "wicked girl" (A). She is not a servant because she won't have to do chores (B). He looks down on her; we know she is not a potential wife and matrimony is never mentioned (C). If it were futile, he would not embark on the project (D). He certainly does not find her to be a tenacious competitor (E).

    General Takeaway: Some drama may seem familiar, particularly if it was adapted at some point for cinema or television. You can use that awareness to help inform your sense of the passage you're looking at, though you still have to look to the passage itself to support answers.

3. **E** According to Higgins, Eliza will "learn how to speak beautifully, like a lady in a florist's shop"; thus (A) and (B) must both be characteristics of the sort of lady Higgins is describing. Since he continues his description of what Eliza will do by telling her that she will be able to "take rides in taxis" and that when she goes to Buckingham Palace she'll be "beautifully dressed," (C) and (D) are also supported. Thus while the notion of an English "lady" from a century ago might conjure for you the image of an upper class woman who "has the leisure not to work," the term "lady" in the context of Higgins' speech describes the "lady in a florist's shop" that Eliza aspires to be.

    General Takeaway: Particularly in more recent drama—in which dialogue tends to be more realistic and conversational—characters may use words in unexpected and idiosyncratic or colloquial ways. Your expectations may be helpful, but you still have to check answers against the particulars of the passage.

4. **B** Higgins is making assumptions and judgments about Eliza based on her social class (B), rather than on her as a person. It is Higgins, not Eliza, who has the military background (A). There is no evidence that Higgins is intimately familiar with Eliza as a person (C), and it is implausible that Higgins' superior attitude expresses sincere insight into what women want (D). Eliza has not expressed a preference (E) in this scene; she just seems confused.

    General Takeaway: Conflict drives drama, so while characters will rarely be so one-dimensional as to be entirely good or entirely bad, in their interactions with others, characters will often reveal some of their own shortcomings.

5. **A** Higgins oversimplifies the matter and talks to Eliza as though she were a child (A). He is not trying to teach her something with the speech (B), (C), nor does the speech really explain anything (D). His words are not apathetic (E).

6. **B** Higgins is making an offer to "improve" Eliza according to his opinion of what makes one person better than another; if he is successful, her reward will be "seven and six pence," which is about 3/8 of a pound of sterling (somewhere between $45 and $250 in present-day value). Since she is threatened with beatings and death for her participation in this project, and her reward is at best $40 per month, it is hard to say that Higgins is generous (B). His condescending speech suggests that he is arrogant (C), and his focus on his own benefit shows self-importance (D); his certainty that Eliza will jump at this opportunity is presumptuous (A). However, from the plan that Higgins describes, it is clear that he is determined (E); he will convince Eliza to participate, and she will be successful (or so he believes).

Drill 2

1. **D** Coyle is bringing up bills from various merchants who are going to take action against Sir Edward because he hasn't paid them, so a judge's decision and a court order are the best paraphrase (D). No one is being branded a criminal (A). The actions are real, not just moral (B). There is no suggestion of a partnership (C). There is no reference to a search of the property (E).

2. **A** Coyle manages Sir Edward's accounts as his "agent" or money manager (A). He is not a lawyer (B). Although Coyle is employed by Sir Edward, he is not a servant (C). Sir Edward's father was a benefactor for Coyle's father, but the current generation does not have this arrangement (D). Coyle and Sir Edward are not related, although Coyle wants to marry Sir Edward's daughter (E).

3. **A** Coyle's father lent Sir Edward's father money and took a property as an assurance that he would pay Coyle's father back, which never happened. In this situation, the property is collateral (A). "Agreement" does not describe the role of the property (B), nor does assurance have the precise meaning (C). Security does not mean "welfare" (D), nor is the property a prize (E).

4. **C** Sir Edward calls the debts "extortion," which means he thinks they are unfair (C). "Infernal" is merely an insult, not a comment on the fairness of the bills (A). "Confound" is an expletive like "darn" (B). "Impudence" describes Coyle's attitude, not the situation (D). "Unencumbered" in this context means "available to mortgage," which does not fit the situation (E).

5. **B** Coyle offers to keep "the Ravensdale estate in the family" if Sir Edward will give Coyle his daughter (B). Coyle does not offer to pay off the creditors—his offer extends only to Ravensdale (A). Coyle wants to marry Sir Edward's daughter, not marry her to a resident of Ravensdale (C). Coyle does not want to marry Sir Edward's daughter to prevent her financial ruin (D). There is no love affair between Coyle and Sir Edward's daughter ("Florence detests him") (E).

6. **D** Sir Edward appears to argue with himself, here, voicing both sides of the argument to accept or deny Coyle's offer (D). Sir Edward is not expressing doubt in his final lines (A). Just because the character is talking to himself does not mean he's going mad (B). The character is not addressing the audience (C). The lines do not explain a plot point; they merely follow Sir Edward's reasoning.

Drill 3

1. **C** Although any of these words can mean "end," in the context of Marina's line, the correct choice is (C). She uses the word in reference to her mother's death, explaining that her mother's life ended when Marina's began. None of the other choices correctly conveys the idea that Marina's mother died in childbirth.

2. **A** At this point in the scene, Pericles' realization that his daughter lives is so overwhelming that he fears the rush of joy will be more than his mortal body can handle. Thus, he asks Helicanus to cause him pain to keep him from dying from this happiness, which is stated in (A). There is no indication that anyone is going to strike Marina (B). The drowning to which Pericles refers is symbolic only (C). Pericles does not want to be relieved of pain (D); he wants to feel pain in order to offset the unbearable joy he is experiencing. Finally, though he speaks figuratively of being in a dream (E) earlier in the scene, Pericles is most definitely awake.

3. **B** Marina is the daughter of Pericles (B). Evidence for this can be found in lines 25, 49, 58, and 86–87. We know (A) is not the correct answer, as Marina ultimately convinces Pericles that she is his daughter, because she knows her mother's name and how she died. She is also clearly not deceased (C). Although Pericles had believed her to be dead, he is now aware that she is alive (line 89). Choice (D) is incorrect, since Marina was rescued by pirates rather than imprisoned by them (line 53). Though Pericles first asks Marina whether she is alive or a fairy (lines 31–32), he then accepts that she is human and alive (line 33). Therefore, (E) is incorrect.

4. **D** Startled to meet someone who shares his daughter's name, Pericles questions Marina throughout the scene, discovering how her story so closely matches his own daughter's, and realizing in the end that she is, in fact, his daughter. He is clearly in awe of this discovery, so (D) is the correct answer. On the other hand, there is nothing in the scene to support the idea that Pericles is old and confused (A). Moreover, he does not try to interrupt Marina (B) but rather encourages her to speak (for example, in lines 3 and 33). Although he has trouble believing her, it is not because he does not trust her (C), but because Marina's story is so astonishing and contrary to what he had believed to be true. And finally, though Pericles is anxious to verify her story (E), there is nothing in the text to support the idea that he is required to do so.

5. **A** In line 21, Pericles explains to Marina how startled he was when she said her name. Therefore, his tone can best be described as disquieted (A) in lines 15–17, as *disquieted* is synonymous with adjectives like perplexed, aghast, or unsettled. Although he mentions laughter, it is not used to describe himself, so *jovial* (B) is not correct. *Irate* (C) could be used to describe the gods that might be mocking him, but it does not describe his tone. Pericles says he is mocked, but he is not being satirical (D). And while Marina asks Pericles to be patient, *impatience* does not describe his tone in lines 15–17.

6. **D** In line 10, Pericles indicates that he had met Marina previously, which she confirms in line 13. He asks her to confirm a comment that she made when he first "perceived" her. Marina replies that she did say that she came "from good descending." From the use of past tense in this exchange, we can infer that the action they are recalling occurred earlier in the play; thus, the audience has already been introduced to these two characters, making statement I an incorrect choice. Therefore, eliminate choices (A), (B), (C), and (E), since they all include statement I. Choice (D) is the correct answer.

Part V
Practice Tests

Chapter 12
Practice Test 2

PRACTICE SAT SUBJECT TEST IN LITERATURE 2

TEST 2

Your responses to the SAT Subject Test in Literature questions should be filled in on Test 2 of your answer sheet.

LITERATURE TEST 2

Directions: This test consists of selections from literary works and questions on their content, form, and style. After reading each passage or poem, choose the best answer to each question and fill in the corresponding oval on the answer sheet.

Note: Pay particular attention to questions that contain the words NOT, LEAST, or EXCEPT.

Questions 1-9. Read the following poem carefully before you choose your answers.

"Promises Like Pie-Crust"

Promise me no promises,
    So will I not promise you:
Keep we both our liberties,
    Never false and never true:
(5) Let us hold the die uncast,
    Free to come as free to go:
For I cannot know your past,
    And of mine what can you know?

You, so warm, may once have been
(10) Warmer towards another one:
I, so cold, may once have seen
    Sunlight, once have felt the sun:
Who shall show us if it was
    Thus indeed in time of old?
(15) Fades the image from the glass,
    And the fortune is not told.

If you promised, you might grieve
    For lost liberty again:
If I promised, I believe
(20) I should fret to break the chain.
Let us be the friends we were,
    Nothing more but nothing less:
Many thrive on frugal fare
    Who would perish of excess.

(1861)

1. The promises referred to in the poem are

(A) pledges to share one another's innermost secrets
(B) articles of incorporation
(C) items in a prenuptial agreement
(D) resolution never to see each other again
(E) vows of undying romantic love

GO ON TO THE NEXT PAGE

2. In the second stanza, the speaker reveals that

    (A) she yearns for the love of someone who is
    oblivious to her
    (B) the listener has expressed more ardent
    sentiments toward her than she has
    expressed toward him
    (C) the listener does not reciprocate her feelings
    (D) she is incapable of deep emotional attachment
    (E) she is heartbroken over the end of a previous
    relationship

3. The speaker compares her current relationship
with the person to whom the poem is addressed to

    (A) one between strangers
    (B) a roll of a die
    (C) one governed by reciprocal obligations
    (D) a restrained diet of plain food
    (E) an image in a crystal ball

4. "Sunlight" (line 12) is used as a symbol for

    (A) innocence
    (B) genuine mutual love
    (C) purity
    (D) absolute confidence in the rightness of a
    decision
    (E) perfect understanding

5. Which of the following is NOT implied in the
poem as a reason to avoid entering into promises?

    (A) One person can never fully know another.
    (B) A promise can be broken without the person
    to whom the promise was made ever
    knowing.
    (C) To make a promise denies one of a degree of
    personal liberty.
    (D) One cannot be judged faithful or unfaithful to
    a commitment that has not been promised.
    (E) One can never fully know the situations or
    feelings of those who made successful and
    binding promises in the past.

6. In context, "fret" (line 20) most nearly means

    (A) irritate
    (B) chafe
    (C) rattle
    (D) worry
    (E) corrode

7. Which of the following best expresses the
meaning of the last two lines of the poem?

    (A) Some people are not meant to enjoy the
    richness of life, just as some cannot digest
    rich food.
    (B) When it comes to relationships, something is
    better than nothing.
    (C) For some people, the potential of happiness is
    more satisfying than the reality of happiness
    because the potential cannot be diminished
    over time.
    (D) Not every relationship is worth the risk
    entailed to the participants.
    (E) Some relationships are better when they are
    not too serious.

8. The tone of the poem as a whole can best be
described as

    (A) delicate but firm
    (B) disappointed but unapologetic
    (C) ambivalent but patronizing
    (D) world-weary and vague
    (E) harsh and unyielding

9. The simile of the title is apt because

    (A) both promises and pie-crust are sweet
    (B) both promises and pie-crust are meant to be
    filled
    (C) both promises and pie-crust are easily broken
    (D) the speaker has overindulged in rich food
    (E) the speaker denies herself all pleasures in life

GO ON TO THE NEXT PAGE

Questions 10-17. Read the following passage carefully before you choose your answers.

Studies serve for delight, for ornament, and for ability. Their chief use for delight is in privateness and retiring; for ornament, is in
Line discourse; and for ability, is in the judgment and
(5) disposition of business. For expert men can execute, and perhaps judge of particulars, one by one; but the general counsels, and the plots and marshalling of affairs come best from those that are learned. To spend too much time in studies
(10) is sloth; to use them too much for ornament is affectation; to make judgment wholly by their rules is the humor of a scholar. They perfect nature, and are perfected by experience: for natural abilities are like natural plants, that need
(15) pruning by study; and studies themselves do give forth directions too much at large, except they be bounded in by experience. Crafty men contemn* studies, simple men admire them, and wise men use them; for they teach not their own
(20) use; but that is a wisdom without them and above them, won by observation. Read not to contradict and confute, nor to believe and take for granted, nor to find talk and discourse, but to weigh and consider.

(c. 1597)

*have contempt for

10. The author's primary purpose is to

(A) demonstrate a display of learned eloquence
(B) encourage pupils to study diligently
(C) discuss the proper approach to book-centered learning
(D) distinguish the more serious from the less dignified motives for study
(E) dissuade students from applying their learning to unethical pursuits

11. By "expert men" (line 5) the author most nearly means

(A) persons with competence in specific activities, but who lack general education
(B) persons who have mastered a craft or trade
(C) persons who carry out the decisions of others
(D) persons who have devoted themselves to their studies
(E) persons who conduct the concrete business of the day

12. The author compares "abilities" and "plants" (line 14) to make the point that

(A) individuals must discipline themselves as they grow to maturity
(B) some students learn profusely while others learn little or slowly
(C) individuals must be nurtured and protected as growing plants must be
(D) education encourages individuals to develop in conformity with one another
(E) education shapes and refines an individual's innate qualities

13. Which of the following cautions is NOT conveyed in the passage?

(A) The organization of large undertakings is best left to persons who have read widely and deeply.
(B) It is possible to be overzealous in the pursuit of knowledge.
(C) One should not flaunt one's learning ostentatiously.
(D) Scholars should live in strict accordance with precepts gained through their study.
(E) The knowledge gained from books must be tested against one's firsthand experience in the world.

GO ON TO THE NEXT PAGE

14. With which of the following words or phrases could "admire" (line 18) be replaced without changing the meaning of the sentence?

    (A) Are awed by
    (B) Profess to respect
    (C) Enjoy
    (D) Are envious of
    (E) Are naturally drawn toward

15. Which of these stylistic devices is most prominent in the author's prose?

    (A) Elaborate metaphor
    (B) Hyperbole
    (C) Neatly balanced syntactic oppositions
    (D) Alliteration
    (E) Long, convoluted sentences

16. Reading, according to the author, is above all else a source for one's

    (A) controversial opinions
    (B) moral and religious beliefs
    (C) quiet amusement
    (D) stimulating conversation
    (E) private deliberation

17. The tone of the passage can best be described as

    (A) pious
    (B) didactic
    (C) satiric
    (D) moralistic
    (E) contentious

GO ON TO THE NEXT PAGE

Questions 18-24. Read the following poem carefully before you choose your answers.

"The Errand"

Dad

"On you go now! Run, son, like the devil
And tell your mother to try
To find me a bubble for the spirit level
And a new knot for this tie."

Line

Hint

(5) But still he was glad, I know, when I stood my ground,
Putting it up to him
With a smile that trumped his smile and his fool's errand,
Waiting for the next move in the game.

(1996)

18. The theme of the poem concerns

(A) rites of passage that mark the beginning of adolescence
(B) the contest of wills between one generation and the next
(C) the futility of needless chores with which parents occupy their children
(D) a boy's developing relationship with his father as the boy matures
(E) the resentment that lingers in the speaker's memory about childhood

19. The errand described in the poem is a quest for

(A) nonsensical components that do not form a coherent whole
(B) tools the speaker needs to continue his work
(C) someone in the neighborhood more foolish than the man's son
(D) degrees of understanding that come with maturity
(E) common ground on which father and son can identify with each other

20. Which of the following distinctions does NOT characterize the difference between the two stanzas?

(A) A shift from perfect rhyme to slant rhyme
(B) A change in speaker
(C) The passage of time
(D) A movement from metaphorical to literal language
(E) A switch from remembered speech to reflection

21. Which of the following is implied by the speaker's use of the word "still" (line 5)?

(A) The father's jovial spirits were not ultimately dampened when his son did not assume the errand.
(B) The father's pleased response to his son's refusal will continue indefinitely.
(C) The game between the father and son will continue indefinitely.
(D) The father did not express his gladness to his son.
(E) The boy's father was disappointed when his son did not assume the errand.

GO ON TO THE NEXT PAGE

22. Which of the following is nearest in meaning to "Putting it up to him" (line 6)?

    (A) Demonstrating to him the poet's awareness of his joke
    (B) Challenging him to find a bubble for himself
    (C) Refusing defiantly to honor his request
    (D) Handing up to him the items he had asked for
    (E) Turning the joke back around on him

23. The poem is best described as the account of

    (A) a young child relating a triumph to his mother
    (B) an adult fondly remembering an incident in his childhood
    (C) a young adult who shares a joke with his father in the midst of a game
    (D) a new father thinking about a lesson his parents taught him
    (E) a boy who is beginning to understand what tools are required for the job his father is working on

24. In the last line the speaker suggests that

    (A) the father will send his son on another, more serious errand
    (B) the father's goal is to make his son appear ridiculous
    (C) the father's response to his son's recognition will be significantly delayed
    (D) the father will continue to good-humoredly tease and test his son
    (E) the father and son will always engage in prankish contests

GO ON TO THE NEXT PAGE ⇒

Questions 25-33. Read the following passage carefully before you choose your answers.

In the second year of the reign of Valentinian and Valens, on the morning of the twenty-first day of July, the greatest part of the Roman world was shaken by a violent and destructive earthquake.

The impression was communicated to the waters; the shores of the Mediterranean were left dry, by the sudden retreat of the sea; great
Line quantities of fish were caught with the hand;
(5) large vessels were stranded on the mud; and a curious spectator amused his eye, or rather his fancy, by contemplating the various appearance of valleys and mountains, which had never, since the formation of the globe, been exposed to the
(10) sun. But the tide soon returned, with the weight of an immense and irresistible deluge, which was severely felt on the coasts of Sicily, of Dalmatia, of Greece, and of Egypt: large boats were transported, and lodged on the roofs of houses,
(15) or at the distance of two miles from the shore; the people, with their habitations, were swept away by the waters; and the city of Alexandria annually commemorated the fatal day, on which fifty thousand persons had lost their lives in the
(20) inundation.
This calamity, the report of which was magnified from one province to another, astonished and terrified the subjects of Rome; and their affrighted imagination enlarged the real
(25) extent of a momentary evil. They recollected the preceding earthquakes, which had subverted the cities of Palestine and Bithynia: they considered these alarming strokes as the prelude only of still more dreadful calamities, and their fearful vanity
(30) was disposed to confound the symptoms of a declining empire and a sinking world.

(1776)

25. Which of the following is NOT a result of the earthquake?

   (A) Beached vessels
   (B) Scorched earth
   (C) Extensive property damage
   (D) Many casualties
   (E) Widespread flooding

26. The sentence "The impression was communicated to the waters" (lines 1-2) most nearly means

   (A) citizens sent distress signals via boats
   (B) the water carried the sound of the earthquake
   (C) the earthquake took place offshore
   (D) the earthquake caused water displacement
   (E) the sea parted with the power of the earthquake

27. It can be inferred from the passage that Rome's citizens

   (A) had never before seen such widespread destruction
   (B) placed a great deal of value on human life
   (C) thought the world was deteriorating
   (D) understood the causes of natural disasters
   (E) were not prone to confabulation

28. The tone of the description of the Romans in the second paragraph can best be described as

   (A) detached
   (B) disparaging
   (C) amused
   (D) frightened
   (E) alarmist

29. All of the following refer to the events that occurred on July 21 EXCEPT:

   (A) "sudden retreat of the sea" (line 3)
   (B) "immense and irresistible deluge" (line 11)
   (C) "the fatal day" (line 18)
   (D) "the calamity" (line 21)
   (E) "alarming strokes" (line 28)

GO ON TO THE NEXT PAGE

30. Which of the following quotes best describes the reason the Romans were so frightened by the earthquake?

    (A) "they considered these alarming strokes as the prelude only of still more dreadful calamities" (lines 27-29)
    (B) "the city of Alexandria annually commemorated the fatal day, on which fifty thousand persons had lost their lives in the inundation" (lines 17-20)
    (C) "a curious spectator amused his eye, or rather his fancy, by contemplating the various appearance of valleys and mountains, which had never, since the formation of the globe, been exposed to the sun" (lines 5-10)
    (D) "great quantities of fish were caught with the hand;" (lines 3-4)
    (E) "But the tide soon returned, with the weight of an immense and irresistible deluge, which was severely felt" (lines 10-12)

31. In context, "declining" (line 31) most nearly means

    (A) sinking
    (B) worsening
    (C) aging
    (D) shrinking
    (E) weary

32. Which of the following is true, according to the passage?

    (A) The Roman Empire lost 50,000 people.
    (B) Homes were destroyed by the rift in the earth.
    (C) The earthquakes in Bithnyia and Palestine were not as destructive as this earthquake.
    (D) The Mediterranean's tides were permanently affected.
    (E) The damage was primarily caused by a surge of water.

33. The line "great quantities of fish were caught with the hand" contains an example of

    (A) figurative language
    (B) colorful adjectives
    (C) passive verb construction
    (D) oxymoronic impossibilities
    (E) pastoral analogies

GO ON TO THE NEXT PAGE

Questions 34-42. Read the following poem carefully before you choose your answers.

"The Mower to the Glowworms"

Ye living lamps, by whose dear light
The nightingale does sit so late,
And studying all the summer night,
Her matchless songs does meditate;

Line
(5)   Ye country comets, that portend
No war nor prince's funeral,
Shining unto no higher end
Than to presage the grass's fall;

Ye glowworms, whose officious flame
(10)   To wandering mowers shows the way,
That in the night have lost their aim,
And after foolish fires do stray;

Your courteous lights in vain you waste,
Since Juliana here is come,
(15)   For she my mind hath so displaced
That I shall never find my home.

(c. 1650)

34. The speaker of the poem first addresses the glowworms by epithets that draw attention to the insects' natural

(A) intelligence
(B) tranquility
(C) luminosity
(D) inconsequence
(E) mortality

35. The speaker of the poem describes glowworms as providing assistance to

   I. nightingales
  II. princes
 III. mowers

(A) I only
(B) II only
(C) III only
(D) I and III only
(E) I, II, and III

36. In its context, the word "portend" (line 5) means

(A) "predict," and alludes to the superstition that the motion of glowworms could be interpreted to foretell future events
(B) "predict," and alludes to the superstition that comets, meteors, and other natural phenomena were omens of evil
(C) "forecast," and alludes to the fact that the behavior of insects can be used to predict the next day's weather
(D) "imitate," and suggests that glowworms mimic the cyclical flight of comets
(E) "weigh," and makes clear that glowworms are oblivious to the dramatic upheavals of human life

GO ON TO THE NEXT PAGE

37. Which of the following best expresses the meaning of "higher end" (line 7)?

    (A) Brighter level
    (B) Greater distance off the ground
    (C) Further boundary
    (D) Secret intention
    (E) Nobler purpose

38. Which of the following is the closest synonym for "officious," as it is used in line 9?

    (A) Helpful
    (B) Dim
    (C) Wandering
    (D) Bureaucratic
    (E) Meddlesome

39. The speaker implies that, without the glowworms, mowers who have "lost their aim" (line 11) would be likely to

    (A) mow the wrong fields
    (B) conduct themselves disgracefully
    (C) fall in love
    (D) be distracted by other, mysterious sources of light
    (E) never find their way home

40. Which of the following is the best paraphrase for the last line of the poem?

    (A) I am blinded by my resentment toward her.
    (B) I will continue wandering forever.
    (C) I will never be myself again.
    (D) I will never go home without her.
    (E) I will never go to heaven.

41. The main verb in the sentence that states the overall theme of the poem is

    (A) "sit" (line 2)
    (B) "waste" (line 13)
    (C) "come" (line 14)
    (D) "displaced" (line 15)
    (E) "find" (line 16)

42. "The Mower to the Glowworms" could most reasonably be considered

    (A) a celebration of fireflies
    (B) an elaborate compliment to a woman
    (C) an analysis of love at first sight
    (D) an allegory about the Holy Spirit
    (E) a commentary on the foolishness of mowers

GO ON TO THE NEXT PAGE

Questions 43-53. Read the following passage carefully before you choose your answers.

ROSE: Times have changed since you was playing baseball, Troy. That was before the war. Times have changed a lot since then.

Line
(5)
TROY: How in hell they done changed?

ROSE: They got lots of colored boys playing ball now. Baseball and football.

BONO: You right about that, Rose. Times have changed, Troy. You just come along too early.

(10) TROY: There ought not never have been no time called too early! Now you take that fellow . . . what's that fellow they had playing right field for the Yankees back then? You know who I'm talking about, Bono. Used to play right field for the Yankees.

(15)

ROSE: Selkirk?

TROY: Selkirk! That's it! Man batting .269, understand? .269. What kind of sense that make? I was hitting .432 with thirty-seven home runs! Man batting .269 and playing right field for the Yankees! I saw Josh Gibson's* daughter yesterday. She walking around with raggedy shoes on her feet. Now I bet you Selkirk's daughter ain't walking around with raggedy shoes on her feet! I bet you that!

(20)

(25)

ROSE: They got a lot of colored baseball players now. Jackie Robinson was the first. Folks had to wait for Jackie Robinson.

(30)

TROY: I done seen a hundred niggers play baseball better than Jackie Robinson. Hell, I know some teams Jackie Robinson couldn't even make! Jackie Robinson wasn't nobody. I'm talking about if you could play ball then they ought to have let you play. Don't care what color you were. Come telling me I come along too early. If you could play . . . then they ought to have let you play.

(35)

(40) *(Troy takes a long drink from the bottle.)*

ROSE: You gonna drink yourself to death. You don't need to be drinking like that.

TROY: Death ain't nothing. I done seen him. Done wrastled with him. You can't tell me nothing about death. Death ain't nothing but a fastball on the outside corner. And you know what I'll do to that! Lookee here, Bono . . .

(45)

(50) am I lying? You get one of them fastballs, about waist height, over the outside corner of the plate where you can get the meat of the bat on it . . . and good god! You can kiss it goodbye. Now, am I lying?

BONO: Naw, you telling the truth there. I seen you do it.

(55) TROY: If I'm lying . . . that 450 feet worth of lying! *(Pause.)* That's all death is to me. A fastball on the outside corner.

ROSE: I don't know why you want to get on talking about death.

(60) TROY: Ain't nothing wrong with talking about death. That's part of life. Everybody gonna die. You gonna die, I'm gonna die. Bono's gonna die. Hell, we all gonna die.

(1986)

*Josh Gibson was a notable baseball player in the Negro Leagues.

43. It can be inferred that Troy played baseball

(A) before the outbreak of World War I
(B) long before the period in which Selkirk played right field for the Yankees
(C) before Jackie Robinson was born
(D) before the major leagues were racially integrated
(E) until his near brush with death

44. Which of the following best expresses the meaning of Troy's statement that "There ought not never have been no time called too early!" (lines 10-11)?

(A) We should judge past conditions in light of their historical context.
(B) It is a shame that we must wait for society's flaws to be corrected by progress and social change.
(C) Most individuals are born before the time period in which they could most prosper or succeed.
(D) The language we use to describe the world affects the way we experience the world.
(E) Despite the appearance of progress, social conditions do not really improve.

GO ON TO THE NEXT PAGE

45. Troy mentions his encounter with Josh Gibson's daughter to

    (A) prove that Selkirk had been unqualified to play right field for the Yankees
    (B) cite an example of a black athlete whose skills in his view exceeded those of Jackie Robinson
    (C) pay tribute to the greatest of right fielders in the Negro Leagues
    (D) illustrate the disparity in the economic rewards available to white and to black professional baseball players before the integration of Major League Baseball
    (E) emphasize his point that times have not changed

46. Troy's tone in lamenting the injustice of his baseball career is one of

    (A) evenhanded objectivity
    (B) harsh political fervor
    (C) lingering resentment
    (D) naïve idealism
    (E) pompous self-pity

47. Troy begins a speech by personifying death and then proceeds to

    (A) ignore Rose's well-meaning advice
    (B) revert to his previous bragging about his prowess as a baseball player
    (C) make a comparison expressing his fearlessness of death
    (D) make an analogy that shows that he believes he can evade death
    (E) explain what he believes it will feel like to die

48. In the context of the passage, the primary effect of "not," "never," and "no" in lines 10 and 11 is to

    (A) suggest that Troy has had limited educational opportunities
    (B) hint that Troy is unduly pessimistic
    (C) emphasize the strength of Troy's feelings on the issue he's discussing
    (D) use alliteration to hint that Troy thinks like a poet
    (E) prove the efficacy of employing nonstandard English

49. Troy's attitude toward death is primarily one of

    (A) contemptuous denial
    (B) naïve self-delusion
    (C) boastful nonchalance
    (D) awed anticipation
    (E) thinly veiled cowardice

50. From the passage, it can be inferred that Troy and Bono are

    (A) opponents in a long-standing dispute
    (B) former teammates of Josh Gibson
    (C) baseball players of two different generations
    (D) flirtatious colleagues
    (E) old friends

51. In context, it appears that Rose's assertion that "Folks had to wait for Jackie Robinson"

    (A) is intended to shut down all further conversation
    (B) causes Bono to stop participating in the discussion
    (C) fails to persuade Troy as she intended it to
    (D) is a deliberate attempt to rile up Troy
    (E) contradicts her claims about the number of black baseball players

GO ON TO THE NEXT PAGE

52. It can be inferred that Rose's feelings for Troy are characterized by

   (A) affectionate concern
   (B) sarcastic mockery
   (C) reverent admiration
   (D) apathetic dismissal
   (E) jealous anxiety

53. Which of the following would most logically precede the discussion excerpted in this passage?

   (A) A discussion about whether Troy's son can expect to be discriminated against in his sports career because he is black
   (B) A debate over whether Troy should compete for a spot at the Yankees' spring training camp
   (C) A debate over the merits of racially integrated neighborhoods
   (D) A discussion of the great moments in Troy's baseball career
   (E) A discussion of persistent racial unrest in American society

Questions 54-61. Read the following passage carefully before you choose your answers.

The guest waked from a dream, and remembering his day's pleasure hurried to dress himself that it might sooner begin. He was
Line sure from the way the shy little girl looked
(5) once or twice yesterday that she had at least seen the white heron, and now she must really be persuaded to tell. Here she comes now, paler than ever, and her worn old frock is torn and tattered, and smeared with pine pitch. The
(10) grandmother and the sportsman stand in the door together and question her, and the splendid moment has come to speak of the dead hemlock-tree by the green marsh.

But Sylvia does not speak after all, though
(15) the old grandmother fretfully rebukes her, and the young man's kind appealing eyes are looking straight in her own. He can make them rich with money; he has promised it, and they are poor now. He is so well worth making
(20) happy, and he waits to hear the story she can tell.

No, she must keep silence! What is it that suddenly forbids her and makes her dumb? Has she been nine years growing, and now, when
(25) the great world for the first time puts out a hand to her, must she thrust it aside for a bird's sake? The murmur of the pine's green branches in her ears, she remembers how the white heron came flying through the golden air and how
(30) they watched the sea and the morning together, and Sylvia cannot speak; she cannot tell the heron's secret and give its life away.

(1886)

54. It can be inferred that the guest's anticipated "day's pleasure" (line 2) centered around

(A) his furthering his acquaintance with Sylvia
(B) his hearing the end of a tale that Sylvia has promised to finish for him
(C) his opportunity to make a carving from a petrified hemlock tree
(D) his opportunity to photograph a white heron in its natural habitat
(E) his opportunity to shoot a white heron

55. Which of the following is NOT an effect of the switch from past-tense narration to present-tense narration in the first paragraph?

(A) It conveys the young man's surprise at the little girl's appearance.
(B) It emphasizes the young man's suspense in waiting for her to speak.
(C) It serves to heighten the reader's anticipation of the little girl's revelation.
(D) It signals the narrator's switch from the guest's point of view to the little girl's.
(E) It intensifies the reader's sense that this is a moment that both the young man and Sylvia have been eagerly awaiting.

56. Which of the following is the strongest enticement for Sylvia to lead the young man to where she has seen the white heron?

(A) Her grandmother's failing health
(B) Her respect for the young man's good intentions toward the heron
(C) Her fear that the young man might take her away from her familiar surroundings
(D) His promise of financial reward
(E) His loyalty to all the wild creatures of the region

57. Which of the following best articulates Sylvia's feelings toward the young man?

(A) She hopes to win his esteem at any cost.
(B) She is torn between her desire to please him and her contrary impulse not to assist him.
(C) She is indifferent to his aims and toward him as a person.
(D) She is repulsed by him personally, although she supports his endeavor.
(E) She despises his mercenary motives.

58. Sylvia's own surprise at her reluctance to speak is best conveyed by

    (A) the narrator's emphasis on her and her grandmother's poverty
    (B) the narrator's admission that Sylvia had never before had the chance to fulfill someone's hopes as she might have fulfilled the young man's
    (C) the short sentences used to convey the choppiness of Sylvia's thoughts
    (D) Sylvia's memory of the pine tree and the view of the sea
    (E) the author's use of rhetorical questions to express Sylvia's own self-questioning

59. Sylvia is described in the passage as

    (A) surprised at her own morality
    (B) failing to honor a promise she had made to her grandmother
    (C) frustrating any hope she might have had of getting to know the young man better
    (D) persistently dismissive of other people's feelings
    (E) remaining faithful to her long-standing beliefs

60. Which of the following phrases from the passage is most nearly the antithesis of what the white heron represents to Sylvia?

    (A) "torn and tattered" (lines 8-9)
    (B) "splendid moment" (line 12)
    (C) "nine years growing" (line 24)
    (D) "the great world" (line 25)
    (E) "the golden air" (line 29)

61. All of the following are functions of the phrase "make them rich with money" (lines 17-18) EXCEPT

    (A) to explain why Sylvia does not speak
    (B) to reflect the colloquial nature of Sylvia's thoughts
    (C) to hint that there is more than one way to be wealthy
    (D) to suggest an opposition to what is represented by the "golden air" (line 29)
    (E) to identify a potential effect of the sportsman's visit

STOP

IF YOU FINISH BEFORE TIME IS CALLED, YOU MAY CHECK YOUR WORK ON THIS SECTION ONLY. DO NOT TURN TO ANY OTHER SECTION IN THE TEST.

Chapter 13
Practice Test 2:
Answers and
Explanations

- Practice Test 2 Answer Key
- Practice Test 2 Explanations
- How to Score Practice Test 2

PRACTICE TEST 2 ANSWER KEY

Question Number	Correct Answer	Right	Wrong
1	E	____	____
2	B	____	____
3	D	____	____
4	B	____	____
5	B	____	____
6	B	____	____
7	E	____	____
8	A	____	____
9	C	____	____
10	C	____	____
11	A	____	____
12	E	____	____
13	D	____	____
14	A	____	____
15	C	____	____
16	E	____	____
17	B	____	____
18	D	____	____
19	A	____	____
20	D	____	____
21	A	____	____
22	A	____	____
23	B	____	____
24	D	____	____
25	B	____	____
26	D	____	____
27	C	____	____
28	B	____	____
29	E	____	____
30	A	____	____
31	B	____	____

Question Number	Correct Answer	Right	Wrong
32	E	____	____
33	C	____	____
34	C	____	____
35	D	____	____
36	B	____	____
37	E	____	____
38	A	____	____
39	D	____	____
40	C	____	____
41	B	____	____
42	B	____	____
43	D	____	____
44	B	____	____
45	D	____	____
46	C	____	____
47	C	____	____
48	C	____	____
49	C	____	____
50	E	____	____
51	C	____	____
52	A	____	____
53	A	____	____
54	E	____	____
55	A	____	____
56	D	____	____
57	B	____	____
58	E	____	____
59	A	____	____
60	D	____	____
61	A	____	____

PRACTICE TEST 2 EXPLANATIONS

1. **E**   The lines "Keep we both our liberties" (line 3) and "Let us be the friends we were" (line 21) suggest that the speaker does not want to be tied down by a romantic entanglement (E). There is no mention of secrets (A) or of articles of incorporation (B). No inventory of items is listed in the poem (C); the narrator wants them to be friends, so presumably they'll see each other (D).

2. **B**   The listener is described as "warm," while the speaker describes herself as "cold," so it is reasonable to infer that the listener feels more than does the speaker (B). The listener is warm, so he is not oblivious to the speaker (A), nor does he not reciprocate her feelings (she may not even have feelings for him) (C). There is no evidence that she is incapable of a relationship—she may "once have felt the sun" (D). There is no evidence that she is grieving another relationship (E).

3. **D**   The last two lines compare the relationship to "fare," which means food (D). The speaker wants to be friends, so the relationship is not compared to strangers (A). Rolling the die is a metaphor for a wedding, which does not occur, so (B) is not the correct answer. No obligations are mentioned (liberties, yes; obligations, no) (C). The speaker says she does not want to know about the past, as symbolized by the crystal ball, but does not compare her relationship to that object (E).

4. **B**   The speaker talks of past romances and suggests she's had one by saying she may have "seen Sunlight," so sunlight is a symbol of love (B). It is not a stand-in for "innocence" (A) or "purity" (C). She is speaking of the past, so the present decision is not the "sunlight" (D). There is no mention that the speaker is thinking about understanding (E).

5. **B**   By Process of Elimination, a broken promise without the knowledge of the other party is the correct answer (it is not implied in the poem) (B). Choice (A) is mentioned in lines 7–8; (C) is discussed in lines 17–20. Choice (D) is mentioned in line 4, and (E) is mentioned in lines 13–14. (Note: You should be circling the "NOT" and putting a "Y" for "yes" and an "N" for "no" next to each choice to find the odd man out.)

6. **B**   The speaker worries that if she promises to be faithful she might want to break her vows, so chafing at her bonds (B) is the best answer. Neither irritating the chain (A) nor rattling it (C) makes sense. "Worry" is too literal a synonym for "fret" (D). And she does not "corrode" the chains of marriage (E).

7. **E**   The speaker wants to just be friends—she warns that trying to be more would destroy the friendship, so (E) is the best answer. There is no discussion of whether people should enjoy the richness of life (A). The speaker warns of too much food, not nothing (B). The diminishment of happiness is not a concern in the poem (C). She does not mention risks in the poem (D).

8. **A**   The speaker lets the listener down gently, so (A) is the best answer. She does not express disappointment (B), nor is she ambivalent or patronizing (condescending) (C). She is not vague (D), nor is she harsh (E).

9. **C** The poem is about broken promises, so (C) is the best answer. The speaker is against promises; they are not "sweet" (A). There is no mention of the filling of promises (B). Choice (D) is a too-literal interpretation of the title, and because of the speaker's mention of her past, it does not seem as though she denies herself pleasure (E).

10. **C** The speaker is arguing for balance in using studies as a complement to both one's natural talents and the wisdom gained by experience. Thus his primary purpose is to put forward an argument about the role that "studies" (or scholarship) should play (C). While he may display learned eloquence (A) and distinguish among motives for studying (D), neither is his primary purpose. Diligent study alone is insufficient to make best use of education (B), and the speaker does not focus on moral issues (E).

11. **A** The sentence beginning on line 5 says that some people with only experience, not education, can make decent decisions, but that the overall plans should be made by people who are educated. "Expert" means more "having experience" (A) than literally having learned a trade (B). The "expert men" "judge of particulars," so they are not merely those who carry out the decisions (C). The author speaks of scholars later on in the passage (D). There is no discussion of what kinds of business "expert men" do (E).

12. **E** According to the author, just as plants need to be pruned to grow correctly, so too does natural ability need education to flourish properly (E). Plants do not prune themselves, and there is no mention of self-discipline (A). The author does not differentiate between kinds of students (B). He speaks of having to tame natural abilities, not having to foster them (C). The author does not talk about making all individuals the same (D).

13. **D** The only choice not mentioned in the passage is (D), that scholars should live according to the morals they find in their studies. Choice (A) is mentioned in lines 7–9, while (B) is talked about in lines 9–10. Lines 10–11 caution against showing off (C), and (E) is discussed in lines 15–17. (Note: You should circle the word "NOT" and put a "Y" for "yes" and an "N" for "no" next to each choice to find the odd man out.)

14. **A** The "simple men" referred to are very impressed with studies (A). There is no evidence that they respect people who are educated (B), nor that they enjoy studies (C). Although choice (D) is tempting, there is no evidence that simple men want to have studies, but just that they are impressed by them (D). There is no evidence in the passage that simple men are drawn toward studies (E).

15. **C** The author mostly compares lists of qualities in each sentence, balancing the opposing parts, so (C) is the best answer. The only metaphor in the passage is actually a simile: the comparison to plants (A). The author does not use hyperbole (exaggeration) (B). There is little alliteration in the piece (D). The sentences are not all convoluted (take the first sentence, for example) (E).

16. **E** Lines 21–24 tell the reader to study in order to "weigh and consider" (E). The author warns against reading to "confute," or find opinions (A). No mention is made of moral or religious beliefs (B). Amusement ("delight"), choice (C), and conversation ("discourse"), choice (D), are mentioned in lines 2–4, but not as the primary reasons for reading.

17. **B** The author is trying to teach the reader something, so the tone can best be described as "didactic" (designed to teach) (B). The narrator is not devout or religious (A), nor is he "satiric" (C). The narrator does not mention ethics or morals in the passage (D), nor does he argue with any other viewpoint (E).

18. **D** The father and the boy are testing each other in this poem, changing their relationship as the boy grows, so (D) is the best answer. The errand on which the father sends the son is not a rite of passage, nor do we know the age of the boy (A). It is not a contest of wills because the boy and his father are smiling (B). The focus of the poem is not on the errand, but on the boy's reaction to it (C). The speaker remembers the exchange fondly, so there is no evidence of resentment (E).

19. **A** The father asks for things that don't have any relationship. Even if this is difficult to see, (A) is the only answer that can't be eliminated. We don't know what the father's work is, and these things cannot be tools (B). Choice (C) is a too-literal interpretation of "fool's errand." The errand is more specifically about the boy and his father, not about degrees of understanding in general (D). The father is not asking for the son to find common ground; the common ground is an outcome of the errand (E).

20. **D** The only one of these answers not found in the poem is (D)—there is a metaphor in the second stanza comparing the errand to a game, and calling the task a "fool's errand." Even if you don't know perfect rhyme from slant rhyme, the rhyme scheme changes between the two stanzas (A). The speaker is the father in the first stanza and his son in the second (B). The narrator is obviously remembering an event that happened in the past (C), and the switch is from the words that he remembers to the thoughts he first had upon hearing those words (E). (Note: You should circle the word "NOT" and put a "Y" for "yes" and an "N" for "no" next to each choice to find the odd man out.)

21. **A** Although the father wanted the boy to go on the errand, his smile at the end shows he was pleased with the boy, so (A) is the best answer. We cannot predict what will happen in the future (B), (C). The father expressed his gladness with a smile (D), so he presumably was not disappointed (E).

22. **A** By "putting it up to him," the boy is showing that he realizes the errand is not meant to be completed, so he understands the joke (A). There is no challenge issued to the father (B), nor is the boy particularly defiant (C). He does not go on the errand, so he cannot hand his father the items (D). And he does not turn the joke back around (E).

23. **B** The speaker describes his own smile as "trump[ing]" his father's and the errand his father tries to send him on as a "fool's errand." Both diction and nature of both descriptions suggest an adult perspective, rather than that of a child (particularly one who has only just come to understand the father's joke), so he is likely to be an adult recounting an incident from his childhood (B) and not a child (A). The moment when the speaker stood his ground occurred when he was a boy and not a young adult (C), and there's no evidence the speaker is a new father (D). The boy's new understanding centered on the nature of his father's joke, not the tools required for a job (E).

24. **D** "The next move in the game" suggests that the game will continue, so (D) is the best answer. We can't know what the nature of the next form of teasing will be (A). There is no evidence that the father wants to make his son appear ridiculous; rather, he is harmlessly teasing his son (B). There is no evidence that the father will delay his response (C). We cannot predict how long this game will last (E).

25. **B** Here you're looking for the thing that is NOT in the passage. Choice (A) is an effect of the earthquake: "large vessels were stranded on the mud" (line 5). Choice (C) is also a result of the earthquake: "the people, with their habitations, were swept away by the waters" (lines 16–17), as is (D), "fifty thousand persons had lost their lives in the inundation" (lines 19–20), and (E) "But the tide soon returned, with the weight of an immense and irresistible deluge, which was severely felt on the coasts of Sicily, of Dalmatia, of Greece, and of Egypt" (lines 10–13). There is no evidence of "scorched earth" (B), as there was no mention of fire.

26. **D** The earthquake caused the water first to retreat, and then to flood the coastal areas, so (D) is the correct answer. There is no mention of distress signals (A). The "impression" refers to the physical movement of the water, not of sound (B). We do not know where the quake took place (C). There is no evidence that the sea parted, merely that it retreated and then flooded (E).

27. **C** The passage makes clear that Roman citizens thought the world was worsening: "their fearful vanity was disposed to confound the symptoms of a declining empire and a sinking world" (lines 29–31), so (C) is the correct answer. There are two other earthquakes mentioned, Palestine and Bithynia, but the current destruction is not compared to them (A). There is no evidence in the passage that Romans placed a great value on human life (B). There is no evidence that they understood the cause of the earthquake; in fact, they thought it was a sign of a worsening world (D). They *were* prone to confabulation (E); the extent of the destruction was exaggerated: "This calamity, the report of which was magnified from one province to another" (lines 21–22).

28. **B** The second paragraph refers to the Romans "affrighted imagination" and "fearful vanity" and points out the mistake they are making in confounding the state of nature with the state of their empire, so the tone is disparaging or deprecating (B). The phrase "fearful vanity" signals that the Romans' behavior is being judged negatively, not that it is being regarded with detachment (A), amusement (C), fear (D), or alarm (E).

29. **E** The "alarming strokes" are the "preceding earthquakes" that affected Palestine and Bithynia and that the Romans saw as precedents that shaped how they responded to the earthquake of July 21 (E). The sea's retreat (A) and deluge (B) were both caused by and occurred shortly after the earthquake itself. The passage uses "fatal day" (C) and "calamity" (D) to refer to the events of July 21.

30. **A** The Romans were afraid because they saw the earthquake as a warning of even more destructive things to come (A). Saying that they were afraid because they commemorated the anniversary does not make sense (B). Because many Romans did not actually witness the flood, the spectator's view is not what scared them (C). Choice (D) is incorrect because it describes a specific moment in the earthquake, but fish caught in hand isn't the reason that the Romans were frightened. The tide was destructive, but not necessarily fear inspiring (E).

31. **B** In the passage, the people are terrified because of the prior earthquakes and are fearful of the "dreadful calamities" still to come; their empire is described as "declining," meaning that it's going downhill. The only choice that has a similar meaning to "going downhill" is "worsening" (B).

32. **E** The sentence "But the tide soon returned, with the weight of an immense and irresistible deluge, which was severely felt on the coasts of Sicily, of Dalmatia, of Greece, and of Egypt: large boats were transported, and lodged on the roofs of houses, or at the distance of two miles from the shore; the people, with their habitations, were swept away by the waters" makes it clear that the damage was primarily caused by a large flood (E). The city of Alexandria lost fifty thousand people; we are not told the total number of casualties (A). Homes were destroyed by the flood, not a tear in the earth (B). There is nothing that compares the severity of this earthquake with the earthquakes in Bithnyia and Palestine (C). There is no evidence that the tides were permanently affected (D).

33. **C** This description contains a passive verb construction (C): the fish "were caught" with the hand. In this sentence, the grammatical subject (the fish) is actually the one receiving the action (being caught); an active-voice construction would say "people caught great quantities of fish by hand." There is no figurative language (A) or colorful adjectives (B) here; the fish can literally be scooped up by hand, since the waters have retreated. Since this actually happened, it is not an impossibility (D). Pastoral analogies (E) are allusions to countryside life, which do not appear in this phrase.

34. **C** The poet calls the glowworms "lamps" (line 1), "comets" (line 5), "flame" (line 9), and "lights" (line 13), so they are naturally luminous (shining) (C). There is no mention of glowworms' intelligence (A) or of their tranquility (B). They are not inconsequential (D), and there is no mention of their death (E).

35. **D** The glowworms help the nightingale (line 2) (Statement I) and the mowers (line 10) (Statement III), but not the princes (Statement II). Choice (D) is correct.

36. **B** The word "portend" means to predict, and the author is drawing attention to the glowworms' innocence to show that, unlike comets, they do not foretell evil (the superstition is elucidated by the line "No war nor prince's funeral") (B). The poet says the glowworms do NOT foretell future events (A). There is no weather mentioned (C). There is no mention of a cyclical flight pattern (D). The word "portend" cannot mean "weigh" in this context (E).

37. **E** The glowworms' light is not of great importance or of any nobler purpose than to shed light (E). Choice (A) is a too-literal interpretation of the phrase, as is choice (B). Choice (C) does not make sense in this context, and there is no "secret intention" (D).

38. **A** The glowworm is helping to light the mower's way (A). If the mower can see by it, it must not be dim (B). There is no evidence that the "officious flame" is bureaucratic (D) or that it is interfering (E). And finally, there is never any context in which *officious* means "wandering" (C).

39. **D** The speaker says that mowers "after foolish fires do stray," meaning they follow other sources of light (D). They would not mow other fields (A) or display poor manners (B). There is no evidence that they would fall in love without the glowworms (C), and although neither the mowers nor the speaker may ever find their way home, it is not because there are no glowworms (E).

40.   C   His mind is so displaced by thoughts of Juliana that it will never go back to its original state (C). He is not resentful (A). He wanders metaphorically, not literally (B), so home is metaphoric, too (D). There is no mention of heaven (E).

41.   B   The question asks for the main verb in the main idea sentence. The first three stanzas are all addressed to the glowworms ("Ye glowworms who…who…who…") and do not state the main idea. Not until the fourth stanza does the reader get to the main-idea sentence ("Your courteous lights …"). The main verb in this sentence—the verb that belongs with the subject "glowworms"— is "waste." So, the best answer is (B). "Sit" refers to the nightingales, not the main subject (A); "come" refers to Juliana, not the main subject (C). "Displaced" is a verb attached to Juliana (D), and the verb "find" refers to the narrator, not the glowworms (E).

42.   B   The whole poem is stating that although the glowworms are powerful lights, they are nothing compared to Juliana, so (B) is the best answer. The poem is not a celebration of fireflies (A). The poem does not mention love at first sight (C). There is no evidence of religious allegory (D), and the fires are considered foolish, not the mowers (which is not the main point of the poem anyway) (E).

43.   D   Troy wasn't allowed to play in the major leagues because he was African American, so he must have played before the major leagues were racially integrated (D). There is no mention of when exactly Troy played (before or after World War I) (A), so we can't know how long it was before Selkirk played (B). Jackie Robinson might already have been born when Troy played baseball, but Robinson hadn't yet broken the color barrier (C). There is no mention of Troy's brush with death (E).

44.   B   Troy thinks that there never should have been a rule that prevented him from playing major league baseball—that he couldn't play because society hadn't progressed enough (B). He does not think that history should be excused just because of its context (A). Choice (C) is not true, as Jackie Robinson prospered as a baseball player. There is no discussion of language (D). The statement quoted does not mention whether social conditions have really improved (E).

45.   D   Gibson was a famous baseball player, but his daughter was poor, so there is a large difference between the money that white players and African American players earned before Major League Baseball was integrated (D). The encounter with Gibson's daughter has nothing to do with Selkirk's qualifications (A). The point of the anecdote was to show the disparate salaries, not to compare black athletes (B). There is no tribute being paid (C). He is not saying that times have not changed—now African Americans can play in the major leagues (E).

46.   C   Troy is still upset that he did not become a professional baseball player: ".269. What kind of sense that make? I was hitting .432 with thirty-seven home runs" (lines 19–21), so (C) is the best answer. He is neither objective (A), nor particularly politically active (B). He is pessimistic, not idealistic (D). And while his tone may seem somewhat self-pitying, it is definitely not pompous (E).

47. C Troy compares death to a fastball that he hits out of the park, meaning he does not fear death (C). He does not begin his speech and then ignore Rose's advice (A), and the main point of his speech is not to brag about his talent as a baseball player (B). He does not believe he can evade death: "I'm gonna die" (line 62) (D). The speech does not say how he thinks death will feel (E).

48. C The first line Troy speaks in this passage—"How the hell they done changed?"—suggests that the subject under discussion agitates him, as do the stage direction about Troy's drinking, Rose's responses to that drinking, and his comments about death. In this context, the triple negation in Troy's exclamation serves to emphasize the strength of his feelings about racial discrimination in professional baseball (C)—not to add poetic style (D) or to demonstrate the efficacy of using triple negatives (E). Troy's agitation and vehement feelings are more significant and central to the passage than his educational attainments (A). Troy's agitation centers on the conditions in the past not in the future so his response doesn't suggest pessimism or that his negative feelings are unwarranted (B).

49. C Troy thinks death is like a fastball—you gotta take what's coming—so (C) is the best answer. He knows he's going to die, so he's not in denial (A), nor is he delusional (B). He is not anxiously awaiting death, nor is he in awe of it (D) or afraid of it (E).

50. E Troy and Bono are old friends—Bono knew him when Troy was a baseball player (E). They don't seem to be in a dispute (A). There is no evidence they played on a team with Gibson (B). There is not enough information to prove that they are of different generations (C). They are not flirtatious (D).

51. C The tension within the passage centers on the negative trajectory of Troy's reactions. The idea that Troy played baseball in a time when racial discrimination unfairly limited his opportunities seems to be a familiar topic to all three characters; in this context, Rose's initial responses seem to be intended to keep him from fully warming to the topic (by asserting that times have changed) and her later ones address Troy's behavior (drinking, talking about death) once he starts talking about the injustice. Thus her comment about Jackie Robinson falls into the earlier category, though it does not achieve this effect (C). The evidence contradicts the claim that she intends to upset Troy (D). There's no evidence that Rose seeks to cut off all conversation (A) or that the mention of Jackie Robinson causes Bono to stop talking (B). The comment is consistent with, not contradicting of, her earlier statement about the number of black athletes (E).

52. A In lines 41–42, Rose says, "You don't need to be drinking like that." She is fond of Troy and doesn't want him to hurt himself, so (A) is the best answer. She is not making fun of him (B), nor does she look up to him (C). She is not apathetic (D), and she is not jealous or anxious (E).

53. A The discussion begins with how times have changed, so it's logical that it would follow a discussion about Troy's son's prospects of becoming a professional athlete (A). Troy is presumably too old (and too drunk) to compete as an athlete (B). They are not discussing the mix of races in neighborhoods (C). If they had been discussing Troy's accomplishments, he would not have reiterated them in the passage (D). They are not discussing current society as a whole, but rather the racial integration of baseball (E).

54. **E** If Sylvia tells, she will "give its life away"—so the man must want to hunt the heron, as he is a "sportsman" (line 10) (E). He does not want to know Sylvia; he only wants her to tell him her secret (A). Sylvia knows where the white heron is; she is not telling him a tale (B). He wants to know about the heron, not about wood (C). He wants to harm the heron, not to photograph it undisturbed—he is a "sportsman" (line 10) (D).

55. **A** The man is not surprised at Sylvia's appearance; he knows that she is coming (A). The man dresses in a hurry, which means he is anxious, so the present tense serves to heighten the suspense he feels (B). The shift affects the anticipation on the reader's part by accelerating the pace from past to present (C). Although the point of view is always omniscient, it goes from a view of the man's thoughts and actions to an interior view of Sylvia's feelings (D). Sylvia has been awaiting this moment as an opportunity to earn money and make the men happy ("the splendid moment has come"), and the switch to the present tense intensifies this suspense. (Note: You should be circling the "NOT" and putting a "Y" for "yes" and an "N" for "no" next to each choice to find the odd man out.)

56. **D** Because "he can make them rich with money" and because her family is so poor (D), Sylvia considers telling him about the heron. There is no mention of her grandmother's health (A). Sylvia does not think the man has good intentions toward the heron. She knows he is a hunter (B). The man does not threaten to take her away (C). He is a hunter, so he is not loyal to animals (E).

57. **B** Sylvia decides to tell him and then changes her mind, so (B) is the best answer. She does want to win his esteem, but the cost is too great (A). He has money and "kind appealing eyes" (line 16), so she is not indifferent to him (C). Because of her observation about his eyes, she is not repulsed (D), and she does not support his endeavor. There is no mention that he will gain money from shooting the heron (E).

58. **E** Sylvia questions what it is that makes her unable to speak, so (E) is the best answer. Sylvia's surprise at her reluctance has nothing to do with the narrator's description of her poverty (A). It is not clear that she wants to fulfill his hopes so much as be rewarded with money (B). The sentences are not particularly short, nor are her thoughts choppy (C). The memory is a calming image; it does not show her surprise (D).

59. **A** She is surprised that she wants to keep silent to help the heron (A). There is no mention of a promise Sylvia made to her grandmother (B). There is no discussion of whether she wants to know the man better or whether her actions prevent her from doing so (C). She is not dismissive in the passage (D). She is surprised at herself, so her beliefs are not long-standing (E).

60. **D** The heron and Sylvia experience an intimate morning together, both naïve and experiencing the world for the first time, so "the great world" is most nearly the opposite (D). The heron does not represent new and clean clothing (A), nor is the heron the opposite of a "splendid moment" (B). She does not think the heron is old, so youth is not the opposite (C). The heron does not represent the earth, so the air is not its antithesis (E).

61. **A** The promise of money is not why Sylvia doesn't speak, but why she rebukes herself for failing to speak (A). Sylvia's indirectly rendered thoughts in the latter half of the passage reveal that the sportsman has promised money in exchange for information about the heron, so the phrase does identify a potential effect of the sportsman's visit (E). The addition of "with money" to modify "rich" is colloquial, or more like everyday speech rather than formal speech (B), but it also serves to hint that it is possible to be rich in things other than money (C). The description of the air the heron flies through as "golden" suggests the value of Sylvia's experience with the heron (D).

HOW TO SCORE PRACTICE TEST 2

When you take the real exam, the proctors will collect your test booklet and bubble sheet and send your answer sheet to a processing center, where a computer looks at the pattern of filled-in ovals on your answer sheet and gives you a score. We couldn't include even a small computer with this book, so we are providing this more primitive way of scoring your exam.

Determining Your Score

STEP 1   Using the answer key, determine how many questions you got right and how many you got wrong on the test. Remember: Questions that you do not answer do not count as either right or wrong answers.

STEP 2   List the number of right answers here.

(A) _58___

STEP 3   List the number of wrong answers here. Now divide that number by 4. (Use a calculator if you're feeling particularly lazy.)

(B) __3___ ÷ 4 = (C) _.75__

STEP 4   Subtract the number of wrong answers divided by 4 from the number of correct answers. Round this score to the nearest whole number. This is your raw score.

(A) – (C) = _57___

STEP 5   To determine your real score, take the number from Step 4 and look it up in the left-hand column of the Score Conversion Table on the next page; the corresponding score on the right is your score on the exam.

PRACTICE TEST 2 SCORE CONVERSION TABLE

Raw Score	College Board Scaled Score	Raw Score	College Board Scaled Score
61	800	25	520
60	800	24	510
59	800	23	500
58	800	22	490
57	800	21	490
56	800	20	480
55	790	19	470
54	780	18	460
53	780	17	450
52	770	16	440
51	760	15	430
50	750	14	420
49	740	13	410
48	730	12	410
47	720	11	400
46	710	10	390
45	700	09	380
44	700	08	370
43	690	07	360
42	680	06	350
41	670	05	350
40	660	04	340
39	650	03	330
38	640	02	320
37	630	01	310
36	620	00	300
35	620	−01	300
34	610	−02	290
33	600	−03	280
32	590	−04	270
31	580	−05	260
30	570	−06	250
29	560	−07	240
28	550	−08	240
27	540	−09	230
26	530	−10	220
		−11	210
		−12	200
		−13	200
		−14	200
		−15	200

Chapter 14
Practice Test 3

PRACTICE SAT SUBJECT TEST IN LITERATURE 3

TEST 3

Your responses to the SAT Subject Test in Literature questions should be filled in on Test 3 of your answer sheet.

LITERATURE TEST 3

Directions: This test consists of selections from literary works and questions on their content, form, and style. After each passage or poem, choose the best answer to each question and fill in the corresponding oval on the answer sheet.

Note: Pay particular attention to questions that contain the words NOT, LEAST, or EXCEPT.

Questions 1-9. Read the following poem carefully before you choose your answers.

"The Author to Her Book"

Thou ill-formed offspring of my feeble brain,
Who after birth didst by my side remain,
Till snatched from thence by friends, less wise than true,
Line Who thee abroad, exposed to public view,
(5) Made thee in rags, halting to th' press to trudge,
Where errors were not lessened (all may judge).
At thy return my blushing was not small,
My rambling brat (in print) should mother call,
I cast thee by as one unfit for light,
(10) Thy visage was so irksome in my sight;
Yet being mine own, at length affection would
Thy blemishes amend, if so I could:
I washed thy face, but more defects I saw,
And rubbing off a spot still made a flaw.
(15) I stretched thy joints to make thee even feet,
Yet still thou run'st more hobbling than is meet;
In better dress to trim thee was my mind,
But nought save homespun cloth i' th' house I find.
In this array 'mongst vulgars may'st thou roam.
(20) In critic's hands beware thou dost not come,
And take thy way where yet thou art not known;
If for thy father asked, say thou hadst none;
And for thy mother, she alas is poor,
Which caused her thus to send thee out of door.

(1678)

GO ON TO THE NEXT PAGE

1. The word "house" (line 18) is a metaphor for the author's

   (A) attic
   (B) book
   (C) brain
   (D) shame
   (E) store

2. According to the poem, how did the author's manuscript come to be published?

   (A) The press demanded it.
   (B) Her friends took it from her on the sly.
   (C) It was stolen by a publisher.
   (D) She showed it to someone who recommended it for publication.
   (E) The poem does not state its publication history.

3. According to the poem, how does the author feel about her manuscript?

   (A) She is thrilled to see it in print.
   (B) She thinks it is too dark.
   (C) She is annoyed at its childishness.
   (D) She is horrified by it.
   (E) She is embarrassed by its quality.

4. The lines "I stretched thy joints to make thee even feet, Yet still thou run'st more hobbling than is meet," (lines 15-16) refer to the author's attempt to

   (A) make the book rhyme better
   (B) trim the book's extraneous parts
   (C) fix the book's meter
   (D) make sure the book has an even number of pages
   (E) make the book less crude

5. The poem as a whole can be considered as

   (A) an extended analogy
   (B) a metaphor for parental worries
   (C) a comparison between two media
   (D) a didactic diatribe
   (E) a discursive exercise

6. The author's tone can best be described as

   (A) cheerless
   (B) antipathetic
   (C) dispassionate
   (D) cavalier
   (E) self-deprecating

7. The word "trim" (line 17) most nearly means

   (A) clothe
   (B) cut
   (C) weave
   (D) hobble
   (E) edit

8. According to the poem, a friend "less wise than true" is most likely to

   (A) mean well but act foolishly
   (B) tell lies in his friend's best interest
   (C) cunningly meddle in his friend's affairs
   (D) sacrifice loyalty for opportunity
   (E) falsely accuse his friend because of lack of knowledge

9. Which of the following is NOT a hope expressed by the author?

   (A) The book will not fall into the hands of critics.
   (B) Someone else will claim authorship.
   (C) The book will fall into obscurity.
   (D) She can fix the book's problems through editing.
   (E) She might make some profit.

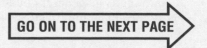

GO ON TO THE NEXT PAGE

Questions 10-17. Read the following passage carefully before you choose your answers.

The principal object of this Work is to remove the erroneous and discreditable notions current in England concerning this City, in common
Line with every thing else connected with the Colony.
(5) We shall endeavour to represent Sydney as it really is—to exhibit its spacious Gas-lit Streets, crowded by an active and thriving Population— its Public Edifices, and its sumptuous Shops, which boldly claim a comparison with those of
(10) London itself: and to shew that the Colonists have not been inattentive to matters of higher import, we shall display to our Readers the beautiful and commodious Buildings raised by piety and industry for the use of Religion. It is true, all
(15) are not yet in a state of completion; but, be it remembered, that what was done gradually in England, in the course of many centuries, has been here effected in the comparatively short period of sixty years. Our object, in setting forth this Work,
(20) is one of no mean moment; and we trust that every Australian, whether this be his native or adopted country, will heartily bid us "God speed!"
It became necessary, after the rebellion of those Colonies now known as the United States, for
(25) Britain to send her convicts elsewhere; and the wide, distant, and almost totally unknown regions of Australia, were adjudged most suitable for the purpose. Accordingly, eleven ships, since known in Colonial History as the "First Fleet," sailed for
(30) New Holland on the 15th of May, 1787, under the command of Captain Arthur Phillip, and arrived in Botany Bay on the 20th day of January in the following year. Finding the spot in many respects unfit for an infant settlement, and but scantily
(35) supplied with water, Captain Phillip determined to explore the coast; and proceeded northward, with a few officers and marines, in three open boats. After passing along a rocky and barren line of shore for several miles, they entered Port Jackson,
(40) which they supposed to be of no great dimensions, it having been marked in the chart of Captain Cook as a boat harbour. Their astonishment may be easily imagined when they found its waters gradually expand, and the full proportions of that
(45) magnificent harbour (capable of containing the whole navy of Britain) burst upon their view. The site of the intended settlement was no longer a matter of doubt; and, after first landing at Manly Beach...they eventually selected a spot on the
(50) banks of a small stream of fresh water, falling into a Cove on the southern side of the estuary....
Sydney, the capital...is situated on the southern shore of Port Jackson, at the distance of seven miles from the Pacific Ocean.... It is built at the
(55) head of the far-famed "Cove"; and, with Darling Harbour as its general boundary to the west, extends, in an unbroken succession of houses, for more than two miles in a southerly direction. As a maritime city its site is unrivalled, possessing at
(60) least three miles of water frontage, at any part of which vessels of the heaviest burden can safely approach the wharves. The stratum on which it stands is chiefly sandstone; and, as it enjoys a considerable elevation, it is remarkably healthy
(65) and dry. The principal thoroughfares run north and south, parallel to Darling Harbour, and are crossed at right angles by shorter streets. This, at first, gives the place an air of unpleasing sameness and formality, to those accustomed to the winding and
(70) romantic streets of an ancient English town; but the eye soon becomes reconciled to the change, and you cease to regret the absence of what is in so many respects undesirable.

(1848)

10. The "Colonists" (line 10) are most likely

(A) prisoners
(B) readers
(C) British sailors
(D) Sydney's citizens
(E) American observers

11. "It is...sixty years" (lines 14-19) serves which of the following purposes in the passage?

(A) It admits a flaw and accepts the argument.
(B) It outlines a counterargument and then provides a mitigating circumstance.
(C) It argues a new point and then returns to the main theme.
(D) It explains a previous point, giving the history behind the argument.
(E) It compares two cities and finds one superior.

GO ON TO THE NEXT PAGE

12. The phrase "mean moment" (line 20) can best be rephrased as

    (A) evil intent
    (B) unhappy time
    (C) average length
    (D) routine description
    (E) small importance

13. The main differences between the three paragraphs can be best described as

    (A) paragraph one addresses the reader, paragraph two continues the argument, and paragraph three summarizes the passage so far
    (B) paragraph one sets the passage's goals, paragraph two tells a history, and paragraph three describes an actual situation
    (C) paragraph one begins the history, paragraph two continues it, and paragraph three concludes it
    (D) paragraph one is descriptive, paragraph two is historical, and paragraph three relates a narrative
    (E) paragraph one is ornate, paragraph two is more subdued, and paragraph three cites examples

14. The second paragraph implies that

    (A) Australia was unsuitable for habitation
    (B) Captain Phillip did not have the backing of the British government
    (C) before the American revolution, Britain used to send its prisoners to America
    (D) Australia had never before been visited by the British
    (E) the "First Fleet" encountered an existing city near Manly Beach

15. Which of the following is NOT a characteristic of Sydney, according to the passage?

    (A) Religious buildings
    (B) Perpendicular side streets
    (C) A long coastline
    (D) A shallow harbor
    (E) Good weather

16. The final sentence, "This, at…respects undesirable" (lines 67-73), most nearly means

    (A) at first, Sydney seems homogenous to people who like England's historical curved streets, but once you get used to it you stop thinking that winding streets are a good thing
    (B) at first, Sydney seems overly formal to people who have studied England's history, but eventually you grow accustomed to it and stop noticing it
    (C) at first, Sydney seems unpleasant to English visitors, but once they accept Sydney for what it is, they grow to love it
    (D) at first, Sydney's streets seem too similar to England's streets; but once you get to know Sydney you find that's not the case
    (E) at first, Sydney seems too rigid to fans of England's historical curved streets, and people are at first apt to regret their visit to Sydney

17. The passages identifies which of the following as a reason the "site of the intended settlement" (lines 46-47) was not determined as soon as the eleven ships reached Botany Bay?

    I.   The conditions in the Botany Bay area were particularly unsuitable for children
    II. The initial site on Botany Bay lacked a good supply of fresh water
    III. Captain Cook's chart misled the sailors about the nature of Port Jackson

    (A) I only
    (B) III only
    (C) II and III only
    (D) I and II only
    (E) I, II, and III

GO ON TO THE NEXT PAGE

Questions 18-27. Read the following passage carefully before you choose your answers.

Enter a Roman and a Volsce [meeting].

ROMAN: I know you well, sir, and you know me. Your name, I think, is Adrian.

VOLSCE: It is so, sir. Truly, I have forgot you.

Line
(5) ROMAN: I am a Roman; and my services are, as you are, against 'em. Know you me yet?

VOLSCE: Nicanor, no?

ROMAN: The same, sir.

VOLSCE: You had more beard when I last saw you; but your favor is well appear'd by your
(10) tongue. What's the news in Rome? I have a note from the Volscian state to find you out there. You have well sav'd me a day's journey.

ROMAN: There hath been in Rome strange
(15) insurrections; the people against the senators, patricians, and nobles.

VOLSCE: Hath been? Is it ended, then? Our state thinks not so. They are in a most warlike preparation, and hope to come upon them
(20) in the heat of their division.

ROMAN: The main blaze of it is past, but a small thing would make it flame again; for the nobles receive so to heart the banishment of that worthy Coriolanus that they are
(25) in a ripe aptness to take all power from the people and to pluck from them their tribunes forever. This lies glowing, I can tell you, and is almost mature for the violent breaking out.

(30) VOLSCE: Coriolanus banish'd?

ROMAN: Banish'd, sir.

VOLSCE: You will be welcome with this intelligence, Nicanor.

ROMAN: The day serves well for them now. I have
(35) heard it said, the fittest time to corrupt a man's wife is when she's fall'n out with her husband. Your noble Tullus Aufidius will appear well in these wars, his great opposer, Coriolanus, being now in no
(40) request of his country.

VOLSCE: He cannot choose. I am most fortunate, thus accidentally to encounter you. You have ended my business, and I will merrily accompany you home.

(45) ROMAN: I shall, between this and supper, tell you most strange things from Rome, all tending to the good of their adversaries. Have you an army ready, say you?

VOLSCE: A most royal one: the centurions and their
(50) charges, distinctly billeted, already in th' entertainment, and to be on foot at an hour's warning.

ROMAN: I am joyful to hear of their readiness, and am the man, I think, that shall set them in
(55) present action. So, sir, heartily well met, and most glad of your company.

VOLSCE: You take my part from me, sir; I have the most cause to be glad of yours.

ROMAN: Well, let us go together.

[Exeunt.] (1623)

18. The meeting between the two men can best be described as

(A) cordial and heartwarming
(B) melodramatic and saccharine
(C) acrimonious and awkward
(D) scandalous and surprising
(E) fortuitous and serendipitous

19. The character of Nicanor is

(A) a Roman spying for the Volscians
(B) Adrian's distant cousin
(C) Adrian's rival for the attentions of a woman
(D) a mercenary in search of Coriolanus
(E) a sworn enemy of Adrian

20. The insurrections spoken of in line 15 are most likely

(A) foreign invasions
(B) military coups
(C) monarchical successions
(D) proletariat uprisings
(E) conflagrations

GO ON TO THE NEXT PAGE

21. It can be inferred from the passage that

    (A) Coriolanus's banishment is the cause of the insurrection
    (B) Coriolanus's banishment was not the nobles' choice
    (C) Coriolanus was the king of Rome
    (D) the two men are supporters of Coriolanus
    (E) the two men dread further war

22. "The main blaze" (line 21) refers to

    (A) a universally quelled rebellion
    (B) public outrage at Coriolanus's banishment
    (C) the fires of purgatory
    (D) incendiary comments
    (E) the people's revolt

23. The plot the men hatch hinges on the fact that

    (A) Tullus Aufidius is romantically involved with Coriolanus's wife
    (B) Roman towns catch fire easily
    (C) the nobles are incensed that Coriolanus has been banished
    (D) there is a ready army
    (E) the senators and patricians are not ready for war

24. The line "You take my part from me, sir" could best be restated as

    (A) "Those were the words I was going to speak."
    (B) "You have usurped my role."
    (C) "You are making fun of me."
    (D) "I would give you a present for your kindness."
    (E) "Yours is the friendship I most cherish."

25. It can be inferred from the passage that the author intended this play most likely to be

    (A) an amusing comedy
    (B) an extended allegory
    (C) a pastoral study
    (D) a historical enactment
    (E) a political satire

26. The words "appear well" (line 38) can best be replaced by

    (A) fight valiantly
    (B) dress for battle
    (C) emerge victorious
    (D) argue persuasively
    (E) feign health

27. The Roman's use of "main blaze" (line 21), "flame again" (line 22), and "lies glowing" (line 27) serves to do which of the following?

    I.   Develop an analogy
    II. Expand on a metaphor employed by the Volsce
    III. Correct a misapprehension

    (A) I only
    (B) III only
    (C) I and II only
    (D) I and III only
    (E) I, II, and III

GO ON TO THE NEXT PAGE

Questions 28-36. Read the following poem carefully before you choose your answers.

"We Too Shall Sleep"

Not, not for thee,
Belovèd child, the burning grasp of life
Shall bruise the tender soul. The noise, and
   strife,
Line And clamor of midday thou shalt not see;
(5) But wrapped for ever in thy quiet grave,
Too little to have known the earthly lot,
Time's clashing hosts above thine innocent
   head,
Wave upon wave,
Shall break, or pass as with an army's tread,
(10) And harm thee not.

A few short years
We of the living flesh and restless brain
Shall plumb the deeps of life and know the
   strain,
The fleeting gleams of joy, the fruitless tears;
(15) And then at last when all is touched and tried,
Our own immutable night shall fall, and deep
In the same silent plot, O little friend,
Side by thy side,
In peace that changeth not, nor knoweth end,
We too shall sleep.

(1899)

28. The use of "Not, not" as the first words and "not" as the last word of the first stanza serves to

(A) prove that the speaker is inconsolable
(B) suggest the complex, knot-like character of family relationships
(C) signal that the speaker refuses to accept what has happened
(D) emphasize that suffering has reduced the speaker's fluency
(E) draw attention to the speaker's shifting sense of what has been lost

29. A difference between the first and second stanzas is

(A) stanza one speaks of memory, while stanza two speaks of the future
(B) stanza one speaks of death, while stanza two speaks of slumber
(C) stanza one speaks of day, while stanza two speaks of night
(D) stanza one speaks of children, while stanza two speaks of the past
(E) stanza one speaks of hurry, while stanza two speaks of patience

30. Which of the following lines contains a simile?

(A) "But wrapped for ever in thy quiet grave,/ Too little to have known the earthly lot" (lines 5-6)
(B) "Shall break, or pass as with an army's tread,/ And harm thee not" (lines 10-11)
(C) "We of the living flesh and restless brain/ Shall plumb the deeps of life and know the strain" (lines 12-14)
(D) "And then at last when all is touched and tried,/ Our own immutable night shall fall, and deep" (lines 15-16)
(E) The poem does not contain a simile.

31. The title symbolically represents

(A) slumber
(B) burial
(C) angels
(D) death
(E) old age

GO ON TO THE NEXT PAGE

32. The author's attitude toward life can best be described as

  (A) life must be endured before death sets us free
  (B) life is sometimes good and sometimes difficult, but it is always short
  (C) life is merely noisy and full of strife
  (D) life is too difficult to be enjoyed
  (E) life's meaning will be forever obscured

33. From the passage, it can be inferred that the author considers that

  (A) it is better to be dead than to suffer fate's cruelty
  (B) death is akin to unconsciousness
  (C) death is like being swept away by waves
  (D) death is the same for soldiers as for children
  (E) it is ridiculous to cry tears for the dead

34. The poem is written from the point of view of

  (A) someone who is grieving
  (B) a congregation of mourners
  (C) someone who is dying
  (D) someone who fears death
  (E) someone who has never before been touched by death

35. Which of the following ideas is NOT implied by the poem?

  (A) Life is joyful or harshly noisy.
  (B) Death is quiet and peaceful.
  (C) Time is like the ocean.
  (D) Life is alternately wonderful and painful.
  (E) The afterlife is superior to our earthly existence.

36. The words "touched and tried" (line 15) represent

  (A) experience
  (B) intensity
  (C) justice
  (D) eternal life
  (E) fruitlessness

GO ON TO THE NEXT PAGE

Questions 37-46. Read the following passage carefully before you choose your answers.

There comes to the house of Yen Chow a Chinese merchant of wealth and influence. His eyes dwell often upon Ah Leen. He whispers to
Line
(5) her father. Yen Chow puffs his pipe and muses: Assuredly a great slight has been put upon his family. A divorce would show proper pride. It was not the Chinese way, but was not the old order passing away and the new order taking its place? Aye, even in China, the old country that had
(10) seemed as if it would ever remain old. He speaks to Ah Leen.

"Nay, father, nay," she returns. "Thou hadst the power to send my love away from me, but thou canst not compel me to hold out my arms to
(15) another."

"But," protests her mother, "thy lover hath forgotten thee. Another hath borne him a child."

A flame rushes over Ah Leen's face; then she becomes white as a water lily. She plucks a leaf of
(20) scented geranium, crushes it between her fingers and casts it away. The perfume clings to the hands she lays on her mother's bosom.

"Thus," says she, "the fragrance of my crushed love will ever cling to Ming Hoan."
(25)   It is evening. The electric lights are shining through the vines. Out of the gloom beyond their radius comes a man. The American girl, seated in a quiet corner of the veranda, sees his face. It is eager and the eyes are full of love and fate. Then
(30) she sees Ah Leen. Tired of women's gossip, the girl has come to gaze upon the moon, hanging in the sky above her like a pale yellow pearl.

There is a cry from the approaching man. It is echoed by the girl. In a moment she is leaning
(35) upon his breast.

"Ah!" she cries, raising her head and looking into his eyes. "I knew that though another had bound you by human ties, to me you were linked by my love divine."
(40)   "Another! Human ties!" exclaims the young man. He exclaims without explaining—for the sins of parents must not be uncovered—why there has been silence between them for so long. Then he lifts her face to his and gently reproaches her. "Ah
(45) Leen, you have dwelt only upon your love for me. Did I not bid thee, 'Forget not to remember that *I* love thee!'"

The American girl steals away. The happy Ming Hoan is unaware that as she flits lightly by
(50) him and his bride she is repeating to herself his words, and hoping that it is not too late to send to someone a message of recall.

(1910)

37. All of the following details suggest that the events in this passage take place in modern times EXCEPT

(A) the story's diction
(B) mention of divorce
(C) an American girl being in China
(D) talk of a "new order"
(E) use of electric lights

38. The line "A flame rushes over Ah Leen's face; then she becomes white as a water lily" provides examples of which two literary devices?

(A) Metaphor and simile
(B) Authorial intrusion and allusion
(C) Simile and comparison
(D) Literary allusion and metaphor
(E) Apostrophe and anaphor

39. It can be inferred from the passage that

(A) Ah Leen has disobeyed her father
(B) Yen Chow is interested only in money
(C) Ah Leen's lover has not been in contact with her
(D) Ah Leen's American friend has stolen her lover
(E) Ah Leen is jealous of her American friend

40. The "great slight" (line 5) of which Yen Chow speaks is

(A) a divorce
(B) an abandonment
(C) an interracial marriage
(D) a deviation from the old ways
(E) the disrespect of elders

41. The "perfume" (line 21) serves as a symbol of

(A) the fragility of human ties
(B) the passing of time
(C) the strength of the marriage bond
(D) the sweetness of mutual love
(E) the endurance of love

GO ON TO THE NEXT PAGE ➡

42. All of the following devices are included within the passage to reveal how characters are thinking and feeling EXCEPT

    (A) anthropomorphism
    (B) indirect discourse
    (C) analogy
    (D) one character's impression of another
    (E) italics

43. Paragraph 6 "It is evening…" contains an example of

    (A) simile
    (B) personification
    (C) alliteration
    (D) parallelism
    (E) anthropomorphism

44. The last paragraph suggests that

    (A) the American girl is going to tell Ming Hoan's parents of the lovers' reunion
    (B) the American girl has a history with Ming Hoan
    (C) Ming Hoan's words are offensive to the American girl
    (D) Ming Hoan's words have caused the American girl to think about her own relationship in a different light
    (E) Chinese morality is incomprehensible to the American girl

45. Why does Ming Hoan not explain his silence?

    (A) He is afraid of hurting Ah Leen.
    (B) He is embarrassed of the reason.
    (C) He wants to protect their parents.
    (D) He doesn't feel he owes her an explanation.
    (E) Ah Leen does not ask him to explain.

46. A main theme of the story is

    (A) old customs are better than new ones
    (B) two people's love is stronger than circumstance
    (C) love can indeed be extinguished by time apart
    (D) absence makes the heart grow fonder
    (E) one can never truly know the heart of another

GO ON TO THE NEXT PAGE

Questions 47-54. Read the following poem carefully before you choose your answers.

"The Triumph of Time"

It will grow not again, this fruit of my heart,
Smitten with sunbeams, ruined with rain.
The singing seasons divide and depart,
Line Winter and summer depart in twain.
(5) It will grow not again, it is ruined at root,
The bloodlike blossom, the dull red fruit;
Though the heart yet sickens, the lips yet smart,
With sullen savour of poisonous pain.

I shall never be friends again with roses;
(10) I shall loathe sweet tunes, where a note grown strong
Relents and recoils, and climbs and closes,
As a wave of the sea turned back by song.
There are sounds where the soul's delight takes fire,
Face to face with its own desire;
(15) A delight that rebels, a desire that reposes;
I shall hate sweet music my whole life long.

The pulse of war and passion of wonder,
The heavens that murmur, the sounds that shine,
The stars that sing and the loves that thunder,
(20) The music burning at heart like wine,
An armed archangel whose hands raise up
All senses mixed in the spirit's cup
Till flesh and spirit are molten in sunder—
These things are over, and no more mine.

(1866)

47. The words "Smitten with" (line 2) could best be replaced with

(A) caressed by
(B) filtered through
(C) in love with
(D) awed by
(E) struck by

48. Which of the following most strongly emphasizes that the speaker does not believe he will ever recover from his misery?

(A) The assertion of extreme claims
(B) The use of alliteration
(C) The personification of the soul
(D) The image of an "armed archangel" (line 21)
(E) The use of oxymoron

49. Which of the following does NOT appear in the poem?

(A) Tidal water
(B) A metaphorical fruit
(C) Parallel phrases
(D) Evocative melody
(E) Exotic reverie

50. Which of the following does the first stanza employ?

(A) Religious iconography
(B) Paired alliteration
(C) Melancholic preaching
(D) Antipathetic musing
(E) Character revelation

51. It is reasonable to assume that the speaker equates music with

(A) a mocking death
(B) sweet fruit
(C) his lost love
(D) original sin
(E) serpentine slyness

52. All of the following lines contain examples of personification EXCEPT

(A) line 3
(B) line 17
(C) line 18
(D) line 19
(E) line 21

53. The third stanza lists examples of
(A) anecdotal evidence
(B) unpleasant memories
(C) inclement weather
(D) fickle fate
(E) love's intensity

54. Which potential replacement for the poem's final line best matches the poem's tone and form?

(A) In love, it's said, one cannot blunder.
(B) Love like an army my heart did plunder.
(C) Neither day nor night can thus resign.
(D) I mourn their passing and decline.
(E) May head and heart now intertwine.

GO ON TO THE NEXT PAGE ➡

Questions 55-61. Read the following passage carefully before you choose your answers.

Once Nanapush began talking, nothing stopped
the spill of his words. The day receded and
darkness broadened. At dusk, the wind picked up
Line and cold poked mercilessly through the chinking
(5) of the cabin. The two wrapped themselves in
quilts and continued to talk. The talk broadened,
deepened. Went back and forth in time and then
stopped time. The talk grew huge, of death and
radiance, then shrunk and narrowed to the making
(10) of soup. The talk was of madness, the stars, sin,
and death. The two spoke of all there was to
know. And although it was in English, during the
talk itself Nanapush taught language to Father
Damien, who took out a small bound notebook
(15) and recorded words and sentences.
In common, they now had the love of music,
though their definition of what composed music
was dissimilar.
"When you hear Chopin," Father Damien
(20) asserted, "you find yourself traveling into your
childhood, then past that, into a time before you
were born, when you were nothing, when the only
truths you knew were sounds."
"Ayiih! Tell me, does this Chopin know love
(25) songs? I have a few I don't sing unless I mean for
sure to capture my woman."
"This Chopin makes songs so beautiful your
knees shake. Dogs cry. The trees moan. Your
thoughts fly up nowhere. You can't think. You
(30) become flooded in the heart."
"Powerful. Powerful. This Chopin," asked
Nanapush, "does he have a drum?"
"No," said Damien, "he uses a piano."
"That great box in your church," said Nanapush.
(35) "How is this thing made?"
Father Damien opened his mouth to say it
was constructed of wood, precious woods, but
in his mind there formed the image of Agnes's
Caramacchione settled in the bed of the river,
(40) unmoved by the rush of water over its keys, and
instead he said, "Time." As soon as he said it, he
knew that it was true.

(2001)

55. The two men are most likely

(A) old friends
(B) of different cultures
(C) future enemies
(D) negotiators
(E) members of the clergy

56. The passage moves from

(A) past to future
(B) general to specific
(C) narration to dialogue
(D) recitation to soliloquy
(E) complexity to simplicity

57. The word "Ayiih!" (line 24) is an example of

(A) Father Damien singing
(B) Father Damien's language
(C) Chopin's music
(D) Father Damien's first name
(E) an interjection

58. The main theme of the passage explores

(A) cultural differences
(B) ironic subtext
(C) the connection between love and music
(D) the nature of relationships
(E) the influence of music

59. From the passage, Nanapush's attitude can be described as one of

(A) intense curiosity
(B) didactic patronization
(C) guarded politeness
(D) affirming sycophancy
(E) scholarly enthusiasm

60. The phrase "flooded in the heart" (line 30) can best be replaced with

(A) overcome by joy
(B) racked with nostalgia
(C) filled with emotion
(D) engorged with blood
(E) momentarily confused

61. In the last paragraph, Father Damien says the piano is made of time because

(A) he does not know the word for "wood" in Nanapush's language
(B) wood seemed too banal for so important an instrument
(C) time seems to be as eternal as the capacity for music
(D) he once saw a piano in a river
(E) he is trying to change the subject to one he feels more comfortable with

STOP

**IF YOU FINISH BEFORE TIME IS CALLED, YOU MAY CHECK YOUR WORK ON THIS SECTION ONLY.
DO NOT TURN TO ANY OTHER SECTION IN THE TEST.**

Chapter 15
Practice Test 3:
Answers and
Explanations

- Practice Test 3 Answer Key
- Practice Test 3 Explanations
- How to Score Practice Test 3

PRACTICE TEST 3 ANSWER KEY

Question Number	Correct Answer	Right	Wrong	Question Number	Correct Answer	Right	Wrong
1	C	____	____	32	B	____	____
2	B	____	____	33	B	____	____
3	E	____	____	34	A	____	____
4	C	____	____	35	E	____	____
5	A	____	____	36	A	____	____
6	E	____	____	37	A	____	____
7	A	____	____	38	A	____	____
8	A	____	____	39	C	____	____
9	B	____	____	40	B	____	____
10	D	____	____	41	E	____	____
11	B	____	____	42	A	____	____
12	E	____	____	43	A	____	____
13	B	____	____	44	D	____	____
14	C	____	____	45	C	____	____
15	D	____	____	46	B	____	____
16	A	____	____	47	E	____	____
17	C	____	____	48	A	____	____
18	E	____	____	49	E	____	____
19	A	____	____	50	B	____	____
20	D	____	____	51	C	____	____
21	B	____	____	52	E	____	____
22	E	____	____	53	E	____	____
23	C	____	____	54	D	____	____
24	A	____	____	55	B	____	____
25	D	____	____	56	C	____	____
26	C	____	____	57	E	____	____
27	C	____	____	58	E	____	____
28	E	____	____	59	A	____	____
29	C	____	____	60	C	____	____
30	B	____	____	61	C	____	____
31	D	____	____				

PRACTICE TEST 3 EXPLANATIONS

1. **C** Choice (C) is correct because the author is racking her brain for ways to make the book better: "In better dress to trim thee" (line 17). Choices (A) and (E) interpret the word *house* too literally. Choice (B) is incorrect because the author is looking for a way to make the book better. She is not looking for the book itself. Searching in her "shame" does not make sense (D).

2. **B** The poem states that the book "didst by my side remain,/Till snatched from thence by friends… Who thee abroad, exposed to public view" (lines 2–4), so (B) is the correct answer. The press did not demand the book (A), nor did the publisher steal it (C). There is no evidence that anyone recommended publishing it to her (D). And the poem does state how the book came to be published (E).

3. **E** The author blushes (line 7), so she is embarrassed, and thus (E) is the correct answer. Blushing does not imply being "thrilled" (A). There is no evidence that she feels it is too dark (B), nor that she considers childishness to be one of its faults (C). "Horrified" is too strong a word for how the author feels (D).

4. **C** The correct answer is (C). Picture someone hobbling, or walking unevenly. Fixing rhyme will not help the book flow more smoothly (A), but fixing the meter will (C). There is "stretching," so no trimming is involved (B). The "even feet" do not refer to the number of pages (D), and although the book is "irksome" and "vulgar," there is no indication that the content of the book is crude; the book itself is merely embarrassing to the author (E).

5. **A** The poem compares a book to a child, so it is an analogy (A). Parental worries are the metaphor, not the poem's point. (B). There is only one medium—the book in question (C). The poem is not intended to instruct, and the word "diatribe" is too strong (D). The poem is not an exercise (E).

6. **E** The author makes light of her abilities and relates her struggles to make things better, so her tone is self-deprecating (E). The poem is funny, so she is not cheerless (A). She is not "antipathetic" or "dispassionate" in the poem (B), (C), and a cavalier attitude is one of carelessness, which does not apply (D).

7. **A** The word "trim" can be replaced with "dress" as in "to dress someone" (A). Be careful not to use the most obvious definition of trim (B). There is no evidence of weaving (C) or of hobbling (why would she want to hobble her book?) (D). Although the line might be a metaphor for editing, the word itself does not mean "edit" (E).

8. **A** The author says her friends took her book and got it published, so they meant well, but did something foolish (A). There are no lies told in the poem (B). Her friends might meddle, but they are not "cunning" (C). According to the poem, the friends do not gain from the publication (D). There is no evidence that (E) is true.

9. **B** The author never hopes that someone else will claim the book (B). She does hope the book will avoid critics (line 20) (A), and that it will be forgotten (line 21) (C). She tries to edit the book, so she hopes it can be fixed (D). She is poor; she hopes she might make some money (lines 23–24) (E).

10. **D** The colonists are the people who live in the city of Sydney, "the colony" (D). They are no longer prisoners (A). The colonists are not the readers (B). The colonists are no longer British sailors (C), nor are they American observers (E).

11. **B** The paragraph states that Sydney is as important as London. The sentence quoted admits the buildings aren't done, but says that England has had several hundred years to build itself up, while Sydney is only sixty years old—(B) is the best answer. The sentence may admit a flaw, but it does not accept it (A). A new point is not argued (C). The sentence does not explain the previous point (D). The sentence compares England to Australia, but does not say one is superior to the other (E).

12. **E** The paragraph is comparing London to Sydney; the writer is obviously a resident of Sydney, so it is very important to him or her that this passage prove Sydney's greatness. The words "small importance" fit nicely into the paraphrased sentence: "Our goal, in writing this, is one of no 'small importance,' and we believe that every Australian…will wish us good luck" (E). There is no reason for the author to refute the accusation of "evil intent" (A). "Unhappy time" does not make sense in the sentence (B). "Average length" is too literal a translation (C), and the goal of the work is not "description" (D).

13. **B** The first paragraph tells the goals of the passage. The second paragraph relates the history of the colonization of Australia, and the third paragraph describes the city of Sydney (B). Although paragraph one does address the reader, paragraph two is not argumentative, and paragraph three is not a summary (A). The paragraphs are not one long narrative (C). Paragraph one is not particularly descriptive, paragraph two is indeed historical, but paragraph three does not tell a story (D). The style of the passage does not change (E).

14. **C** The first sentence of the paragraph says that because the United States rebelled, Britain had to send its convicts elsewhere, implying that previously it had sent its convicts to the United States (C). Although Botany Bay was unsuitable, Manly Beach was very suitable for habitation (because Sydney was erected there) (A). There is no evidence that Captain Phillip was not backed by the government (B). Australia had obviously been previously visited as Captain Cook had made a map, which Captain Phillip carried (D). The passage does not state that anyone lived near Manly Beach (E).

15. **D** The passage says that even "vessels of the heaviest burden can safely approach the wharves," which means that the harbor must be deep for heavy boats to be able to sail there (D). Religious buildings are mentioned in lines 13-14 (A). The streets "are crossed at right angles," so they are perpendicular (B). Sydney is "unrivaled" in its three-mile coastline (C). The climate is "healthy and dry" (E).

16. **A** The sentence boils down to "first you think it's too 'homogenous' but 'you get used to it.'" This is closest to (A). The sentence does not suggest that you "stop noticing" the difference between Australia and England (B). The author does not suggest that people grow to "love" the city (C). Sydney does not seem similar to London (D). The author does not say that people will regret visiting Sydney (E).

17.   C   The passage's statement that the site on Botany Bay was "unfit for an infant settlement" does not mean it was unsuitable for infants but that it was unsuitable for a young or new settlement; as the first statement is not supported, choices (A), (D), and (E) can be eliminated. That initial site was "but scantily supplied with water," which supports the second statement, so choice (B) can be eliminated. That leaves choice (C); the third statement is supported by reference to the sailors' "astonishment" when they discovered that Port Jackson was much larger than Captain Cook's label of "boat harbour" had suggested, so (C) is correct.

18.   E   Adrian is "sav'd…a day's journey" by the meeting, so it is "fortuitous" (lucky) (E). There is nothing particularly heartwarming about the meeting of spies (A), nor is there any notion of melodrama (B). The men are friendly; there is nothing "acrimonious" (C). We don't know enough about the passage/play to judge it "scandalous" or "surprising" (D).

19.   A   This is a good example of picking the least bad answer. "My services are, as you are, against 'em" (lines 4-5) proves that Nicanor is a spy, but all of the other answers are easily proved false (A). There is no mention of a family relationship or of a relationship with a woman, eliminating (B) and (C). Nicanor is not looking for Coriolanus (D). The two men are friendly; they are not enemies (E).

20.   D   "The people against the senators, patricians, and nobles" (lines 15–16) show that (D) is the correct answer. There is no foreign invasion (A), the military is not overthrowing the government (B), and there is no mention of a royal family (C). A fire is not an insurrection (E).

21.   B   The nobles "receive so to heart the banishment" and are ready to take all power away from the people, so they are not happy about his banishment (B). There is no evidence that the banishment is the cause of the insurrection (A). There is nothing to tell us what role Coriolanus played in the government (C). The men do not support Coriolanus; they are using his absence to their advantage (D). The men are plotting war, so they do not dread it (E).

22.   E   "The main blaze" is the people's revolt (E). The insurrection is not quite over: "a small thing would make it flame again" (line 21–22) (A). It can be inferred that the public wanted Coriolanus banished (B). There is no evidence that the flames refer to purgatory (C) or to comments (D).

23.   C   The nobles are so mad about Coriolanus, according to the men, that they are about to dissolve the government (lines 23–27) (C). There is no evidence of a romantic entanglement (A). They are not planning to burn the Roman towns (B). The ready army is a plus, but the plan can be hatched without it (D). There is no evidence that the nobles are not ready for war (E).

24.   A   Adrian is saying that he is also glad to have met Nicador (in other words, the feeling is mutual), so (A) is the best answer. There is no notion of rivalry between the men (B), nor is one making fun of the other (C). There is no mention of any present (D). There is nothing to suggest they have a cherished friendship (E).

25.   D   It's hard to tell much from this short passage, but it's about two men planning a war, so it's most likely historical (D). There's nothing particularly funny (A), nor is it allegorical (B). It doesn't take place in the country (C), and there is nothing that makes it satirical (E).

26. C Without "his great opposer," Tullus will probably win (C). We do not know whether he will do the fighting (A). "Appear" does not refer to his dress (B). There is no evidence that says he'll be required to argue (D) or that he'll need to pretend to be healthy (E).

27. C The Volsce remarks that his state hopes to come upon the Romans "in the heat of their division." In his reply to that remark, the Roman uses fire imagery to characterize the relations between "the people" of Rome and Rome's "senators, patricians, and nobles"; thus he both builds on metaphorical language first used by the Volsce and further develops the analogy comparing the Roman political situation to a fire. This support for the first and second statements means that choices (A), (B), and (D) can be eliminated. In their exchange, the Volsce asks whether it is correct to say that "the insurrections" have ended, as his state "thinks not so." The Roman's reply reassures him that the disagreement "lies glowing" and that "a small thing" could "make it flame again." Those statements corroborate the opinion of the Volsce state, which is therefore not operating under a misapprehension and there is nothing to correct. As the third statement is not supported, (E) can be eliminated and the remaining answer, (C), is correct.

28. E The stanza begins and ends with the same word, but in the lines between, the speaker moves from emphasizing that the "Belovèd child" will not experience "the burning grasp of life" to listing other things the child will not experience—bruising of the soul, noise, and strife. This in turn leads to the acknowledgement that because the child was "too little to have known the earthly lot," the action of "Time's clashing hosts" will not ever harm the child. The repetition of "not" serves to frame this shift in emphasis from the fact that the child has lost the chance to live to the fact that the child has consequently also lost the experience of suffering that human life entails (E). The evidence does suggest the speaker has found some consolation (A) and is trying to come to terms with what has happened (C). There's no evidence the speaker intends a pun on not/knot (B), though he does demonstrate good command of language (D).

29. C The imagery in the first stanza is of "midday" (line 5) while the second stanza speaks of "night" (line 16), so choice (C) is correct. Both stanzas talk of the future (A). Slumber is a metaphor for death, so both stanzas are about death (B). Stanza two is not about the past (D). Patience and hurry are not mentioned in the poem (E).

30. B Time is compared to "an army's tread" using "as" (B). There are no similes in (A), (C), or (D). Because there is a simile, (E) cannot be correct.

31. D "Sleep," the title action, is a symbol for death (D). Sleep cannot be a symbol for slumber because the two words mean the same thing (A). It is not a symbol for burial (B). There are no angels in the poem (C). Sleep represents death, not old age (E).

32. B The author describes life using the words "joy" and "tears" and mentions "a few short years," so (B) is correct. There is no sense in the poem that death creates freedom (A). The author enjoys parts of life, so (C) is too extreme, as is (D). The poem does not contemplate the meaning of life (E).

33. **B** The author says that the dead cannot hear and are not harmed by time; death is like sleep, so it is like unconsciousness (B). The author does not describe life as cruel (A), nor does he compare death to being swept away by waves (C). He does not compare different kinds of death (D). Tears are not described as ridiculous (E).

34. **A** The author addresses the poem to someone who has died, so it is safe to assume it is written by someone who is grieving (A). Although the author uses "we," he means the human race, not a specific "we" (B). There is no evidence that the author is dying (C). The author describes death as peaceful, so he does not fear it (D). We cannot know whether the author has been previously touched by death (E).

35. **E** There is no afterlife suggested in the poem (E). Joy and noise (A) are mentioned in lines 3–5 and 14. Quiet and peace (B) are mentioned in lines 6 and 19. Time is compared to an ocean in lines 10–11 (C), and (D) is suggested in line 13.

36. **A** The line "when all is touched and tried" (line 15) means "when life has been fully lived" (A). It does not refer to intensity (B) or justice (C). There is no discussion of eternal life in the poem (D). The lines refer to the end of life, not whether it is fruitless (E).

37. **A** The language in the characters' speech is very archaic (A). However, divorce (B), Americans in China (C), the coming of a "new order" (D), and use of electric lights (E) are all signs that the story is relatively contemporary.

38. **A** The first line describes a blush as being a flame, and then describes Ah Leen's face as being white like a flower. The first comparison does not use a word such as "like" or "as," which makes it metaphorical; the second uses an explicit comparison word, which makes it a simile (A). "Authorial intrusion" (B) is the author interrupting the narrative to speak directly to the reader, which does not happen here. "Comparison" (C) is too vague a word, and this choice incorrectly identifies the flame as being a simile. "Literary allusion" (D) is a reference to another literary work, which does not occur here. Apostophe (E) is an author speaking directly to one of the characters, while anaphor or anaphora is a literary device that emphasizes words by repeating them at the beginning of consecutive phrases.

39. **C** "There has been silence between them for so long" (lines 42–43) proves that Ming Hoan has not been in contact (C). There is no evidence that Ah Leen has disobeyed her father (A). Although money is mentioned, it is not Yen Chow's only concern (the affront to his family is in his mind) (B). There is no evidence that Ah Leen's American friend has stolen her lover or that Ah Leen is jealous of her, so eliminate (D) and (E).

40. **B** The slight is an affront that a divorce will remedy, and Ah Leen's mother says her lover has forgotten her and had a child with another woman, so (B) is the correct answer. The divorce is the remedy, not the insult (A). There is no evidence of an interracial marriage (C). A divorce would be the deviation from custom; it hasn't occurred (D). No elders have been disrespected (E).

41. **E** Ah Leen says that they can send her lover away, but they can't make her love anyone else (E). The perfume is a symbol of love, not marriage (C). Perfume does not symbolize time (B) or fragility (A). It does not represent mutual love (D).

42. **A** In the first paragraph, as Yen Chow "muses" about the Chinese merchant's whispers, his thoughts are rendered in indirect discourse (B). Ah Leen compares the way her "crushed love" clings to Ming Hoan to the way the scent of a crushed leaf clings to her hands (C). The American girl's impression of Ming Hoan—with his eyes "full of love and fate"—provides insight into how he is feeling as he arrives (D). Ming Hoan emphasizes "I" (and the emphasis is denoted by italics) to remind Ah Leen that she has not remembered to dwell on his love for her (E). There is no example of anthropomorphism in the passage (A).

43. **A** "Like a pale yellow pearl" (line 32) is a simile (A). Nothing is given human characteristics, so eliminate (B) and (E). There is no example of alliteration (C), and nothing is particularly parallel (D).

44. **D** "A message of recall" (line 52) would suggest that the girl wants to send a message to someone; Ming Hoan's words (which she is repeating) have made her rethink a relationship (D). There is no evidence that the American girl even knows Ming Hoan's parents (A) or that she has a history with Ming Hoan (B). The girl does not take offense (C). The girl does not repeat his words in incomprehension (E).

45. **C** Ming Hoan does not explain because "the sins of parents must not be uncovered" (lines 41–42) (C). It is not because he is afraid of hurting his love (A) or that he is embarrassed (B). There is no evidence that he doesn't feel he needs to explain (D), and the fact that she doesn't ask is not the reason the story gives (E).

46. **B** Ah Leen says in lines 37–39, "Though another had bound you by human ties, to me you were linked by my love divine" (B). There is no preference for old customs (A). The passage would tend to suggest that true love cannot be forgotten, the opposite of choice (C). There is no evidence that their love has grown (D) or that the heart of another is unknowable (E).

47. **E** The words are parallel to "ruined by rain," so the answer must be equally destructive (E). Choices (A) and (B) are not strong enough, while (C) and (D) have the opposite meaning from the one the poem intends.

48. **A** The speaker makes extreme or absolute claims in lines 1, 5, 9, 16, and 24; if these assertions were to prove true, then in the speaker's case, misery would have overcome time's capacity to heal wounds (A). The poem features much alliteration, but the use of poetic language suggests that the speaker is not so miserable as to be entirely inured to beauty (B). The speaker does personify the soul but primarily to explain the effects of certain kinds of music (C). The speaker does mention an "armed archangel," but the image is primarily an element of the speaker's description of passionate rhapsody (D). The speaker does not employ oxymoron (E).

49. **E** There are no exotic images, and the poet does not appear to dream (E). "A wave of the sea" is a reference to tidal water (A). The "fruit of my heart" is a metaphor (B). Lines 2 and 11, among others, provide examples of parallel phrases (C). The "sweet tunes" do evoke a strong response (D).

50. **B**   "Smitten with sunbeams, ruined with rain" and "sullen savor of poisonous pain" are examples of paired alliteration (B). There are no religious images in the first stanza (A). The author does not preach (C). He is not antipathetic (D), and character is not really revealed (the poem is more about emotions in general than in this poet's specific feelings) (E).

51. **C**   The poem is about how he has lost his love, and music is what he now hates (C). Death is not a theme in the poem (A). Music and fruit are both symbols, but the poet does not compare music to fruit (B). There is no mention of original sin in the poem (D), and the poet does not talk about slyness or snakes (E).

52. **E**   An archangel is a human-like being who would have hands that could "raise up," so this is *not* an example of giving human characteristics to an inhuman object (E). Personification is present in "singing seasons" (A), "pulse of war" (B), "heavens that murmur" (C), and "stars that sing" (D). Choose (E).

53. **E**   These "things are over" (line 24) according to the author, so they are examples of how love feels (E). There are no anecdotes (A). The memories are not necessarily unpleasant (B). The stanza does not literally speak of weather (C). Fate is not a part of the poem (D).

54. **D**   The eighth line must rhyme with the second and fourth lines and lament the loss of love (D). Choices (A) and (B) do not rhyme with the correct lines. Choice (C) does not make sense in the context; day and night are not mentioned in the poem. Choice (E) is incorrect, as the poet never mentions the wish for head and heart to mingle.

55. **B**   Both men love music, although their ideas of what compose it are "dissimilar" (line 18) because they are of different cultures; also, Nanapush is teaching his language to Father Damien, so (B) is the correct answer. There is no evidence that they are old friends (A). We cannot predict the future, and there is nothing to suggest the men don't get along (C). They are not negotiators (D). Only Father Damien is clearly part of a church (E).

56. **C**   The first paragraph is reported dialogue, while after line 18 all but the last paragraph is quoted dialogue (C). The future is never discussed (A). There is no movement from general to specific or from complexity to simplicity, so eliminate (B) and (E). No one recites or utters a soliloquy (D).

57. **E**   The word "Ayiih" is a sound of surprise and understanding, an interjection (E). It is not singing (A). Father Damien speaks English; this word is not English (B). It does not try to mimic the sound of Chopin (C). It is not Father Damien's first name (D).

58. **E**   Music's influence is discussed throughout the passage (E). The cultural differences exist but are not the main theme of the passage (A). There is no ironic subtext (B). Although Nanapush uses music to pursue women, this is not the main theme of the passage (C), nor are relationships (D).

59. **A** Nanapush asks many questions, so (A) is the correct answer. He does not patronize Father Damien—in fact, he asks him questions (B). He is not overly guarded or polite (C). He is not "kissing up" to Father Damien (D). And his passion is not clearly scholarly (E).

60. **C** Father Damien is describing the emotion he feels when he hears Chopin (C). The emotion is not necessarily joy ("Dogs cry," line 28) (A). There is no sense of nostalgia mentioned (B). (D) is too literal an answer. Although "you can't think," "flooded in the heart" is more of an infusion of emotion than confusion (E).

61. **C** The image of the piano sitting in the river bed while the river rushes around it shows that Father Damien considers time eternal and that the piano (music) is, too (C). The men are speaking in English (A). He does not think that wood is too common a material; he even calls it "precious." (B). The image of the piano is foremost in his mind, but it is not the reason he says the piano is made of "time" (D). There is no evidence that he feels uncomfortable with the topic (E).

HOW TO SCORE PRACTICE TEST 3

When you take the real exam, the proctors will collect your test booklet and bubble sheet and send your answer sheet to a processing center, where a computer looks at the pattern of filled-in ovals on your answer sheet and gives you a score. We couldn't include even a small computer with this book, so we are providing this more primitive way of scoring your exam.

Determining Your Score

STEP 1   Using the answer key, determine how many questions you got right and how many you got wrong on the test. Remember: Questions that you do not answer do not count as either right or wrong answers.

STEP 2   List the number of right answers here.

(A) _____

STEP 3   List the number of wrong answers here. Now divide that number by 4. (Use a calculator if you're feeling particularly lazy.)

(B) _____ ÷ 4 = (C) _____

STEP 4   Subtract the number of wrong answers divided by 4 from the number of correct answers. Round this score to the nearest whole number. This is your raw score.

(A) – (C) = _____

STEP 5   To determine your real score, take the number from Step 4 and look it up in the left-hand column of the Score Conversion Table on the next page; the corresponding score on the right is your score on the exam.

PRACTICE TEST 3 SCORE CONVERSION TABLE

Raw Score	College Board Scaled Score	Raw Score	College Board Scaled Score
61	800	25	520
60	800	24	510
59	800	23	500
58	800	22	490
57	800	21	490
56	800	20	480
55	790	19	470
54	780	18	460
53	780	17	450
52	770	16	440
51	760	15	430
50	750	14	420
49	740	13	410
48	730	12	410
47	720	11	400
46	710	10	390
45	700	09	380
44	700	08	370
43	690	07	360
42	680	06	350
41	670	05	350
40	660	04	340
39	650	03	330
38	640	02	320
37	630	01	310
36	620	00	300
35	620	−01	300
34	610	−02	290
33	600	−03	280
32	590	−04	270
31	580	−05	260
30	570	−06	250
29	560	−07	240
28	550	−08	240
27	540	−09	230
26	530	−10	220
		−11	210
		−12	200
		−13	200
		−14	200
		−15	200

Chapter 16
Practice Test 4

PRACTICE SAT SUBJECT TEST IN LITERATURE 4

TEST 4

Your responses to the SAT Subject Test in Literature questions should be filled in on Test 4 of your answer sheet.

LITERATURE TEST 4

Directions: This test consists of selections from literary works and questions on their content, form, and style. After reading each passage or poem, choose the best answer to each question and fill in the corresponding oval on the answer sheet.

Note: Pay particular attention to questions that contain the words NOT, LEAST, or EXCEPT.

Questions 1-9. Read the following passage carefully before you choose your answers.

While they had been young, no event in the
social world of Elsinore had been a success
without the lovely De Coninck sisters. They were
Line the heart and soul of all the gayety of the town.
(5) When they entered its ballrooms, the ceilings of
sedate old merchants' houses seemed to lift a little,
and the walls to spring out in luminous Ionian
columns, bound with vine. When one of them
opened the ball, light as a bird, bold as a thought,
(10) she consecrated the gathering to the gods of true
joy of life, from whose presence care and envy
are banished. They could sing duets like a pair of
nightingales in a tree, and imitate without effort
and without the slightest malice the voices of all
(15) the *beau monde* of Elsinore, so as to make the
paunches of their father's friends, the matadors of
the town, shake with laughter around their card
tables. They could make up a charade or a game
of forfeits in no time, and when they had been out
(20) for their music lessons, or to the Promenade, they
came back brimful of tales of what had happened,
or of tales out of their own imaginations, one
whim stumbling over the other.
And then, within their own rooms, they would
(25) walk up and down the floor and weep, or sit in the
window and look out over the harbor and wring
their hands in their laps, or lie in bed at night
and cry bitterly, for no reason in the world. They
would talk, then, of life with the black bitterness
(30) of two Timons of Athens, and give Madam
Baek an uncanny feeling, as in an atmosphere of
corrodent rust. Their mother, who did not have
the curse in her blood, would have been badly
frightened had she been present at these moments,
(35) and would have suspected some unhappy love
affair. Their father would have understood them,
and have grieved on their behalf, but he was
occupied with his affairs, and did not come into
his daughters' rooms. Only this elderly female
(40) servant, whose temperament was as different as
possible from theirs, would understand them in
her way, and would keep it all within her heart,
as they did themselves, with mingled despair and
pride. Sometimes she would try to comfort them.
(45) When they cried out, "Hanne, is it not terrible
that there is so much lying, so much falsehood, in
the world?" she said, "Well, what of it? It would
be worse still if it were actually true, all that they
tell."
(50) Then again the girls would get up, dry their
tears, try on their new bonnets before the glass,

plan their theatricals and sleighing parties, shock
and gladden the hearts of their friends, and have
the whole thing over again. They seemed as unable
(55) to keep from one extremity as from the other.
In short, they were born melancholiacs, such as
make others happy and are themselves helplessly
unhappy, creatures of playfulness, charm and salt
tears, of fine fun and everlasting loneliness.

(1934)

1. It can be inferred from the passage that Hanne's response to the sisters in lines 47-49 is

   (A) a purely rhetorical question that she does not expect them to consider seriously
   (B) a reflection of Hanne's more idealistic perspective
   (C) an attempt to alleviate the sisters' distress
   (D) an indication of how frustrated Hanne has become at her inability to comfort the sisters
   (E) an attempt to fill an awkward silence

2. The sisters can best be described as

   (A) vivacious yet standoffish
   (B) joyful yet impolite
   (C) beloved yet acrimonious
   (D) popular yet superficial
   (E) amusing yet despairing

3. The "curse in her blood" (line 33) refers to

   (A) bad luck in romance
   (B) the strain of melancholy inherited by the sisters
   (C) the mother's lack of talent
   (D) the girls' overreaction to events
   (E) the mother's constant fear

GO ON TO THE NEXT PAGE

LITERATURE TEST 4—*Continued*

4. The style of the last line can best be described as

   (A) a description of contrasts
   (B) an extended analogy
   (C) authorial intrusion
   (D) ironic detachment
   (E) subtle differentiation

5. In contrast to the sisters, Hanne is

   (A) practical
   (B) reassuring
   (C) dismissive
   (D) uncaring
   (E) even-tempered

6. The sentence "When one of them opened the ball, light as a bird, bold as a thought, she consecrated the gathering to the gods of true joy of life, from whose presence care and envy are banished" (lines 8-12) can best be restated as

   (A) the sisters acted as religious figures, blessing events
   (B) the sisters were anxious hosts, making sure their guests were enjoying themselves
   (C) if the sisters were at the ball, it could be considered a success
   (D) the sisters were so delightful that many in their presence had a good time
   (E) the girls never worried about or were jealous of others

7. Which of the following is NOT mentioned as a talent of the sisters?

   (A) Storytelling
   (B) Singing
   (C) Impersonations
   (D) Organizing games
   (E) Decorating

8. In this context, "uncanny" (line 31) most nearly means

   (A) concerned
   (B) uncomfortable
   (C) preoccupied
   (D) poisonous
   (E) invigorating

9. It can be inferred from the use of words such as *"beau monde"* (line 15) and "matadors" (line 16) that the sisters

   (A) were members of the upper class
   (B) suffered from crippling clinical depression
   (C) were in search of appropriate husbands
   (D) were easily frightened
   (E) were indifferent to male attention

GO ON TO THE NEXT PAGE

Questions 10-18. Read the following passage carefully before you choose your answers.

Joe's funeral was the finest thing Orange County had ever seen with Negro eyes. The motor hearse, the Cadillac and Buick carriages;
Line Dr. Henderson there in his Lincoln; the hosts
(5) from far and wide. Then again the gold and red and purple, the gloat and glamor of the secret orders, each with its insinuations of power and glory undreamed of by the uninitiated. People on farm horses and mules;
(10) babies riding astride of brothers' and sisters' backs. The Elks band ranked at the church door and playing "Safe in the Arms of Jesus" with such a dominant drum rhythm that it could be stepped off smartly by the long line as it
(15) filed inside. The Little Emperor of the crossroads was leaving Orange County as he had come—with the out-stretched hand of power.
Janie starched and ironed her face and came set in the funeral behind her veil. It was like a
(20) wall of stone and steel. The funeral was going on outside. All things concerning death and burial were said and done. Finish. End. Nevermore. Darkness. Deep hole. Dissolution. Eternity. Weeping and wailing
(25) outside. Inside the expensive black folds were resurrection and life. She did not reach outside for anything, nor did the things of death reach inside to disturb her calm. She sent her face to Joe's funeral, and herself went rollicking with
(30) the springtime across the world. After a while the people finished their celebration and Janie went on home.

(1937)

10. Which of the following is the closest paraphrase of the first sentence of the passage?

(A) Joe's funeral was the finest display the black people of Orange County had ever seen.
(B) Joe's funeral was the finest display of black people that the white people of Orange County had ever seen.
(C) The finest-looking black people in Orange County were all in evidence at Joe's funeral.
(D) The ceremony of Joe's funeral was not much compared to an average funeral for a white person in Orange County.
(E) Joe's funeral gave the white people in attendance a chance to experience the world from a black point of view.

11. The effect of the first paragraph is to

(A) contrast the pomp and display of the assembled mourners with Janie's genuine grief
(B) show how Joe's funeral was not in keeping with the tendencies of his life
(C) demonstrate the importance with which Joe was viewed in his community
(D) illustrate the fruitless nature of our attempts to disguise the starkness of death
(E) emphasize the ephemerality of life

12. It can be inferred that the mourners at Joe's funeral

(A) are deeply grieved by Joe's death
(B) are exaggerating their respect for Joe out of sympathy for Janie
(C) are insincerely using Joe's funeral as an excuse for a flamboyant celebration
(D) are all members of a single, tight-knit community
(E) would be surprised to learn of Janie's sense of detachment from the proceedings

13. "Secret orders" (line 7) most probably refers to

(A) the self-importance felt by those driving expensive automobiles to the funeral
(B) the silent commands governing the conduct of some attendees at the funeral
(C) members of fraternal organizations who came to the funeral dressed in their clubs' regalia
(D) the haughty behavior of people attending the funeral whom the other attendees had never met or seen
(E) the majestic, heavenly hosts of which Joe is now presumably a member

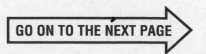

GO ON TO THE NEXT PAGE

14. Why is Janie's veil described as "a wall of stone and steel" (lines 19-20)?

    (A) The veil allows Janie to suppress her anguish and maintain her composure during the funeral.
    (B) The veil screens Janie from the accusing stares of the mourners at the funeral.
    (C) The veil represents the solidity of Janie's emotional state.
    (D) The veil allows Janie to endure the formal pretense of mourning at Joe's funeral, which is not in keeping with her true feelings.
    (E) The veil allows Janie to hide her true feelings from herself until after the funeral.

15. What is the primary effect of the phrase "the people finished their celebration" (line 31)?

    (A) It draws attention to the funeral's emphasis on the virtues of Joe's life and achievements.
    (B) It emphasizes the communal nature of the funeral, which brings together individuals from all ranks of society.
    (C) It emphasizes Janie's isolation from the others at the funeral.
    (D) It emphasizes the distances from which people had traveled to attend the funeral.
    (E) It points out that celebrations are by nature temporary and must give way to the routines of daily life.

16. The style of the passage is characterized by the repeated use of

    (A) African American Vernacular
    (B) grammatically incomplete sentences
    (C) religious imagery
    (D) ironic turns of phrase
    (E) oxymoron

17. Which of the following phrases from the passage best expresses Janie's emotional state during the funeral?

    (A) "gloat and glamor" (line 6)
    (B) "starched and ironed" (line 18)
    (C) "Darkness. Deep hole." (line 23)
    (D) "Weeping and wailing" (line 24)
    (E) "resurrection and life" (line 26)

18. Which of the following inferences can be made about Janie's relationship to Joe?

    (A) Janie knew Joe only as a casual acquaintance and is unmoved by his death.
    (B) Janie cared deeply for Joe and has not yet fully experienced the shock of his death.
    (C) Janie felt a strong dislike for Joe and must disguise her antipathy at his funeral.
    (D) Janie's relationship with Joe was such that she feels unburdened and revitalized by his death.
    (E) Janie's feelings for Joe were a secret to the community and must be suppressed at his funeral.

GO ON TO THE NEXT PAGE

Questions 19-28. Read the following poem carefully before you choose your answers.

"To my Honoured Kinsman John Driden, of Chesterton, in the County of Huntingdon, Esq."

How blessed is he, who leads a country life,
Unvexed with anxious cares, and void of strife!
Who, studying peace, and shunning civil rage,
Line Enjoyed his youth, and now enjoys his age:
(5) All who deserve his love, he makes his own;
And, to be loved himself, needs only to be known.
Just, good, and wise, contending neighbors come,
From your award to wait their final doom;
And, foes before, return in friendship home
(10) Without their cost, you terminate the cause,
And save the expense of long litigious laws;
Where suits are traversed, and so little won,
That he who conquers is but last undone:
Such are not your decrees; but so designed,
(15) The sanction leaves a lasting peace behind;
Like your own soul, serene, a pattern of your mind.
   Promoting concord, and composing strife,
Lord of yourself, uncumbered with a wife;
Where, for a year, a month, perhaps a night,
(20) Long penitence succeeds a short delight:
Minds are so hardly matched, that even the first,
Though paired by heaven, in Paradise were cursed.

                                      (1697)

19. In context "void of" (line 2) most nearly means

   (A) rejecting
   (B) lacking
   (C) reversed in
   (D) canceled from
   (E) disqualified for

20. Lines 12 and 13 refer to

   (A) the importance of fine clothing when attempting to get a legal award
   (B) the subject's approach to disputes, which gave few rewards to the victor
   (C) the way a court case under the legal system could bankrupt even the winner
   (D) the method through which Driden's justice gave victory to the most patient
   (E) the subject's attitude toward military victory, which he felt was hollow

21. It can be inferred from the poem that the speaker considers country life to be

   (A) tedious
   (B) onerous
   (C) momentous
   (D) undesirable
   (E) idyllic

22. Which of the following is NOT mentioned by the speaker as a benefit of country living?

   (A) A calm mind
   (B) Old age
   (C) Many friends
   (D) Wisdom
   (E) Good health

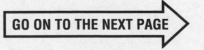
GO ON TO THE NEXT PAGE

23. It can be inferred from the poem that the speaker thinks of marriage as

    (A) a necessary evil
    (B) an unavoidable concession
    (C) a protracted lawsuit
    (D) a source of aggravation
    (E) a prison sentence

24. Which of the following best describes the difference between lines 1-6 and lines 7-23?

    (A) Generalization to direct address
    (B) Present tense to past tense
    (C) Positive discourse to negative discourse
    (D) Simple description to extended simile
    (E) Terrestrial presence to divine intervention

25. The word "their" (line 8) refers to

    (A) suits
    (B) expenses
    (C) foes
    (D) neighbors
    (E) laws

26. Which of the following best describes the role played by the subject of the poem in his community?

    (A) Farmer
    (B) Judge
    (C) Religious leader
    (D) Writer
    (E) Scholar

27. Which of the following contains an example of alliteration?

    I. "And, foes before, return in friendship home" (line 9)
    II. "And save the expense of long litigious laws" (line 11)
    III. "Long penitence succeeds a short delight" (line 20)

    (A) I only
    (B) II only
    (C) III only
    (D) I and III only
    (E) I, II, and III

28. Lines 21-22 can be restated as

    (A) True equality is hard to come by; and whenever it does occur, it is cursed by God.
    (B) It's difficult to get along with someone else; even God's original creations fought.
    (C) The more alike two people are, the more they're prone to argue.
    (D) Soul mates are rare; the rest of humanity lives outside Paradise with incompatible spouses.
    (E) It is wise to disguise intelligence—those who are exceptional are often cast out of society.

GO ON TO THE NEXT PAGE

Questions 29-36. Read the following poem carefully before you choose your answers.

"To My Own Soul"

Hold yet a while, Strong Heart,
Not part a lifelong yoke
Though blighted looks the present, future gloom.

Line
(5)
And age it seems since you and I began our
March up hill or down. Sailing smooth o'er
Seas that are so rare—
Thou nearer unto me, than oft-times I myself—
Proclaiming mental moves before they were!

Reflector true—Thy pulse so timed to mine,
(10)
Thou perfect note of thoughts, however fine—
Shall we now part, Recorder, say?

In thee is friendship, faith,
For thou didst warn when evil thoughts were
                    brewing—
(15)
And though, alas, thy warning thrown away,
Went on the same as ever—good and true.

                              (1847)

29. In the poem, the speaker uses all of the following as terms to name the subject of his address EXCEPT

    (A) Thou (line 7)
    (B) Reflector (line 9)
    (C) Recorder (line 11)
    (D) Heart (line 1)
    (E) faith (line 12)

30. In this context "brewing" (line 14) most nearly means

    (A) threatening
    (B) forming
    (C) clouding
    (D) imbibing
    (E) foreshadowing

31. It is clear from the first three lines that the speaker regards his heart as

    (A) aching for the love of another
    (B) failing and ceasing to function
    (C) a separate entity
    (D) wanting to separate from his body
    (E) an enemy of his soul

32. The lines "And age it seems since you and I began our March up hill or down. Sailing smooth o'er Seas that are so rare—" (lines 4-6) can best be restated as

    (A) "We've been through many travails, some easy, some more difficult."
    (B) "Our journey will take a long while and range over land and sea."
    (C) "We are prisoners of an army from across the ocean."
    (D) "It is unfortunate that most of our journey has not been on the water."
    (E) "We are now too old to hike; sailing is easier on our frail limbs."

33. All of the following are themes of the poem EXCEPT

    (A) the pitfalls of romantic love
    (B) the steadfast nature of the soul
    (C) the difficulty of doing what one knows one should
    (D) the divided nature of human consciousness
    (E) the challenges of being human

34. The speaker employs which of the following techniques?

    I.   Apostrophe
    II. A rigid rhyme scheme
    III. Challenging syntax

    (A) I only
    (B) III only
    (C) I and II only
    (D) I and III only
    (E) II and III only

35. The speaker's tone can best be described as

    (A) excited
    (B) begging
    (C) resigned
    (D) proud
    (E) questioning

36. "Thou perfect note of thoughts" (line 10) is an example of

    (A) alliteration
    (B) personification
    (C) metaphor
    (D) paradox
    (E) allegory

GO ON TO THE NEXT PAGE

Questions 37-44. Read the following passage carefully before you choose your answers.

Eugene Coristine and Farquhar Wilkinson were youngish bachelors and fellow members of the Victoria and Albert Literary Society. Thither, on
Line Wednesday evenings, when respectable church-
(5) members were wending their way to weekly service, they hastened regularly, to meet with a band of like-minded young men, and spend a literary hour or two. In various degrees of fluency they debated the questions of the day; they read
(10) essays with a wide range of style and topic; they gave readings from popular authors, and contributed airy creations in prose and in verse to the Society's manuscript magazine. Wilkinson, the older and more sedate of the two, who wore a
(15) tightly-buttoned blue frock coat and an eyeglass, was a schoolmaster, pretty well up in the Toronto Public Schools. Coristine was a lawyer in full practice, but his name did not appear on the card of the firm which profited by his services. He was
(20) taller than his friend, more jauntily dressed, and was of a more mercurial temperament than the schoolmaster, for whom, however, he entertained a profound respect. Different as they were, they were linked together by an ardent love of
(25) literature, especially poetry, by scientific pursuits, Coristine as a botanist, and Wilkinson as a dabbler in geology, and by a firm determination to resist, or rather to shun, the allurements of female society. Many lady teachers wielded the pointer in
(30) rooms not far removed from those in which Mr. Wilkinson held sway, but he did not condescend to be on terms even of bowing acquaintance with any one of them. There were several young lady typewriters of respectable city connections in the
(35) offices of Messrs. Tyler, Woodruff and White, but the young Irish lawyer passed them by without a glance. These bachelors were of the opinion that women were bringing the dignity of law and education to the dogs.

(1892)

37. The two men have all of the following in common EXCEPT:

(A) They are both unmarried.
(B) They both look down upon women.
(C) They are both professionals.
(D) They are both bibliophiles.
(E) They both speak foreign languages.

38. The phrase "well up" (line 16) in this context most nearly means

(A) handsomely paid
(B) generally liked
(C) professionally advanced
(D) comfortably sated
(E) nattily dressed

39. The sentence "Thither, on Wednesday evenings, when respectable church-members were wending their way to weekly service, they hastened regularly, to meet with a band of like-minded young men, and spend a literary hour or two" (lines 3-8) suggests the men are

(A) chauvinists
(B) talented authors
(C) lapsed church-members
(D) rebellious
(E) pious

40. In this context, "mercurial" (line 21) most nearly means

(A) excitable
(B) overheated
(C) incorrigible
(D) embarrassed
(E) self-confident

41. From the passage it is reasonable to conclude that the two men

(A) had little opportunity to meet women
(B) felt threatened by female influence
(C) feared their jobs would be taken by women
(D) considered women generally inferior to men
(E) felt that women were fit only for teaching and clerical work

GO ON TO THE NEXT PAGE

42. By the phrase, "Coristine was a lawyer in full practice, but his name did not appear on the card of the firm which profited by his services" the author suggests that

    (A) Coristine is not valued by his firm
    (B) Coristine does not have enough money to have business cards made
    (C) although he was part of a firm, he worked independently
    (D) Coristine did not contribute sufficiently to his company's earnings
    (E) Coristine's temperament kept him from advancing in his firm

43. The tone of the passage can best be described as

    (A) indignantly offended
    (B) gently mocking
    (C) hesitantly critical
    (D) unflinchingly honest
    (E) offhandedly distant

44. As it is used in the passage, the phrase "wending their way" (line 5) can best be replaced with the words

    (A) journeying to
    (B) hastening to
    (C) retiring from
    (D) returning from
    (E) late to

GO ON TO THE NEXT PAGE

Questions 45-53. Read the following poem carefully before you choose your answers.

How vain have prov'd the Labours of the Stage,
In striving to reclaim a vitious Age!
Poets may write the Mischief to impeach,
Line You care as little what the Poets teach,
(5) As you regard at Church what Parsons preach.
But where such Follies, and such Vices reign,
What honest Pen has Patience to refrain?
At Church, in Pews, ye most devoutly snore;
And here, got dully drunk, ye come to roar:
(10) Ye go to Church to glout*, and ogle there,
And come to meet more leud convenient here

With equal Zeal ye honour either Place,
And run so very evenly your Race,
Y' improve in Wit just as you do in Grace
(15) It must be so, some Doemon** has possest
Our Land, and we have never since been blest.

   *to pout or look sullen
   **demon
      (1682)

45. In this context, "vitious" (line 2) most nearly means

   (A) boastful
   (B) desperate
   (C) vicious
   (D) capricious
   (E) complex

46. The first two lines "How vain have prov'd the Labours of the Stage, In striving to reclaim a vitious Age!" suggest that

   (A) the speaker considers actors a self-important group
   (B) the speaker considers the theater world to be full of back-stabbing heathens
   (C) the speaker considers that the theater's attempt to improve society's lack of morality has failed
   (D) acting requires more work than most common citizens understand
   (E) through good theater, people can be metaphorically transported back in time

47. Which of the following is an example of personification?

   (A) "Poets may write the Mischief to impeach" (line 3)
   (B) "What honest Pen has Patience to refrain?" (line 7)
   (C) "And run so very evenly your Race" (line 13)
   (D) "Y' improve in Wit just as you do in Grace" (line 14)
   (E) "It must be so, some Doemon has possest" (line 15)

48. The poem consists of

   (A) arrhythmic rhyme
   (B) rhyming couplets only
   (C) rhyming couplets and triplets
   (D) epic hyperbole
   (E) passive verbs only

49. From the poem, it is reasonable to infer that the speaker regards the church as

   (A) intensely boring
   (B) ineffective in its teachings
   (C) a den of gossip
   (D) the domain of hypocrites
   (E) inferior to theater

50. The tone of lines 13-14, "And run so very evenly your Race, / Y' improve in Wit just as you do in Grace," can best be described as

   (A) hyperbolic
   (B) sarcastic
   (C) condemning
   (D) admiring
   (E) parodical

51. According to the speaker, people do all of the following in church and/or the theater EXCEPT

   (A) look at others
   (B) nap soundly
   (C) heckle the stage
   (D) conduct contests
   (E) become inebriated

GO ON TO THE NEXT PAGE →

52. In the context, what is the narrative effect of the phrase "devoutly snore" (line 8)?

    (A) It indicates that the people are so pious as to be devout even while asleep.
    (B) It is an ironic attack on the people's lack of attention to services.
    (C) It is an attack on church services, which have become less interesting than the theater.
    (D) It rebukes people who carouse so late that they cannot stay awake at church.
    (E) It contrasts the respectful quietude of people in church with the commotion they make at plays.

53. Overall, the tone of the poem is best characterized as

    (A) excessively priggish
    (B) overtly apocalyptic
    (C) cautiously optimistic
    (D) harshly critical
    (E) blatantly hypocritical

GO ON TO THE NEXT PAGE

Questions 54-62. Read the following passage carefully before you choose your answers.

In the mind of the mariner, there is a superstitious horror connected with the name of Pirate; and there are few subjects that interest and excite the curiosity of mankind generally,
Line
(5) more than the desperate exploits, foul doings, and diabolical career of these monsters in human form. A piratical crew is generally formed of the desperadoes and runagates of every clime and nation. The pirate, from the perilous nature of his
(10) occupation, when not cruising on the ocean, the great highway of nations, selects the most lonely isles of the sea for his retreat, or secretes himself near the shores of rivers, bays and lagoons of thickly wooded and uninhabited countries, so
(15) that if pursued he can escape to the woods and mountain glens of the interior. The islands of the Indian Ocean, and the east and west coasts of Africa, as well as the West Indies, have been their haunts for centuries; and vessels navigating the
(20) Atlantic and Indian Oceans, are often captured by them, the passengers and crew murdered, the money and most valuable part of the cargo plundered, the vessel destroyed, thus obliterating all trace of their unhappy fate, and leaving
(25) friends and relatives to mourn their loss from the inclemencies of the elements, when they were butchered in cold blood by their fellow men, who by practically adopting the maxim that "dead men tell no tales," enable themselves to pursue their
(30) diabolical career with impunity....
But the apprehension and foreboding of the mind, when under the influence of remorse, are powerful, and every man, whether civilized or savage, has interwoven in his constitution a moral
(35) sense, which secretly condemns him when he has committed an atrocious action, even when he is placed in situations which raise him above the fear of human punishment, for "Conscience, the torturer of the soul, unseen. Does fiercely brandish
(40) a sharp scourge within; Severe decrees may keep our tongues in awe, but to our minds what edicts can give law? Even you yourself to your own breast shall tell Your crimes, and your own conscience be your hell."

(1837)

54. Which of the following sentences best describes the passage's structure?

(A) Paragraph one introduces a topic, while paragraph two further elaborates, citing poetic evidence.
(B) Paragraph one states a point of view, while paragraph two opposes it.
(C) Paragraph one states the general perception of a profession, while paragraph two delves into the actual emotions of the individuals in that profession.
(D) Paragraph one explains atrocities, and paragraph two justifies them.
(E) Paragraph one provides background on a topic, while paragraph two gives a contemporary popular culture example.

55. Which of the following situations would be most analogous to the passage's suppositions about pirates' emotions?

(A) A student who cheated on a test but felt so bad about it that he turned himself in
(B) A student who cheated on a test and gave her transgression no more than a passing thought
(C) A student who falsely accused another student of cheating, and then retracted his statement because of guilt
(D) A student who cheated on a test but felt so ashamed that he was unable to enjoy the high grade he received
(E) A student who cheated on a test but felt justified in doing so because the teacher had not properly prepared her for the material on the test

56. Which of the following is an example of a metaphor?

(A) "their haunts for centuries" (lines 18-19)
(B) "the desperate exploits, foul doings, and diabolical career" (lines 5-6)
(C) "the great highway of nations" (lines 10-11)
(D) "the desperadoes and runagates of every clime and nation" (lines 7-9)
(E) "the apprehension and foreboding of the mind" (lines 31-32)

GO ON TO THE NEXT PAGE

57. The passage's prose can be characterized as

    (A) descriptively complex, using extensive modifiers and subordinate clauses
    (B) deceptively ornate, couching a simple subject in complicated language
    (C) rhetorically interrogative, raising questions that the author never answers
    (D) narrowly biased, providing a unilateral viewpoint
    (E) defensively argumentative, anticipating critical objections and rejecting them

58. The word "secretes" (line 12) as it is used in the passage most nearly means

    (A) admits
    (B) ensconces
    (C) emanates
    (D) entertains
    (E) silences

59. According to the passage, what do relatives of the victims believe happened to the victims?

    (A) They died of scurvy or other shipborne diseases.
    (B) They were murdered by pirates.
    (C) They were kidnapped by foreign cultures to be sold as slaves.
    (D) They succumbed to the lure of the open ocean.
    (E) They capsized in a large storm and drowned.

60. The author most likely believes in

    (A) a universal conscience that transcends cultures
    (B) a supreme deity who governs all actions
    (C) a higher court to which murderers are held accountable
    (D) the potential power of international law
    (E) the importance of nurture in the development of a moral code

61. The use of the word "practically" (line 28)

    (A) proves that murderers are always haunted by remorse
    (B) suggests that not all victims were killed
    (C) insinuates that the pirates were motivated only by greed
    (D) explains the logic behind murder
    (E) implies that the author is not exactly sure of the pirates' actions

62. According to the passage, "adopting the maxim that 'dead men tell no tales'" (lines 28-29) encourages the pirates to

    (A) ignore the human cost of piracy
    (B) eliminate all witnesses
    (C) successfully challenge charges brought against them in court
    (D) lie to their victims' friends and family without repercussions
    (E) rationalize their most vicious behavior

STOP

**IF YOU FINISH BEFORE TIME IS CALLED, YOU MAY CHECK YOUR WORK ON THIS SECTION ONLY.
DO NOT TURN TO ANY OTHER SECTION IN THE TEST.**

Chapter 17
Practice Test 4:
Answers and
Explanations

- Practice Test 4 Answer Key
- Practice Test 4 Explanations
- How to Score Practice Test 4

PRACTICE TEST 4 ANSWER KEY

Question Number	Correct Answer	Right	Wrong	Question Number	Correct Answer	Right	Wrong
1	C	___	___	32	A	___	___
2	E	___	___	33	A	___	___
3	B	___	___	34	D	___	___
4	A	___	___	35	B	___	___
5	E	___	___	36	C	___	___
6	D	___	___	37	E	___	___
7	E	___	___	38	C	___	___
8	B	___	___	39	D	___	___
9	A	___	___	40	A	___	___
10	A	___	___	41	D	___	___
11	C	___	___	42	A	___	___
12	E	___	___	43	B	___	___
13	C	___	___	44	A	___	___
14	D	___	___	45	C	___	___
15	C	___	___	46	C	___	___
16	B	___	___	47	B	___	___
17	E	___	___	48	C	___	___
18	D	___	___	49	B	___	___
19	B	___	___	50	B	___	___
20	C	___	___	51	D	___	___
21	E	___	___	52	B	___	___
22	E	___	___	53	D	___	___
23	D	___	___	54	C	___	___
24	A	___	___	55	D	___	___
25	D	___	___	56	C	___	___
26	B	___	___	57	A	___	___
27	B	___	___	58	B	___	___
28	B	___	___	59	E	___	___
29	E	___	___	60	A	___	___
30	B	___	___	61	D	___	___
31	D	___	___	62	B	___	___

PRACTICE TEST 4 EXPLANATIONS

1. **C** Hanne's response to the sisters is presented following the statement that "Sometimes [Hanne] would try to comfort them," so her remark that the world would be worse if people weren't lying is an attempt to alleviate the sisters' concerns (C). The passage suggests that only Hanne "would understand them in her way" and hold their worries "all within her heart, as they did themselves" (lines 41-42), so it seems unlikely that Hanne does not expect the sisters to take her response seriously (A) or that Hanne is frustrated by the sisters' melancholy (D). Her reaction isn't an attempt to fill silence, because it follows the sisters' asking her a question (E). Hanne doesn't suggest that the world is a more ideal place than the sisters' concerns characterize it (B)—she just points out that it could be worse.

2. **E** The sisters are said to make their father's friends "shake with laughter" (line 17) but often "weep" (line 25), so they are "amusing yet despairing." They may be "vivacious," but they are not "standoffish" (A). They may be "joyful," but they are not "impolite" (B). They are "beloved" but not "acrimonious" (hostile) (C), and they are not "superficial" (D).

3. **B** The curse refers to the melancholy the sisters suffered from, which their mother did not have. Additional support is provided in line 56 for the idea that the sisters inherited it: "they were born melancholiacs" (B). There is no evidence that the girls were unlucky in romance (A). The mother's talent (or lack thereof) is not mentioned (C). The "curse" is not an overreaction to events (D), and the mother's fear is not described as "constant" (E).

4. **A** The last sentence describes contrasts: the girls make people happy, but they themselves are unhappy; they are fun but are themselves lonely (A). There is no analogy (B). The author does not make an appearance in the passage, nor does the voice change (C). The narrator is not particularly detached (D). The differentiation between "happy" and "sad" is not subtle (E).

5. **E** The sisters are prone to wild mood swings, but Hanne's "temperament was as different as possible from theirs" (lines 40–41) (E). There is no evidence that the sisters are not practical (A), so Hanne being practical cannot be the contrast. Although Hanne attempts to comfort/reassure the sisters, her attempts do not directly contrast with any quality possessed by the sisters (B). Hanne is not "dismissive" (C), nor is she "uncaring" (D).

6. **D** The sentence states that the girls were the life of the party (D). The "gods of true joy" do not refer to Christian religion (A). The sisters are not the hostesses of these parties (B). Although (C) is mentioned in lines 1–3, the question is referring to a different sentence in the passages (lines 8–12), where a different point is made—one that does not suggest that the girls' mere presence guaranteed social success. The girls banish "care and envy," but there is no evidence that they themselves were never worried or jealous (E).

7. **E** The girls are never described as decorators (E). They are good storytellers: "brimful of tales" (line 21) (A). They sing like "a pair of nightingales" (lines 12–13) (B). They were excellent imitators (line 13) (C), and they could "make up a charade or a game of forfeits" (lines 18–19) (D).

8. **B** The girls make Madam Baek feel as though she was in an "atmosphere of corrodent rust" (that is, uncomfortable) (B). Although she may be concerned, this is not the meaning of uncanny (A). Nor is "preoccupied" a good synonym for her feeling of unease (C). Neither "poisonous" (D) nor "invigorating" (E) makes sense here.

9. **A**   The term *beau monde* marks the sisters' social group as "high society," while describing their father's friends as "matadors" is an example of figurative language emphasizing the men's relative social power, so (A) is the best answer. The terms referenced in the question have nothing to do with whether or not the sisters have received a clinical diagnosis regarding their melancholia (B) or whether they were indifferent to male attention (E). The passage's descriptions of the sisters' socializing don't mention that the girls are searching for husbands (C) or are easily frightened (D).

10. **A**   "Negro eyes" refers to the black people watching the funeral (A). White people are not the ones watching (B). The funeral refers to the finest event in general, not the finest-looking people (C). There is no mention of what white funerals are like (D). There is no evidence that there were any white people in attendance at the funeral (E).

11. **C**   All of the community's important people came to Joe's funeral, so he must have been well regarded (C). Janie does not necessarily feel genuine grief, and she's not mentioned in the first paragraph (A). There is no information in the passage about Joe's life (B). There is no generalization being drawn from this particular funeral (D) and (E).

12. **E**   Janie's outside appearance gives no clue to her inner feelings: "She sent her face to Joe's funeral, and herself went rollicking with the springtime across the world"; so she is detached (E). We do not know what the mourners are really feeling (A) and (B). We cannot judge their sincerity (C). And we don't know enough to be able to tell whether they are a single community (D).

13. **C**   To be in the secret orders, you must be "initiated," and they are wearing certain colors, so it is reasonable to assume that they are members of fraternal organizations (C). There is only one car mentioned (A). There is nothing in the passage about governing commands (B). There is no evidence that anyone at the funeral was a stranger (D). There is no mention of heaven or life after death (E).

14. **D**   Janie is obviously not grieving at Joe's death, and her veil allows her to go to the funeral without letting on (D). Janie is not anguished (A). No one is staring at her accusingly (B). Janie's emotional state cannot be described as "solid" (C). Janie knows what her true feelings are (E).

15. **C**   Everyone is celebrating, but Janie is not; she is isolated (C). The funeral does not emphasize Joe's life (A). The primary effect of the phrase is not to emphasize the "community" of the funeral (B). There is no mention of distances traveled (D). There is no larger lesson that the passage is attempting to draw parallels to (E).

16. **B**   The most obvious style is the use of incomplete sentences (B). There is no dialect in the passage (A), nor is there much religious imagery (C). There are no ironies in the passage (D), and although there are some contrasts, there are no oxymorons (E).

17. **E**   Janie is herself "behind her veil" and "inside the expensive black folds" (line 25), where her emotional state is described as "resurrection and life" (E). "Gloat and glamor" refers to the secret orders (A); "starched and ironed" refers to Janie's facial expressions/outward appearance, not her emotional state (B). "Darkness. Deep hole" refers to the funeral proceedings, not Janie's emotions (C); she is not "weeping and wailing" (D).

18. **D** Janie feels as though she is reborn, brought to life by Joe's death (lines 25–26) (D). Janie is inwardly celebrating, so his death has had some effect on her (A). We have no evidence that Janie cared for Joe (B). We don't know Janie's exact feelings, but she feels calm, not antipathetic (C). We have no evidence that the community knows or doesn't know about Janie's feelings for Joe (E).

19. **B** The country life is without anxious cares and strife. "Lacking" has the closest meaning to "without," so (B) is the best answer.

20. **C** Lines 12 and 13 describe the circumstances under the "long litigious laws" (line 11), which ultimately are the undoing of both the victor and the vanquished; the speaker says that those kinds of exhausting legal proceedings are "not your decrees" (line 14), because this is not the approach which Driden takes to justice (B), (D). "Suits" in line 12 does not refer to clothing (A), but to lawsuits; and "conquers" (line 13) is not referring to military victory (E) but to victory in court. Therefore, (C) is the best answer.

21. **E** The speaker considers the country dweller to be "blessed" and "unvexed" so the speaker thinks that country life is excellent. Only "idyllic" fits this description (E).

22. **E** The speaker never mentions the effect of country life on health (E)—"Enjoyed his youth, and now enjoys his age" does not refer to health but rather longevity (B). The speaker does talk about a calm mind: "Like your own soul, serene, a pattern of your mind" (A). The speaker does speak of friendship: "All who deserve his love, he makes his own; And, to be loved himself, needs only to be known" (C), and says that the country-dweller is "wise" (D).

23. **D** The speaker describes the subject as "uncumbered with a wife," so he finds a wife to be a burden and a source of strife (D). Marriage is not a necessity; the subject of the poem is not married (A), (B). The protracted lawsuit does not refer to marriage (C), nor is there evidence that the speaker considers marriage to be a prison sentence (E).

24. **A** The first six lines speak of a general "he," while the rest of the poem addresses the subject using "you" (A). There is no switch in tense (B), nor is there a general switch in attitude (C). There is no extended simile (D), and although God is mentioned in the last lines, there is no divine intervention (E).

25. **D** The sentence reads, "Just, good, and wise, contending neighbors come, From your award to wait their final doom," so "their" refers to the contending neighbors (D). None of the others is the correct antecedent.

26. **B** The "contending" (disagreeing) neighbors come for advice and to avoid lawsuits, so the subject must play the role of a judge (B). There is no evidence that he is a farmer (A) or a religious leader (C). Similarly, nowhere in the poem does it suggest the subject is a writer (D) or scholar (E).

27. **B** The second sentence has alliteration in "long litigious laws," so eliminate (A), (C), and (D). The third sentence does not contain alliteration, so eliminate (E). Therefore, the correct answer is (B).

28. **B** The speaker is making the point that it's difficult to get along, and even Adam and Eve disagreed (B). The speaker does not suggest that God punishes all couples, nor is equality the issue in the poem (A). "Matched" means "coupled," not necessarily "similar" (C). Choice (D) is too general a statement for the poem. Intelligence is not mentioned as a reason for being ostracized (E).

29. **E** The speaker uses all the listed words except "faith" as symbols of "heart" (E). The speaker calls his heart "thou" in line 7 (A). "Reflector" is located in line 9 (B) and "Recorder" in line 11 (C). The speaker addresses his "Strong Heart" in line 1 (D).

30. **B** The speaker says his heart warned him when he began to think of evil thoughts, so "forming" is the best synonym (B). None of the others accurately fits the meaning.

31. **D** The speaker wants his heart to stay put and not break their bond. ("Hold yet a while, Strong Heart, Not part a lifelong yoke") (D). There is nothing in the passage that suggests an outside love (A). There is no mention of a failing heart ("Strong Heart") (B). "Even though the speaker is talking metaphorically to his heart (and he is asking it not to break a "lifelong yoke"), his heart is still inside his body and, therefore, is not a separate being (C). He considers his heart a friend ("In thee is friendship"), not an enemy (E).

32. **A** The speaker speaks of rare smooth sailing and marching up and downhill for a long time, so (A) is the best answer. There is not a literal journey (and it is in the past) (B). There is no evidence of prison (C). Although the speaker seems to find the water easier, there is no expression of regret (D). The speaker speaks of a metaphoric journey, not a literal one (E).

33. **A** The poem does not discuss romantic love (A). The speaker does ask the soul to "Not part a lifelong yoke" (line 2), so the soul's steadfast nature is key to the poem's argumentation (B), in part because of the "up hill or down" nature of the speaker's human experiences (E). The speaker notes that the soul sometimes acted as a moral compass—"thou didst warn when evil thoughts were brewing" (line 13–14) (C)—and the fact that the speaker addresses his own soul in the first place suggests that the poem is exploring the divided nature of consciousness (D).

34. **D** This is an instance in which the poem's title can help you answer questions: "To My Own Soul" is clearly an apostrophe directed to the speaker's soul (Statement I), so you can eliminate (B) and (E). While occasionally pairs of lines rhyme, the poem is not organized according to a rigid rhyme scheme (Statement II), so you can eliminate (C). The lines do, however, display challenging syntax, punctuated with many dashes that sometimes muddle whether the soul is the subject or the object of a particular verb's action (Statement III). Thus, (D) is the correct answer.

35. **B** The speaker appears to be thanking his heart and coaxing it to stay, so "begging" is the best answer (B). The speaker is not "excited" (A), nor is he "resigned" (C). There is no evidence of pride (D), and although there is a question mark, the speaker does not employ a "questioning" tone (E).

36. **C** The speaker is comparing his heart to a recorder of thoughts, so it is a metaphor (C). There is no alliteration (A), paradox (D), or allegory (E). In this particular line, there is also no personification (B).

37. **E** There is no evidence the men speak foreign languages ("various degrees of fluency" refers to their skill levels in the subjects, not foreign languages) (E). They are "youngish bachelors" and, therefore, unmarried (line 2) (A). Wilkinson did not "condescend" to speak with female teachers, and Coristine won't look at the women who work in his firm (B). Wilkinson is a teacher, and Coristine is a lawyer (C). They both like books: "they were linked together by an ardent love of literature" (lines 24–25) (D).

38. **C** Because Wilkinson is compared to Coristine, and "Coristine was a lawyer in full practice," then Wilkinson must have a position of responsibility in the school system (C). There is no mention of how well he is paid (A). There is also no discussion about how people feel about them (B). They are not eating, so they are not "sated" (D). Although they are well-dressed, this is not the focus of this line (E).

39. **D** The young men are being contrasted with "respectable church members." They are "rebellious" (D) because they are not doing what "respectable" people do on Wednesdays. Although they may be "chauvinists," this sentence does not say that (A). There is no discussion of how talented they are (B). There is no evidence that the young men used to go to church, nor was "respectable" emphasized in the passage, which would suggest that the young men were a different type of church member than the "respectable" ones (C). And because they are not going to church, we cannot say that they are "pious" (E).

40. **A** Wilkinson is described as "sedate" (line 14), so Coristine is in comparison the opposite, which is "excitable" (A). None of the other words conveys this meaning.

41. **D** According to the men, women were "bringing the dignity of law and education to the dogs," so the men thought they were inferior (D). They had opportunities to meet women at work (A). There is no evidence in the passage that they felt threatened (B) or feared their jobs would be taken from them (C); although that may have been their subconscious fear, the passage never states this. They object to female teachers and clerks (E).

42. **A** This is a good example of a "least bad" answer. The only plausible choice is that Coristine is apparently not valued by his firm (A), since he is a practicing lawyer and his name is not part of the firm's name. There is no discussion of finances (B), (D). There is nothing to suggest that he works independently (C). The passage states that Coristine is "mercurial"; however, there is no evidence that his temperament has anything to do with his standing within his firm (E).

43. **B** The narrator makes fun of the characters as he paints them as snobs who consider themselves superior (B). The narrator is not offended (A), nor is the writing hesitant or overtly critical (C). The passage is not marked by extreme honesty (D), nor is it distant (E).

44. **A** People were making their way to church as the young men were hurrying to their literary society, so the manner in which the two groups were going to their respective destinations is contrasted. Therefore, "journeying to" is the best match (A). There is no evidence that the people were also in a hurry (B) or that they were late (E). And they were going to the meeting, not coming from it (C), (D).

45. **C** Context for this archaic word comes from the rest of the poem. Writers are trying to bring back a vicious age, but grace wins out in the end, so (C) is the best answer. None of the other words fits the sentence.

46. **C** The line can be restated as "in trying to reclaim some viciousness, the theater world's efforts have been wasted" so (C) is the best answer. The speaker does not think that actors are conceited (A), nor does the speaker claim that the theater is a home to those who don't believe in God (B). Although the passage speaks of labor, it is not the labor of acting (D). There is no evidence that the speaker is talking about the transformative power of theater (E).

47. **B** A pen writing ("refrain"-ing) and having patience is an example of personification (B). None of the other phrases contains an example of personification.

48. **C** Even if you don't know what triplets are, you can tell which answers are wrong. The poem has pairs of rhyming phrases and some phrases that come in rhyming sets of threes (C). There is a regular rhythm to the poem (A). There are triplets (also called tercets) as well as couplets (B). Nothing is epic about the poem (D), and there are active as well as passive verbs (E).

49. **B** From the lines "You care as little what the Poets teach, As you regard at Church what Parsons preach" (lines 4–5), it is clear that the speaker thinks people disregard what's said in church (B). It is not clear from the poem that the speaker thinks church is boring, only that he or she is aware that others do (A). There is no evidence that there is gossip in the church (C) or that the speaker considers the church a place for hypocrites (D). The speaker does not state the superiority of either the church or theater—he or she suggests only that people learn little from either (E).

50. **B** The lines are sarcastic in that the speaker is mocking the people by saying that they learn as little from theater as they do from church (B). They are not an exaggeration (A). Although the tone is negative, it is not condemning (C). The speaker does not admire the theatergoers (D). In order for something to be parodical, it must be copying something else (E).

51. **D** The poem states that people do everything in church and theater except conduct contests (D). They "ogle" (line 10) (A). They "snore" (line 8) (B). They "roar" (heckle the stage) (line 9) (C). They "get dully drunk" (line 9) (E).

52. **B** The phrase "devoutly snore" is an ironic, satirical attack on the people (B), whom the speaker believes are insufficiently attentive at church services and the theater both. The speaker does not sincerely believe that sleeping is a pious act (A), nor that people sleeping in pews are being respectfully quiet (E). The speaker is lamenting the lack of respect that people show for church and the theater, but not criticizing people for staying up too late at night (D), and the speaker believes that the problem lies with the people, not the services themselves (C).

53. **D** The poem's harsh judgment of the theatergoers can be characterized in the lines, "where such Follies, and such Vices reign, / What honest Pen has Patience to refrain?" (lines 6-7)—the speaker, for one, is writing a critical response to the theatergoers' perceived vices (D). The speaker is not optimistic about the theatergoers' likelihood of being reformed (C), nor is the speaker being obviously hypocritical in opposing their behavior (E). While the speaker does condemn the theatergoers' vices, the speaker makes no claims about whether his/her own conduct is actually superior, so the tone can't be characterized as excessively priggish (A). The poem does not include overt apocalyptic imagery or proclamations (B).

54. **C** The first paragraph introduces what people think about pirates. The second paragraph is about how pirates feel guilty, so (C) is the best answer. Choice (A) is too general; the second paragraph doesn't really elaborate. There are no opposing viewpoints (B). The second paragraph does not justify the pirates' actions (D). The purpose of the second paragraph is not to cite popular culture but rather to talk about pirates' feelings of guilt (E).

55. **D** The passage suggests that pirates feel so guilty that they live with the constant hell of their consciences, so (D) is the best answer, in that the student is wracked with guilt. The pirates do not atone for their actions or turn themselves into the police (A). According to the passage, the pirates think a lot about their actions (B). There are no accusations in the passage (C). There is no evidence that the pirates feel justified in their actions (E).

56. **C** The sea is compared to a highway, so (C) is the correct answer. None of the other answers is a comparison between two things.

57. **A** Complex sentence structures and vivid descriptions appear throughout the text (for example, lines 9–16), so (A) is the best answer. The subject is not particularly simple (B). There are no unanswered questions (C). Although the author does seem to be against the pirates, the prose itself is not biased (D). The argument of the passage does not anticipate any objections or alternative interpretations (E).

58. **B** The pirates hide out when they are not plundering, so "ensconces" is the best answer (B). None of the other words has the correct meaning.

59. **E** The victims' relatives believe they were lost "from the inclemencies of the elements," or the harsh weather (a storm) (E). There is no evidence that the relatives believe the victims died of disease (A) or that they were murdered by pirates (B). There is no mention of slavery (C) or that the victims ran away (D).

60. **A** The author says "every man, whether civilized or savage, has interwoven in his constitution a moral sense," so it is clear that he believes in a general conscience that all humans have (A). There is no mention of God or a deity (B) or a higher court (C). The only punishment the author talks about is the punishment of the pirates' consciences (D). The author does not discuss how upbringing (or nurture) affects a moral code (E).

61. **D** The line can be translated as "pirates act on the saying 'dead men tell no tales' and kill all their victims so they won't be around to bear witness to the crime." Therefore, the word "practically" tells us that there is logic behind the killings (D). This part of the passage does not speak of remorse (A). All the victims were indeed killed (B). The pirates were motivated by greed, yes, but they killed their victims so they (the pirates) wouldn't get caught (C). The word "practically" means "in a practical way" here, not "an uncertain amount" (E).

62. **B** If, as the passage suggests, pirates "adopt" the maxim that dead men won't talk, the pirates are neither ignoring that their piracy comes at the cost of lost lives (A) nor rationalizing their behavior by trivializing its consequences, especially since the passage notes that adopting the maxim allows the pirates to "pursue their diabolical career with impunity" (lines 29-30) (E). The pirates in the passage don't actively lie to their victims' friends and family, but rather they leave their victims' loved ones to assume that weather was responsible for their losses (D). The passage does not discuss pirates challenging charges brought against them in court, whether by adopting a maxim or by any other means (C). When the pirates act on the quoted maxim, however, they do so by leaving no survivors of their attacks, so (B) is the correct answer.

HOW TO SCORE PRACTICE TEST 4

When you take the real exam, the proctors will collect your test booklet and bubble sheet and send your answer sheet to a processing center, where a computer looks at the pattern of filled-in ovals on your answer sheet and gives you a score. We couldn't include even a small computer with this book, so we are providing this more primitive way of scoring your exam.

Determining Your Score

STEP 1 Using the answer key, determine how many questions you got right and how many you got wrong on the test. Remember: Questions that you do not answer do not count as either right or wrong answers.

STEP 2 List the number of right answers here.

(A) __59__

STEP 3 List the number of wrong answers here. Now divide that number by 4. (Use a calculator if you're feeling particularly lazy.)

(B) __3__ ÷ 4 = (C) __.75__

STEP 4 Subtract the number of wrong answers divided by 4 from the number of correct answers. Round this score to the nearest whole number. This is your raw score.

(A) − (C) = __58__

STEP 5 To determine your real score, take the number from Step 4 and look it up in the left-hand column of the Score Conversion Table on the next page; the corresponding score on the right is your score on the exam.

PRACTICE TEST 4 SCORE CONVERSION TABLE

Raw Score	College Board Scaled Score	Raw Score	College Board Scaled Score
62	800	23	500
61	800	22	490
60	800	21	490
59	800	20	480
58	800	19	470
57	800	18	460
56	800	17	450
55	790	16	440
54	780	15	430
53	780	14	420
52	770	13	410
51	760	12	410
50	750	11	400
49	740	10	390
48	730	09	380
47	720	08	370
46	710	07	360
45	700	06	350
44	700	05	350
43	690	04	340
42	680	03	330
41	670	02	320
40	660	01	310
39	650	00	300
38	640	−01	300
37	630	−02	290
36	620	−03	280
35	620	−04	270
34	610	−05	260
33	600	−06	250
32	590	−07	240
31	580	−08	240
30	570	−09	230
29	560	−10	220
28	550	−11	210
27	540	−12	200
26	530	−13	200
27	540	−14	200
26	530	−15	200
25	520		
24	510		

Completely darken bubbles with a No. 2 pencil. If you make a mistake, be sure to erase mark completely. Erase all stray marks.

1. YOUR NAME: _____
(Print)   Last   First   M.I.

SIGNATURE: _____   **DATE:** ___ / ___ / ___

HOME ADDRESS: _____
(Print)   Number and Street

_____
City   State   Zip Code

PHONE NO. : _____
(Print)

IMPORTANT: Please fill in these boxes exactly as shown on the back cover of your test book.

2. TEST FORM

6. DATE OF BIRTH

Month	Day	Year
○ JAN		
○ FEB		
○ MAR	⓪ ⓪	⓪ ⓪
○ APR	① ①	① ①
○ MAY	② ②	② ②
○ JUN	③ ③	③ ③
○ JUL		④ ④
○ AUG		⑤ ⑤
○ SEP	⑥	⑥ ⑥
○ OCT	⑦	⑦ ⑦
○ NOV	⑧	⑧ ⑧
○ DEC	⑨	⑨ ⑨

3. TEST CODE   **4. REGISTRATION NUMBER**

7. SEX
○ MALE
○ FEMALE

The **Princeton Review**®
© TPR Education IP Holdings, LLC
FORM NO. 00001-PR

5. YOUR NAME

First 4 letters of last name				FIRST INIT	MID INIT

(bubble grid A–Z for each column)

Test 1 Start with number 1 for each new section. If a section has fewer questions than answer spaces, leave the extra answer spaces blank.

1. Ⓐ Ⓑ Ⓒ Ⓓ Ⓔ
2. Ⓐ Ⓑ Ⓒ Ⓓ Ⓔ
3. Ⓐ Ⓑ Ⓒ Ⓓ Ⓔ
4. Ⓐ Ⓑ Ⓒ Ⓓ Ⓔ
5. Ⓐ Ⓑ Ⓒ Ⓓ Ⓔ
6. Ⓐ Ⓑ Ⓒ Ⓓ Ⓔ
7. Ⓐ Ⓑ Ⓒ Ⓓ Ⓔ
8. Ⓐ Ⓑ Ⓒ Ⓓ Ⓔ
9. Ⓐ Ⓑ Ⓒ Ⓓ Ⓔ
10. Ⓐ Ⓑ Ⓒ Ⓓ Ⓔ
11. Ⓐ Ⓑ Ⓒ Ⓓ Ⓔ
12. Ⓐ Ⓑ Ⓒ Ⓓ Ⓔ
13. Ⓐ Ⓑ Ⓒ Ⓓ Ⓔ
14. Ⓐ Ⓑ Ⓒ Ⓓ Ⓔ
15. Ⓐ Ⓑ Ⓒ Ⓓ Ⓔ
16. Ⓐ Ⓑ Ⓒ Ⓓ Ⓔ
17. Ⓐ Ⓑ Ⓒ Ⓓ Ⓔ
18. Ⓐ Ⓑ Ⓒ Ⓓ Ⓔ
19. Ⓐ Ⓑ Ⓒ Ⓓ Ⓔ
20. Ⓐ Ⓑ Ⓒ Ⓓ Ⓔ
21. Ⓐ Ⓑ Ⓒ Ⓓ Ⓔ
22. Ⓐ Ⓑ Ⓒ Ⓓ Ⓔ
23. Ⓐ Ⓑ Ⓒ Ⓓ Ⓔ
24. Ⓐ Ⓑ Ⓒ Ⓓ Ⓔ
25. Ⓐ Ⓑ Ⓒ Ⓓ Ⓔ
26. Ⓐ Ⓑ Ⓒ Ⓓ Ⓔ
27. Ⓐ Ⓑ Ⓒ Ⓓ Ⓔ
28. Ⓐ Ⓑ Ⓒ Ⓓ Ⓔ
29. Ⓐ Ⓑ Ⓒ Ⓓ Ⓔ
30. Ⓐ Ⓑ Ⓒ Ⓓ Ⓔ
31. Ⓐ Ⓑ Ⓒ Ⓓ Ⓔ
32. Ⓐ Ⓑ Ⓒ Ⓓ Ⓔ
33. Ⓐ Ⓑ Ⓒ Ⓓ Ⓔ
34. Ⓐ Ⓑ Ⓒ Ⓓ Ⓔ
35. Ⓐ Ⓑ Ⓒ Ⓓ Ⓔ
36. Ⓐ Ⓑ Ⓒ Ⓓ Ⓔ
37. Ⓐ Ⓑ Ⓒ Ⓓ Ⓔ
38. Ⓐ Ⓑ Ⓒ Ⓓ Ⓔ
39. Ⓐ Ⓑ Ⓒ Ⓓ Ⓔ
40. Ⓐ Ⓑ Ⓒ Ⓓ Ⓔ
41. Ⓐ Ⓑ Ⓒ Ⓓ Ⓔ
42. Ⓐ Ⓑ Ⓒ Ⓓ Ⓔ
43. Ⓐ Ⓑ Ⓒ Ⓓ Ⓔ
44. Ⓐ Ⓑ Ⓒ Ⓓ Ⓔ
45. Ⓐ Ⓑ Ⓒ Ⓓ Ⓔ
46. Ⓐ Ⓑ Ⓒ Ⓓ Ⓔ
47. Ⓐ Ⓑ Ⓒ Ⓓ Ⓔ
48. Ⓐ Ⓑ Ⓒ Ⓓ Ⓔ
49. Ⓐ Ⓑ Ⓒ Ⓓ Ⓔ
50. Ⓐ Ⓑ Ⓒ Ⓓ Ⓔ
51. Ⓐ Ⓑ Ⓒ Ⓓ Ⓔ
52. Ⓐ Ⓑ Ⓒ Ⓓ Ⓔ
53. Ⓐ Ⓑ Ⓒ Ⓓ Ⓔ
54. Ⓐ Ⓑ Ⓒ Ⓓ Ⓔ
55. Ⓐ Ⓑ Ⓒ Ⓓ Ⓔ
56. Ⓐ Ⓑ Ⓒ Ⓓ Ⓔ
57. Ⓐ Ⓑ Ⓒ Ⓓ Ⓔ
58. Ⓐ Ⓑ Ⓒ Ⓓ Ⓔ
59. Ⓐ Ⓑ Ⓒ Ⓓ Ⓔ
60. Ⓐ Ⓑ Ⓒ Ⓓ Ⓔ
61. Ⓐ Ⓑ Ⓒ Ⓓ Ⓔ

Test 2

1. Ⓐ Ⓑ Ⓒ Ⓓ Ⓔ
2. Ⓐ Ⓑ Ⓒ Ⓓ Ⓔ
3. Ⓐ Ⓑ Ⓒ Ⓓ Ⓔ
4. Ⓐ Ⓑ Ⓒ Ⓓ Ⓔ
5. Ⓐ Ⓑ Ⓒ Ⓓ Ⓔ
6. Ⓐ Ⓑ Ⓒ Ⓓ Ⓔ
7. Ⓐ Ⓑ Ⓒ Ⓓ Ⓔ
8. Ⓐ Ⓑ Ⓒ Ⓓ Ⓔ
9. Ⓐ Ⓑ Ⓒ Ⓓ Ⓔ
10. Ⓐ Ⓑ Ⓒ Ⓓ Ⓔ
11. Ⓐ Ⓑ Ⓒ Ⓓ Ⓔ
12. Ⓐ Ⓑ Ⓒ Ⓓ Ⓔ
13. Ⓐ Ⓑ Ⓒ Ⓓ Ⓔ
14. Ⓐ Ⓑ Ⓒ Ⓓ Ⓔ
15. Ⓐ Ⓑ Ⓒ Ⓓ Ⓔ
16. Ⓐ Ⓑ Ⓒ Ⓓ Ⓔ
17. Ⓐ Ⓑ Ⓒ Ⓓ Ⓔ
18. Ⓐ Ⓑ Ⓒ Ⓓ Ⓔ
19. Ⓐ Ⓑ Ⓒ Ⓓ Ⓔ
20. Ⓐ Ⓑ Ⓒ Ⓓ Ⓔ
21. Ⓐ Ⓑ Ⓒ Ⓓ Ⓔ
22. Ⓐ Ⓑ Ⓒ Ⓓ Ⓔ
23. Ⓐ Ⓑ Ⓒ Ⓓ Ⓔ
24. Ⓐ Ⓑ Ⓒ Ⓓ Ⓔ
25. Ⓐ Ⓑ Ⓒ Ⓓ Ⓔ
26. Ⓐ Ⓑ Ⓒ Ⓓ Ⓔ
27. Ⓐ Ⓑ Ⓒ Ⓓ Ⓔ
28. Ⓐ Ⓑ Ⓒ Ⓓ Ⓔ
29. Ⓐ Ⓑ Ⓒ Ⓓ Ⓔ
30. Ⓐ Ⓑ Ⓒ Ⓓ Ⓔ
31. Ⓐ Ⓑ Ⓒ Ⓓ Ⓔ
32. Ⓐ Ⓑ Ⓒ Ⓓ Ⓔ
33. Ⓐ Ⓑ Ⓒ Ⓓ Ⓔ
34. Ⓐ Ⓑ Ⓒ Ⓓ Ⓔ
35. Ⓐ Ⓑ Ⓒ Ⓓ Ⓔ
36. Ⓐ Ⓑ Ⓒ Ⓓ Ⓔ
37. Ⓐ Ⓑ Ⓒ Ⓓ Ⓔ
38. Ⓐ Ⓑ Ⓒ Ⓓ Ⓔ
39. Ⓐ Ⓑ Ⓒ Ⓓ Ⓔ
40. Ⓐ Ⓑ Ⓒ Ⓓ Ⓔ
41. Ⓐ Ⓑ Ⓒ Ⓓ Ⓔ
42. Ⓐ Ⓑ Ⓒ Ⓓ Ⓔ
43. Ⓐ Ⓑ Ⓒ Ⓓ Ⓔ
44. Ⓐ Ⓑ Ⓒ Ⓓ Ⓔ
45. Ⓐ Ⓑ Ⓒ Ⓓ Ⓔ
46. Ⓐ Ⓑ Ⓒ Ⓓ Ⓔ
47. Ⓐ Ⓑ Ⓒ Ⓓ Ⓔ
48. Ⓐ Ⓑ Ⓒ Ⓓ Ⓔ
49. Ⓐ Ⓑ Ⓒ Ⓓ Ⓔ
50. Ⓐ Ⓑ Ⓒ Ⓓ Ⓔ
51. Ⓐ Ⓑ Ⓒ Ⓓ Ⓔ
52. Ⓐ Ⓑ Ⓒ Ⓓ Ⓔ
53. Ⓐ Ⓑ Ⓒ Ⓓ Ⓔ
54. Ⓐ Ⓑ Ⓒ Ⓓ Ⓔ
55. Ⓐ Ⓑ Ⓒ Ⓓ Ⓔ
56. Ⓐ Ⓑ Ⓒ Ⓓ Ⓔ
57. Ⓐ Ⓑ Ⓒ Ⓓ Ⓔ
58. Ⓐ Ⓑ Ⓒ Ⓓ Ⓔ
59. Ⓐ Ⓑ Ⓒ Ⓓ Ⓔ
60. Ⓐ Ⓑ Ⓒ Ⓓ Ⓔ
61. Ⓐ Ⓑ Ⓒ Ⓓ Ⓔ

Completely darken bubbles with a No. 2 pencil. If you make a mistake, be sure to erase mark completely. Erase all stray marks.

1. YOUR NAME: _____
(Print)   Last   First   M.I.

SIGNATURE: _____   DATE: ___/___/___

HOME ADDRESS: _____
(Print)   Number and Street

_____
City   State   Zip Code

PHONE NO. : _____
(Print)

5. YOUR NAME

First 4 letters of last name				FIRST INIT	MID INIT
Ⓐ	Ⓐ	Ⓐ	Ⓐ	Ⓐ	Ⓐ
Ⓑ	Ⓑ	Ⓑ	Ⓑ	Ⓑ	Ⓑ
Ⓒ	Ⓒ	Ⓒ	Ⓒ	Ⓒ	Ⓒ
Ⓓ	Ⓓ	Ⓓ	Ⓓ	Ⓓ	Ⓓ
Ⓔ	Ⓔ	Ⓔ	Ⓔ	Ⓔ	Ⓔ
Ⓕ	Ⓕ	Ⓕ	Ⓕ	Ⓕ	Ⓕ
Ⓖ	Ⓖ	Ⓖ	Ⓖ	Ⓖ	Ⓖ
Ⓗ	Ⓗ	Ⓗ	Ⓗ	Ⓗ	Ⓗ
Ⓘ	Ⓘ	Ⓘ	Ⓘ	Ⓘ	Ⓘ
Ⓙ	Ⓙ	Ⓙ	Ⓙ	Ⓙ	Ⓙ
Ⓚ	Ⓚ	Ⓚ	Ⓚ	Ⓚ	Ⓚ
Ⓛ	Ⓛ	Ⓛ	Ⓛ	Ⓛ	Ⓛ
Ⓜ	Ⓜ	Ⓜ	Ⓜ	Ⓜ	Ⓜ
Ⓝ	Ⓝ	Ⓝ	Ⓝ	Ⓝ	Ⓝ
Ⓞ	Ⓞ	Ⓞ	Ⓞ	Ⓞ	Ⓞ
Ⓟ	Ⓟ	Ⓟ	Ⓟ	Ⓟ	Ⓟ
Ⓠ	Ⓠ	Ⓠ	Ⓠ	Ⓠ	Ⓠ
Ⓡ	Ⓡ	Ⓡ	Ⓡ	Ⓡ	Ⓡ
Ⓢ	Ⓢ	Ⓢ	Ⓢ	Ⓢ	Ⓢ
Ⓣ	Ⓣ	Ⓣ	Ⓣ	Ⓣ	Ⓣ
Ⓤ	Ⓤ	Ⓤ	Ⓤ	Ⓤ	Ⓤ
Ⓥ	Ⓥ	Ⓥ	Ⓥ	Ⓥ	Ⓥ
Ⓦ	Ⓦ	Ⓦ	Ⓦ	Ⓦ	Ⓦ
Ⓧ	Ⓧ	Ⓧ	Ⓧ	Ⓧ	Ⓧ
Ⓨ	Ⓨ	Ⓨ	Ⓨ	Ⓨ	Ⓨ
Ⓩ	Ⓩ	Ⓩ	Ⓩ	Ⓩ	Ⓩ

IMPORTANT: Please fill in these boxes exactly as shown on the back cover of your test book.

2. TEST FORM

3. TEST CODE

4. REGISTRATION NUMBER

6. DATE OF BIRTH

Month	Day		Year	
◯ JAN				
◯ FEB				
◯ MAR	⓪	⓪	⓪	⓪
◯ APR	①	①	①	①
◯ MAY	②	②	②	②
◯ JUN	③	③	③	③
◯ JUL		④	④	④
◯ AUG		⑤	⑤	⑤
◯ SEP		⑥	⑥	⑥
◯ OCT		⑦	⑦	⑦
◯ NOV		⑧	⑧	⑧
◯ DEC		⑨	⑨	⑨

Test code bubbles: 0 A, 1 B, 2 C, 3 D, 4 E, 5 F, 6 G, 7, 8, 9

Registration number bubbles: 0 through 9 in each column

7. SEX
◯ MALE
◯ FEMALE

The Princeton Review®
© TPR Education IP Holdings, LLC
FORM NO. 00001-PR

Test 3
Start with number 1 for each new section. If a section has fewer questions than answer spaces, leave the extra answer spaces blank.

1. Ⓐ Ⓑ Ⓒ Ⓓ Ⓔ   16. Ⓐ Ⓑ Ⓒ Ⓓ Ⓔ   31. Ⓐ Ⓑ Ⓒ Ⓓ Ⓔ   46. Ⓐ Ⓑ Ⓒ Ⓓ Ⓔ
2. Ⓐ Ⓑ Ⓒ Ⓓ Ⓔ   17. Ⓐ Ⓑ Ⓒ Ⓓ Ⓔ   32. Ⓐ Ⓑ Ⓒ Ⓓ Ⓔ   47. Ⓐ Ⓑ Ⓒ Ⓓ Ⓔ
3. Ⓐ Ⓑ Ⓒ Ⓓ Ⓔ   18. Ⓐ Ⓑ Ⓒ Ⓓ Ⓔ   33. Ⓐ Ⓑ Ⓒ Ⓓ Ⓔ   48. Ⓐ Ⓑ Ⓒ Ⓓ Ⓔ
4. Ⓐ Ⓑ Ⓒ Ⓓ Ⓔ   19. Ⓐ Ⓑ Ⓒ Ⓓ Ⓔ   34. Ⓐ Ⓑ Ⓒ Ⓓ Ⓔ   49. Ⓐ Ⓑ Ⓒ Ⓓ Ⓔ
5. Ⓐ Ⓑ Ⓒ Ⓓ Ⓔ   20. Ⓐ Ⓑ Ⓒ Ⓓ Ⓔ   35. Ⓐ Ⓑ Ⓒ Ⓓ Ⓔ   50. Ⓐ Ⓑ Ⓒ Ⓓ Ⓔ
6. Ⓐ Ⓑ Ⓒ Ⓓ Ⓔ   21. Ⓐ Ⓑ Ⓒ Ⓓ Ⓔ   36. Ⓐ Ⓑ Ⓒ Ⓓ Ⓔ   51. Ⓐ Ⓑ Ⓒ Ⓓ Ⓔ
7. Ⓐ Ⓑ Ⓒ Ⓓ Ⓔ   22. Ⓐ Ⓑ Ⓒ Ⓓ Ⓔ   37. Ⓐ Ⓑ Ⓒ Ⓓ Ⓔ   52. Ⓐ Ⓑ Ⓒ Ⓓ Ⓔ
8. Ⓐ Ⓑ Ⓒ Ⓓ Ⓔ   23. Ⓐ Ⓑ Ⓒ Ⓓ Ⓔ   38. Ⓐ Ⓑ Ⓒ Ⓓ Ⓔ   53. Ⓐ Ⓑ Ⓒ Ⓓ Ⓔ
9. Ⓐ Ⓑ Ⓒ Ⓓ Ⓔ   24. Ⓐ Ⓑ Ⓒ Ⓓ Ⓔ   39. Ⓐ Ⓑ Ⓒ Ⓓ Ⓔ   54. Ⓐ Ⓑ Ⓒ Ⓓ Ⓔ
10. Ⓐ Ⓑ Ⓒ Ⓓ Ⓔ   25. Ⓐ Ⓑ Ⓒ Ⓓ Ⓔ   40. Ⓐ Ⓑ Ⓒ Ⓓ Ⓔ   55. Ⓐ Ⓑ Ⓒ Ⓓ Ⓔ
11. Ⓐ Ⓑ Ⓒ Ⓓ Ⓔ   26. Ⓐ Ⓑ Ⓒ Ⓓ Ⓔ   41. Ⓐ Ⓑ Ⓒ Ⓓ Ⓔ   56. Ⓐ Ⓑ Ⓒ Ⓓ Ⓔ
12. Ⓐ Ⓑ Ⓒ Ⓓ Ⓔ   27. Ⓐ Ⓑ Ⓒ Ⓓ Ⓔ   42. Ⓐ Ⓑ Ⓒ Ⓓ Ⓔ   57. Ⓐ Ⓑ Ⓒ Ⓓ Ⓔ
13. Ⓐ Ⓑ Ⓒ Ⓓ Ⓔ   28. Ⓐ Ⓑ Ⓒ Ⓓ Ⓔ   43. Ⓐ Ⓑ Ⓒ Ⓓ Ⓔ   58. Ⓐ Ⓑ Ⓒ Ⓓ Ⓔ
14. Ⓐ Ⓑ Ⓒ Ⓓ Ⓔ   29. Ⓐ Ⓑ Ⓒ Ⓓ Ⓔ   44. Ⓐ Ⓑ Ⓒ Ⓓ Ⓔ   59. Ⓐ Ⓑ Ⓒ Ⓓ Ⓔ
15. Ⓐ Ⓑ Ⓒ Ⓓ Ⓔ   30. Ⓐ Ⓑ Ⓒ Ⓓ Ⓔ   45. Ⓐ Ⓑ Ⓒ Ⓓ Ⓔ   60. Ⓐ Ⓑ Ⓒ Ⓓ Ⓔ
                                                                61. Ⓐ Ⓑ Ⓒ Ⓓ Ⓔ

Test 4

1. Ⓐ Ⓑ Ⓒ Ⓓ Ⓔ   16. Ⓐ Ⓑ Ⓒ Ⓓ Ⓔ   31. Ⓐ Ⓑ Ⓒ Ⓓ Ⓔ   47. Ⓐ Ⓑ Ⓒ Ⓓ Ⓔ
2. Ⓐ Ⓑ Ⓒ Ⓓ Ⓔ   17. Ⓐ Ⓑ Ⓒ Ⓓ Ⓔ   32. Ⓐ Ⓑ Ⓒ Ⓓ Ⓔ   48. Ⓐ Ⓑ Ⓒ Ⓓ Ⓔ
3. Ⓐ Ⓑ Ⓒ Ⓓ Ⓔ   18. Ⓐ Ⓑ Ⓒ Ⓓ Ⓔ   33. Ⓐ Ⓑ Ⓒ Ⓓ Ⓔ   49. Ⓐ Ⓑ Ⓒ Ⓓ Ⓔ
4. Ⓐ Ⓑ Ⓒ Ⓓ Ⓔ   19. Ⓐ Ⓑ Ⓒ Ⓓ Ⓔ   34. Ⓐ Ⓑ Ⓒ Ⓓ Ⓔ   50. Ⓐ Ⓑ Ⓒ Ⓓ Ⓔ
5. Ⓐ Ⓑ Ⓒ Ⓓ Ⓔ   20. Ⓐ Ⓑ Ⓒ Ⓓ Ⓔ   35. Ⓐ Ⓑ Ⓒ Ⓓ Ⓔ   51. Ⓐ Ⓑ Ⓒ Ⓓ Ⓔ
6. Ⓐ Ⓑ Ⓒ Ⓓ Ⓔ   21. Ⓐ Ⓑ Ⓒ Ⓓ Ⓔ   36. Ⓐ Ⓑ Ⓒ Ⓓ Ⓔ   52. Ⓐ Ⓑ Ⓒ Ⓓ Ⓔ
7. Ⓐ Ⓑ Ⓒ Ⓓ Ⓔ   22. Ⓐ Ⓑ Ⓒ Ⓓ Ⓔ   37. Ⓐ Ⓑ Ⓒ Ⓓ Ⓔ   53. Ⓐ Ⓑ Ⓒ Ⓓ Ⓔ
8. Ⓐ Ⓑ Ⓒ Ⓓ Ⓔ   23. Ⓐ Ⓑ Ⓒ Ⓓ Ⓔ   38. Ⓐ Ⓑ Ⓒ Ⓓ Ⓔ   54. Ⓐ Ⓑ Ⓒ Ⓓ Ⓔ
9. Ⓐ Ⓑ Ⓒ Ⓓ Ⓔ   24. Ⓐ Ⓑ Ⓒ Ⓓ Ⓔ   39. Ⓐ Ⓑ Ⓒ Ⓓ Ⓔ   55. Ⓐ Ⓑ Ⓒ Ⓓ Ⓔ
10. Ⓐ Ⓑ Ⓒ Ⓓ Ⓔ   25. Ⓐ Ⓑ Ⓒ Ⓓ Ⓔ   40. Ⓐ Ⓑ Ⓒ Ⓓ Ⓔ   56. Ⓐ Ⓑ Ⓒ Ⓓ Ⓔ
11. Ⓐ Ⓑ Ⓒ Ⓓ Ⓔ   26. Ⓐ Ⓑ Ⓒ Ⓓ Ⓔ   41. Ⓐ Ⓑ Ⓒ Ⓓ Ⓔ   57. Ⓐ Ⓑ Ⓒ Ⓓ Ⓔ
12. Ⓐ Ⓑ Ⓒ Ⓓ Ⓔ   27. Ⓐ Ⓑ Ⓒ Ⓓ Ⓔ   42. Ⓐ Ⓑ Ⓒ Ⓓ Ⓔ   58. Ⓐ Ⓑ Ⓒ Ⓓ Ⓔ
13. Ⓐ Ⓑ Ⓒ Ⓓ Ⓔ   28. Ⓐ Ⓑ Ⓒ Ⓓ Ⓔ   43. Ⓐ Ⓑ Ⓒ Ⓓ Ⓔ   59. Ⓐ Ⓑ Ⓒ Ⓓ Ⓔ
14. Ⓐ Ⓑ Ⓒ Ⓓ Ⓔ   29. Ⓐ Ⓑ Ⓒ Ⓓ Ⓔ   44. Ⓐ Ⓑ Ⓒ Ⓓ Ⓔ   60. Ⓐ Ⓑ Ⓒ Ⓓ Ⓔ
15. Ⓐ Ⓑ Ⓒ Ⓓ Ⓔ   30. Ⓐ Ⓑ Ⓒ Ⓓ Ⓔ   45. Ⓐ Ⓑ Ⓒ Ⓓ Ⓔ   61. Ⓐ Ⓑ Ⓒ Ⓓ Ⓔ
                                    46. Ⓐ Ⓑ Ⓒ Ⓓ Ⓔ   62. Ⓐ Ⓑ Ⓒ Ⓓ Ⓔ